Gender and History:
Retrospect and Prospect

Gender and History: Retrospect and Prospect

Leonore Davidoff, Keith McClelland and Eleni Varikas

Copyright © Blackwell Publishers Ltd 2000

This edition first published in 1999

Transferred to digital print 2004

Blackwell Publishers Ltd
108 Cowley Road
Oxford OX4 1JF, UK

Blackwell Publishers Inc
350 Main Street
Malden, Massachusetts 02148, USA

British Library Cataloguing in Publication Data has been applied for

Library of Congress Cataloging-in-Publication Data has been applied for

ISBN: 0-631-21998-6 (pbk)

Typeset by Advance Typesetting, Long Hanborough
Printed and bound in Great Britain by
Marston Book Services Limited, Oxford

This book is printed on acid-free paper

CONTENTS

        Åsa Lundqvist   165

14 Gender and the Categories of Experienced History
        Selma Leydesdorff   179

15 Writing Gender into History and History in Gender:
        Creating A Nation and Australian Historiography
        Joy Damousi   194

        Notes on Contributors   207

        Index   209

Preface

Leonore Davidoff, Keith McClelland and Eleni Varikas

In 1999 the journal *Gender & History* entered a second decade of publication. To mark the event the editorial collective decided to invite a wide range of contributors to reflect upon how the history of gender relations has developed in their particular fields and national cultures and what issues command attention. This volume is the result.

Since 1989 both the subject of gender relations in history and the journal itself have grown in strength and importance. *Gender & History* has become established as the leading international journal in the field. We have published more than 150 articles and a very large number of review articles and book reviews – all of which are testimony to both the growing strength of the field and to the liveliness of exploration and debate. Indeed, part of the achievement of the journal and of historians working on gender history is the sheer growth of the subject. The range and volume of work is now considerable: many leading journals publish articles; the flood of books is to be measured in hundreds of titles a year; and gender history is often an established part of the agenda of many historical conferences and congresses.

When we started the journal, we wrote in the editorial ('Why Gender and History?', vol. 1 [1989], p. 1):

> *Gender & History* brings to the study of history the centrality of gender relations and to the study of gender a sense of history. As its editors, we seek to examine all historical social relations from a feminist perspective, to construct a comprehensive analysis of all institutions that take their gender-specific characters into account. In addressing men and masculinity as well as women and femininity, the journal will illuminate the ways in which societies have been shaped by the relations of power between women and men.

We further suggested (p. 4) that:

> Although we are an English language publication, we are committed to cutting across boundaries of time and place, and we encourage contributions from scholars whatever their nationality or language. Our definition of the historical stretches back into antiquity as well as incorporating living memory.

We have been fairly successful in achieving these objectives. A commitment to feminist social and political analysis has remained a central spring of the journal's content and purposes, not least in taking relations of power, in all their complexity and unevenness, as of paramount importance. We have published a considerable body of work which examines masculinities as well as femininities. In the journal's pages we have read analyses ranging from state institutions and political movements to the domestic, familial and personal. We have also carried articles on a wide range of places and periods stretching from the ancient world to the present, from Latin America to Northern Europe. However, it remains the case that the overwhelming bulk of the material we have published has been on the 'western' world, particularly Britain and the United States, over the last 200 years. Perhaps inevitably, as based in Anglo-American institutions, we have not been entirely successful in fulfilling our initial objectives of becoming a truly international journal.

In part this reflects the field itself. Gender history has developed rapidly but very unevenly. Clearly it flourishes, even as a minority subject, within regions such as Britain, North America, Australia, and India. Yet within Europe, for instance, while important work has been undertaken in many countries, in some, such as France, there are very considerable institutional and cultural obstacles to the field, while the subject has only very recently begun to develop within Eastern Europe and Russia. Moreover, work often comes from the established centres of the subject even when the content relates to other places. *Gender & History* has not been alone in publishing material on, say, African history by African historians who have had to migrate to the metropolitan heartlands of the west, above all in the United States, in order to secure jobs and research opportunities. Similarly, the spread of work terms of periods has been very uneven: it is no detriment to the work undertaken by many historians of earlier periods to say that the bulk of research has probably been on the period since the late eighteenth century.

The field has also been marked by lively and extensive debate over the last decade. Gender history, like historical scholarship in general, has been marked by widespread and often sharp discussion about methodological and theoretical issues. One clearly important element of this has been the so-called 'linguistic turn' or the turn to culture. This is clear in culture as an object of study, the description and analysis of difference embedded in language and cultural forms. It has also focused on language, or culture more widely defined, as the pivot of explanations of change. Feminist historians and gender history have been major contributions to these debates and have often been in the forefront of raising crucial and difficult conceptual issues. For example, there has been much discussion on the relationship between 'language' and 'experience' or the ways in which the social and political identities of men and women have been constructed, broken and re-shaped in relation to the discourses and structures of political, social, economic and cultural power.

Gender & History has been both informed by debates such as these and contributed to them: many of the chapters in this book are directly engaged with such issues. But the journal has never sought to impose a 'line'. Our commitment to studying the diversity of relations between men and women in the past starts from the axiom that these have been typically, though not inevitably, relations of unequal power. Beyond that we seek only to encourage a plurality of voices in accounting for how those relations are made or re-made over time.

Related to this is the issue of the place of gender in relation to other forms of social difference and division. In our commitment to publishing work which is exploratory of gender relations is a necessary implication that we believe that relations of gender are threaded through other forms of social relations – notably those of class, of race and of ethnicity. However, this does not entail an a priori assumption that gender is always of primary importance in describing or analysing particular historical moments. This is not a theoretical question but rather an historical one, for only in the analysis of the historical moment can the importance of gender be assessed. Whereas, for instance, most forms of Marxism have insisted that relations of class are paramount, over-determining all other social relations, the analysis of gender requires examining the mutual determinations of, say, class and gender, or of race and gender or, most difficult of all, the inter-relation of all these dimensions. Yet, again, *how* this work is done by historians is not something which *Gender & History* is or can be prescriptive about.

The insistence that gender does matter to the study of history, even where we do not yet always know the precise ways in which this is the case, is amply demonstrated by the expanding range of subjects treated by gender historians over the last decade and by work in progress. When we began the journal there was already valuable work available in such areas as women and employment, women and the family, issues of social policy, the history of women in particular political movements such as suffrage campaigns. Other less conventional areas of study, such as the history of masculinities, were beginning to emerge.

Much of that work built upon 'recovery history' – that is the pioneering work of feminist historians in many countries in uncovering the hidden history of women. This work does and must continue, and not only in those countries where even the most basic facts of women's pasts are ignored. It is still true in those supposedly advanced and sophisticated historiographies in countries like Britain and the United States it is too often assumed that mainstream subjects like economic growth or the histories of state politics can be safely pursued without reference to women's existence, let alone the relations of gender. One of the major developments of the past decade has been the broadening of gender history to include work on what was formerly often considered to be such traditional historical areas. For example, recognising gender relations widens the definition of politics and the political. It remains the ambition of *Gender & History* to continue to encourage such work in the belief that it is necessary to assault the skies and challenge existing historical narratives in their central structures of thought.

The essays in this volume all seek to pose such challenges in diverse ways. They are focused on the nineteenth and twentieth centuries, in a variety of national and thematic contexts. There are restrictions of both place and period here, which would appear to confirm one of the limits of the journal's achievement which we noted earlier. However, this book should be seen as part of a cumulative body of work, not least in relation to other past and forthcoming book special issues which we have published, including those on *Presentations of the Self in Early Modern England*, ed. Amy Louise Erickson and Ross Balzaretti (1995), *Gendered Colonialisms in African History*, ed. Nancy Rose Hunt, Tessie R. Liu, and Jean Quataert (1996), *Gender and the Body in the Ancient Mediterranean*, ed. Maria Wyke (1997) and the book special issue being planned for 2000 on medieval history.

The contributors to this volume come from a wide range of countries and include both senior scholars and younger historians. We hope that their essays, with their diverse topics and approaches, will be read as both engaging with very particular issues but also as contributing to wider questions. To commence a new decade of publishing in the field, these are *essays*: exploratory and often speculative rather than offering definitive conclusions. We intend and hope that they will stimulate readers to not only further empirical work and to challenge the arguments voiced in these pages but also to reflect more widely on where histories of gender have come from and where they are going.

1

Woman in Nineteenth-Century America

Christine Stansell

In 1845, the brilliant American journalist Margaret Fuller published a portentously titled book, *Woman in the Nineteenth Century*. A pastiche of high-flown Transcendentalist mysticism, literary musings and social commentary, Fuller called for the removal of 'every arbitrary barrier' to women's full development and buttressed her argument with a stream of examples of both the impediments and the triumphs that had accrued to humankind when women surmounted them. There were plenty of books around with women in the title in the 1840s – the cult of true womanhood was in full swing – but Fuller's was not a tract of prescriptions for ladies, but rather an exalted investigation of the possibilities for a broader, more complex female life.

There was not a lot of material at hand for her vision in the middle-class New England society she lived in, so Fuller rummaged through such work about women as she had available. She was looking for what we might call women's agency. How had women acted in and upon the world, despite their being housebound, denied education, hemmed in by laws? Fuller's central figure, Woman, reverberated across culture and time, coming to rest in the moment of realisation and redemption, the nineteenth century. In the nineteenth-century manner, she used what sources she had at hand to do women's history, calling upon the stories of women in the Bible, Greek and Roman mythology and history, and stories of European noblewomen and queens for her examples. She even dipped into proto-ethnography with sympathetic reflections on the Amerindian women she had met on a trip to the Canadian border. Woman was not just a social referent, it was a discursive point, laden with meaning, charged with force. It was an expression of a female penchant for what Natalie Zemon Davis has called, in another context, extravagant universalising. The habit would gather terrific force over the next half century.[1]

The structures of universalising – she, so different from me in most respects, is really like me in fundamental ways, because we are both women – has fallen into low repute with the advent of identity politics and critiques of the Enlightenment. Readers and scholars now look with jaundiced eyes at the universal Woman invented by women's rights advocates like Fuller, among others, in Anglo-America in the early nineteenth century. Those early paradigms of sisterhood were recuperated in the 1970s to inspire and structure the founding of a history just for women. But quickly the commonality of womanhood seemed to scholars to partake of sentimentality, obfuscation, and pretensions on the part of the universalisers. Historians of class relations pointed out the self-serving elements in middle-class women's efforts to help their working-class sisters. Historians of race pointed out that, in slave societies, slave-owning women (and men) saw enslaved women as female, but of a different species than white 'ladies'. Later, scholars of empire have alerted us to the uses to which ruling nations have put normative definitions of woman in their colonising enterprises. Attempts to understand others across divides of nation, culture, language, religion seem easier when assumptions about the shared vulnerabilities and strengths of women are invoked, but we have seen in case after case how misguided such attempts can be. In the spirit of the times, the editor of my volume of *Woman in the Nineteenth Century* even takes care to take Margaret Fuller to task for her biases toward and stereotypes of 'other' women – the Amerindians, the Chinese, the Turks – she used to bolster her argument.

This scholarly turn was necessary and important, bringing us to a shrewder and more realistic appraisal of the power relations embedded in the women's rights tradition of which Fuller was a part. But like the race/class/gender triad to which it is moored, the critique has its own essentialising pitfalls. In US scholarship, an overweening stress on identity formation and separate feminisms (Afro-American feminism, working-class feminism, Latin feminism) has created some predictable plot lines and, at times, the perspective obscures more than it reveals. Separate group identities, ever forming, take on an intractable quality, not all that different from a much earlier historiography's use of social role theory. It is time to re-evaluate the universalising impulse, to assess its effects and analyse its origins and political effects. Two approaches are involved: an intellectual and political history of the uses of Woman and a social and cultural history of mixture, of those heterogeneous colloquies of women from different social groups which can generate the powerful intellectual construct Woman and give it a political momentum.

Extravagant universalising is a notion that Natalie Zemon Davis uses to analyse Marie de l'Incarnation, a French nun who became a missionary to Amerindian villages near Quebec in 1639. Davis describes Marie's deep and passionate identification with the *filles sauvages* she befriended and instructed. Marie set out for Quebec with a hope she might clasp the savage girls to her breast. How did the hope fare and what did she learn, Davis asks, from those whom she had come to teach? Davis argues for a transformative chemistry which the colonial mixture – French nuns, Amerindian women – effected, a reaction between cultures more volatile than Marie imposing her culture on her charges or her students resisting her colonising impulses. Marie saw likenesses between herself and the girls and women she taught, Davis suggests, and in coming to see those likenesses, she changed her ideas and methods. The Amerindian women, too, changed in their encounter with her in the all-female space of the mission.

Taking care not to romanticise the French réligieuse, Davis teases out some threads of similarities between the nuns and the Amerindian women. Christianity brought to the Amerindians some of the same consolations it brought to Marie, freedom from the cares of the world and an ability to accept life on its own terms. Marie's sense of how God's grace could exist at the core of a busy domestic female life, both hard-working and spiritual, was reinforced by the Indian women. The life histories of a number of her converts resembled her own in their pleasure in the education which religion gave them and in their subsequent religious activism. The portrait is nuanced, and here I cannot do it justice, but its importance for historians of gender lies in Davis's success in breaking with categorical approaches. While avoiding the trap of idealising shared ties of sex, she also suggests that the very construct of universal womanhood has the power to render cultural identities more labile and permeable to others.

The recent 150th anniversary of the first Convention for Women's Rights in the United States gives an occasion to look again at 'woman in the nineteenth century', in all her complexity. The grand sweep of the tradition, its enormous achievements, its dispiriting failures, throws up its own sense of likeness, sometimes modest, sometimes extravagant, but always loaded with the redolent meanings attached to the term Woman. With the help of some new American scholarship, it is possible, I believe, to look at Woman from another angle. Even with all we know now about divisions, antagonisms and real enmities between different groups of women, we can still conceive of the universalist impulse as a fructifying mixture rather than dead weight, a political and intellectual point where women sometimes drew otherwise unattainable benefits, intellectual and social, and created politics in the name of likeness.

The place to begin is in 1848, in the little country town of Seneca Falls in upstate New York, where several dozen excited women and a few interested men held the first meeting in the world devoted solely to women's rights. It was the 'springtime of the peoples' in Europe and, although far removed geographically and imaginatively, the Americans caught some of the fever of emancipatory proclamations with one of their own, the Declaration of Rights and Sentiments. The propositions it offered the world were remarkable.

The Declaration turned upon a rhetorical personage who was close kin to Margaret Fuller's Woman. 'The history of mankind is a history of repeated injuries and usurpations on the part of man toward woman, having in direct object the establishment of an absolute tyranny over her.'[2] Now we know that the manifesto was an entry in a long, fitfully articulated history of women's grievances, but the participants were not aware of it at the time. They thought they were doing something entirely new. They probably had

read Margaret Fuller's best selling *Woman*, and they most certainly would
have read Sarah Grimké's incredible *Letters on the Equality of the Sexes*
(1837), since it was a book circulating in anti-slavery circles in which most
of them were active. But most certainly they would not have known about
women's agitation for rights in the early years of the French Revolution or
the sporadic protests that extended as far back as the late Middle Ages, to
Christine de Pizan's *Book of the City of Ladies*. And few would have read
the most salient book for their purposes, Mary Wollstonecraft's *Vindication
of the Rights of Woman* (1792), which had passed out of print and general
discussion, along with any knowledge that a woman had spent concentrated intellectual labour thinking about how odd it was that her sex was
unable to profit from the universal rights of man.

The absence of an accessible tradition makes the Americans' inventive-
ness all the more striking. And perhaps there were benefits. For in the
Declaration of Rights and Sentiments, the character Woman has an explosive polemical power she lacks in Mary Wollstonecraft's book. There are
many differences between the Americans and Wollstonecraft fifty years
earlier, but, put briefly, one could say that Woman in Wollstonecraft's work
is always extrapolated from a set of premises about Reason; she exists as a
logical counter in a debate with the revolutionary republicans and Rousseau
more than she does as a character in an actual narrative situation. She
vibrates slightly to life and its daily burdens – there is talk in the *Vindication*
of the obligations of childrearing, the indignities of the marriage market –
but mostly she is moved here and there, a pawn in a set of propositions
about character, virtue, and citizenship.

But at Seneca Falls, and in the subsequent writing from women's rights
stalwarts in the early 1850s the convention prompted, we see more concrete preoccupations, a nascent sense of likeness with women in different
life situations. True, the Seneca Falls deliberations also turn on a series of
abstract proposals about Woman. In lofty rhetoric, the signers point out
that women were legally the subjects of their husbands and fathers, that
wives could not hold property in their own names, that divorce was an economic and social disaster for women, that they could not go to college or
become doctors, lawyers, ministers or clergy, that no decently paid work
was open to them, and so forth.

Yet there is a trace of knowledge of a wider provenance to women's
troubles than those of the small circle of respectable ladies who attended
the convention. The belief that a number of different but connected lives
made up womanhood, and endowed it with urgency and wide applic-
ability, would gain great strength over the next two decades. This was in
large measure because of the origins of women's rights in the anti-slavery
movement. As early as the 1830s, women in the inner circles of abolition-
ism stretched the metaphor of enslavement to encompass their own situations. The energy of extrapolation galvanised their thinking. Here was a
sense of likeness that was truly extravagant: the analogy of the abolitionist

lady with the woman slave. 'Am I not a woman and a sister?' implores the kneeling, chained, half-naked woman on the emblem of the female anti-slavery societies.[3] The identification was by turns histrionic, sentimental and brilliantly revealing for the women's rights movement, given all the actual ways in which men had the ability to coerce and constrain wives and daughters and the legal fact that wives and daughters were, to some degree, the property of their husbands and fathers. 'Yours in the bonds of woman-hood', the Southern ex-slaveholding renegade Sarah Grimke signed each of her *Letters*, a paraphrase of the bonds of slavery, designed to detonate regular provocations throughout the text.

This strain of universalising, carried through women's rights and strength-ened in the political culture of the 1850s, provided audiences with an enor-mous sense of political efficacy, even for disenfranchised women, and a rich repertoire of versatile metaphors and images: of 'bondage' for instance, which Elizabeth Cady Stanton, who had emerged from the Seneca Falls Convention a leader of the nascent movement, translated into the 'mental bondage' of undereducated, housebound women, of 'universal democracy', the rich term for a consortium of rights-bearing individuals. The school of anti-slavery was a huge pedagogical effort in reasoning, arguing, writing, orating and storytelling and they learned its lessons well for their new cause. The resources of melodrama, anecdote, and narrative identification used to soften up scornful or indifferent Northern audiences to the plight of the slave proved useful to the women too. Some of the same sociological interest that went into stripping away myth and revealing 'slavery as it is' resulted in a curiosity about and compulsion to tell the different stories of women.

We can see how deftly Stanton used the figure of Woman to broaden radically the reach of her politics. The rectification of civil disabilities for married women were mainstays of the movement since Seneca Falls. But Stanton sailed past the campaign against coverture law to a hard-edged critique of the structural limitations of marriage itself. She argued her case by telling little stories of women in different situations of conjugal vulner-ability, drumming up, through the strategies of sentimental fiction, empathy for women quite different from her mostly-affluent contemporaries in the movement. In speeches and writing, she staged melodramas about 'the drunkard's wife' and 'the poor widow', the unfortunate woman in the work-house or the lunatic asylum, the labouring woman in the garret. This sort of sentimental narrative is often associated with conservative gender im-pulses, but in the political climate of the mid nineteenth century, as the late Elizabeth Clark argued brilliantly, Victorian sentimentalism was enor-mously efficacious in creating identifications which overrode deep structures of class and racial arrogance by employing ideas of a shared humanity.[4] To know another woman, to believe you might feel her pain as your pain, to comprehend frailties that, however different they might seem, bore some rela-tion to your own: this was the core impulse of mid-century woman's rights.

It is in this context we can place Sojourner Truth's impressive speech, when she stepped up to the platform of one of the early conventions that followed Seneca Falls and inquired of the audience 'Arn't I a woman?' Truth was a former slave, a travelling preacher and a personage on the fringe of the mostly white abolitionist world. She had sat silently, so the story went, for two days listening to arguments go back and forth about the proper nature of Woman and her Rights (the audience had a vocal contingent of conservative men). She finally stood to speak and – again, as one reminiscence claimed – pulled up her sleeve and lifted her bared arm to remind her listeners of her own sex.

> That man over there says that women need to be helped into carriages, and lifted over ditches, and to have the best place everywhere. Nobody ever helps me into carriages … And arn't I a woman? Look at me! Look at my arm. I have ploughed and planted, and gathered into barns, and no man could head me! And arn't I a woman?

This version of Truth's words, reconstructed by a white woman from memory many years later, is less dependable than the less sensationalistic, more reasoned and plainspoken speech recorded at the time, in which Truth calmly stepped into the spot marked for woman.

> I am a woman's rights. I have as much muscle as any man … I have ploughed and reaped and husked and chopped and mowed, and can any man do more than that?

Nell Irvin Painter has precisely excavated the many layers of audience reaction, expectation, representations and misrepresentations that made up this racial moment. But whatever the quotient of rhetorical skill, oratorical finesse, showmanship, aggravation, and abiding grief in Truth's oratory, one can say, most simply, that she had seen Woman striding about in the oratory for a number of days and she wanted to wrap herself in Her folds. And what's more she succeeded – if only in the moment. She was not hustled off the stage, booed, or subjected to racist taunts. True, her intervention would have little effect in opening up women's rights to the black women abolitionists who could have brought their own political finesse and experiences of gender to the movement. But the resonance of Truth's speech nonetheless shows the elasticity of the universalising structures, ideas about 'the sex' which could be stretched, albeit not without difficulty.[5]

Where did the possibilities for identification come from? Not from political liberalism, which while supple enough to allow women's rights to coalesce in the 1850s, cannot account for the explosive elements of the tradition, its historically unprecedented valuation of the female person and the ability of its leaders to ally themselves, in practice and in imagination, with women *as they were*, in a variety of places. For the ability to see likeness we must look to sources outside liberalism, to the freshets which dissolved inherited limits of the imagination. In Stanton, in particular, is evident an admixture of influences. Although she would in time become a militant secularist, her Protestant heritage always undergirded a radical faith that the soul had no sex. But the influences of nineteenth-century Romantic writers are also evident. Her wonderful profession of woman's rights as spiritual vocation beats with a Romantic passion – Fuller's mysticism, heated up – that merges body and soul, imagination and intellect: 'Nothing, nobody could abate the all-absorbing, agonising interest I feel in the redemption of woman. I could not wash my hands of woman's rights, for they are dyed clear through to the marrow of the bone'.[6]

But for all the excitement this early movement generated, débâcle was in the wings. The line of vulnerability was precisely that sense of extravagant likeness across the colour line. When the Civil War came, women's rights activists threw themselves into the effort, expecting universal suffrage as their payoff once the war was won. This did not happen. The Reconstruction amendments, which marked a turning point that might have enshrined universal democracy as the law of the land, had the paradoxical effect of explicitly repudiating woman suffrage by introducing the qualification 'male' in the Constitution for the first time.

When politically traduced women need defend themselves, who, exactly, to call to the defence? Stanton and Anthony have been accused, not without justice, of restricting the campaign for woman suffrage to white women, but right after the war their universalism held for a time: they worked from the premises of votes for everyone. The real question was universal citizenship and they and their supporters believed that 'the same despotism which tramples on the negro will trample on woman, and revolution after revolution shall go on, until we have established our institutions on the broad basis of justice to all classes and colours'.[7] Most of their one-time allies, however, divided the issues. Black men, especially Republican supporters and returning soldiers in the South, required immediate help. Every once in a while Stanton protested that women were black as well, but it was a weak retort. Woman's rights paid the price for the lack of connections to the free black women in anti-slavery organisations in the 1850s who, after the war, might have helped create a politics which joined the plight of the freed-people to that of women. Finally, when virtually all their allies in the Republican Party had defected to universal male suffrage, Stanton and Anthony turned to bolster the cause of women with racist and nativist arguments. Old friends were appalled.

The split is familiar, and it is generally understood as the defection of the strongest wing of the woman's movement from a commitment to racial equality, a lesson in the flimsiness of feminist cross-race – and even cross-class – identifications. Some American scholars, however, have found a more complicated story: in which political mixing – of groups and of issues – produced transactions between women that did retain a tinge of integration and reciprocity. A few historians of Afro-American women have turned up stories of intense and productive contacts with white female activists, not simplistic acts of solidarity between sisters, surely, but ambiguous (and shrewd) political exchanges that involved discoveries of likeness. The impulse of this new work is not to dismiss cross-racial contact as implicitly racist – although racism was never absent – but to investigate the transformative effects of encounters among women.

One of the finest of these efforts is Amy Dru Stanley's *From Bondage to Contract*, a beautifully delineated intellectual and cultural history of the consecration of wage labour as the pre-eminent model of social relations in the wake of the emancipation of the slaves.[8] The Sea Islands, a fertile rice-growing region off the coast of South Carolina and Georgia, held a huge population of freedpeople and became a focus, early on in emancipation, for the creation of a new free black society. Mingling with the former slaves were cadres of abolitionists from the North, free black and white teachers, ministers and advisers come to help (and uplift), to prove to the country that African Americans were capable of living in freedom. Among the Northerners were women, white and black.

Strikingly, the freedwomen's particular notions of freedom – visceral and bred-in-the-bone – meshed with the women's rights concerns of some Northern leaders. While government agents thought freedom meant one thing for a man – self-ownership, the ability to sell his labour and to make contracts – they assumed it meant quite another for a woman. Northern agents and male slaves alike believed that the right to marry, and have a wife and her labour at one's disposal, was a bequest of emancipation. But many freedwomen thought differently, and their distinct version of emancipation resonated with the helpers and teachers from the North who circulated among them. They believed, powerfully, that freedom meant that now they owned themselves and their own bodies. 'I am my own woman and I will do as I please', a Georgia woman declared in a divorce petition in 1876. The Northern women, too, who had been exposed to quite a few years of debate on the marriage question, were compelled by arguments that endowed the female self – including the physical self – with utter integrity, an inviolable protection from mastery of any sort – especially in marriage. So, while Elizabeth Stanton criss-crossed the North speaking on marriage reform to circles of white women, the African American Frances Harper travelled the South in the same years talking about some of the same things to the freedwomen.

Stanley is fastidious in showing that the intellectual encounter between bookish Northern ladies, raised on a diet of intense political reading and debating, and illiterate Southern fieldworkers was reciprocal. Freedwomen were not blank tablets for the Northerners' ideas, but they may well have grown more confident with those ideas in their contacts with women's rights activists, especially those of their own race. And as for the Northerners, the experience of seeing the abstraction 'freedom' settle into the bones of women as an adamantine bodily autonomy gave depth and urgency to their own understanding of Woman, and the self-entitlement the figure could entail, their own included.

This cross-racial strain was recessive, Amy Stanley insists. Exchanges between the freedwomen and the (mostly white) woman's rights movement were quiet – one could say even subliminal, simmering in the political consciousness of women's rights. Ideas born in the refugee camps did not enter the manifest content of thought about women – nor did the subjectivity of the impoverished black originators register in the consciousness of those who wrote most prolifically about women. Still, Stanley's perspective alerts us to what may be gained by eschewing rigid notions of exclusive camps of identity. A particularly rich nineteenth-century female sympathy, with all the flaws of projection that sympathy can involve, created a political space for the freedwomen and an intellectual reserve for the Northerners.

Against Stanley's work on the immediate post-war period, we can place Evelyn Brooks Higginbotham's study of cross-racial missionary efforts from 1880 to 1920. In *Righteous Discontent,* Higginbotham examines the records of women's organisations in the black Baptist church, the leading denomination for Southern Afro-Americans.[9] Northern white female supporters, she finds, created opportunities for black women that were closed off elsewhere, by sending money to Southern churchwomen, reading their missives from the field, and sponsoring their visits to the North. Missionary efforts in the nineteenth century, no less than the early modern Catholic missions which Natalie Davis studied, have not won good press in historical scholarship. Higginbotham, however, re-evaluates their political effects in a society where racial segregation was hardening. 'Women's missions created structured avenues along which black and white women travelled together, heard each other's voices, and learned of each other's struggles and values.'

White women went South to preach, moralise and judge, but black women went North, too (note again the mobility that enlisting in the troops of Woman could bring), to face racial slights, yes, but also to find, at times, appreciative, praiseful contemporaries, eager audiences, and much-needed money. Taking care to note the mixed motives of the white women, who were never free of racial condescension, Brooks-Higginbotham still argues that they created in tandem with black churchwomen an important space of agency and perhaps even resistance. At a time when Social Darwinism ran rife, the women's shared work defied reigning assumptions about the preternatural lowness of the Negro race. Constituting a single-sex bloc of support, the white women aided their black contemporaries in articulating distinct goals of their own, over and beyond those of African-American men.

The period Higginbotham studies is judged the nadir of race relations in the US and she never forgets the ironclad existence of the Jim Crow system of racial segregation. Yet, without soft pedalling the racism of white women's politics, she locates historical ground where an extravagant (or even tentative) sense of likeness allowed seeds of change to be planted and grow.

Glenda Gilmore's *Gender and Jim Crow* also covers this period, judged to be the nadir of US race relations.[10] Gilmore finds temperance, that most conservative of women's movements, to be a point of racial mixing, one of the few interracial movements in the country, in fact. Although temperance was in tune with conventional ideas of middle-class white women's superior morality and the degraded morals of the poor (white and black), still, middle-class black women pushed their way into white women's crusade against drink. Their success challenged and undercut racial codes, since Southern society provided only one template for an interracial relationship between women: the white female employer and her black maid. Temperance work, its Victorian ideas notwithstanding, provided a narrow path into some kind of modern relationship between black and white women. Black women who worked in the Women's Christian Temperance Union saw, for the first time, a chance to create a community of Christian women who might look past skin colour to acknowledge a common humanity, a model of interracial cooperation that might expand and encourage shared labours in the future.

None of these historians are sentimentalists. The conversations and meetings they sketch are no sweet domain of sisterhood. The temperance movement, for example, involved black women in the same regimen of slights, insults, and prejudice that black men faced in the Republican Party in the South. While black women saw themselves, in the universalising mode, as mothers joined with other mothers to make the world better for their families, white women saw them as their younger sisters, to be instructed and helped. Like much interracial work that followed, the proceedings depended upon black women's equanimity and patience in the face of the condescension and the smug theatrics of race tolerance the white women dished out.

Woman in the nineteenth century was not a monolith, she was a shape-shifter. She took on different attributes and appearances – that was her charm and power – in order to contain and stabilise identifications, especially as the woman's movement grew larger and more politically hetero-geneous. The changes are complicated, but, loosely, one can identify two competing points of attachment and likeness, Woman as Mother and Woman as Daughter.

The interracial politics examined by Gilmore and Higginbotham, like the rest of the women's movement in the late nineteenth century, was a feminism of the mothers. It leaned towards responsibility and propriety, accepted the constraints of custom, acknowledged the compensations of traditional families, wanted to make men more accountable to their wives and children: in sum, it was a politics that sought to augment women's power within existing patriarchal structures. The Woman who is the point of identification is older, aware of her vulnerabilities and those of the people she loves; she knows the value of accommodation and compromise and the difficulties of holding onto power once you get it. This could be said of both Afro-American and white women and, indeed, suggests one reason for their temperamental affinities despite the social forces that separated them.

But by 1900 a feminism of the daughters was gathering force, and with it a sense of likeness that was as prolific as that of the 1850s, but with a modern gloss. Distinct from the network of late-Victorian and matronly activists was an inchoate milieu of young New Women who defined themselves by the modernist term 'feminism'. Imported from France, the word denoted youth, psychology, sex, financial independence, self. The feminism of the daughters tended towards contempt for the way things are, was utopian in the way things could be, flamboyant, defiant, and insistent on claiming the privileges of men: intent on a bold imagination of equality, springing women loose to act in the world. For its adherents, Woman had the world before her; she was energetic, contemptuous of obstacles, willing to forego the protections of husbands and fathers. Power was there for the bold and energetic to take. This was the politics of a second generation of New Women, and it activated a busy traffic, not across race lines but certainly across class divisions and national boundaries. New Women in the United States battened off their contemporaries in Britain; variants crop up in the Continental cities – Munich, Berlin, Prague, Budapest. We still need to understand the exchanges across these lines and to see how far afield they ranged: what were the specific connections between agitation for women's rights in China, for example, and in Turkey? Iran? But in the British-American case, both gender and class hierarchies buckled under the to-ings and fro-ings of New Women – independent-minded and often marriage-spurning daughters with an extravagant sense of identification with other young women in the same situation. They were in settlement houses and the professions, but they were also in the trade unions.[11]

Ellen DuBois's political biography of Harriot Stanton Blatch shows how a young woman who had inherited the universalising impulse (she was Elizabeth Stanton's daughter) renovated it for twentieth-century uses. Returning to New York City in 1902 after a productive decade in England spent in Fabian activism and suffrage work, Blatch found the suffrage movement virtually moribund, a cause for true believers with little chance of real success. In short order she tapped into a milieu of self-employed, politically ingenuous but interested working women and reinvigorated the suffrage scene in the city. Blatch's Equality League, a small but influential group, brought together some of New York's most brilliant young professionals with gifted workingwomen and labour organisers from the trades. The focus was on the bonds that connected employed women across the class lines: a faith in paid work as emancipation from marital dependence and a necessary basis for sex equality. Early twentieth-century feminists held up a spirited, youthful workingwoman as exemplar of emancipation,

the spirited rebel girl of the picket lines to be admired, emulated and supported. The tincture of youthful hope, the emphasis on a destiny outside of
marriage, and the scornful rejection of conventional womanhood all figured
in the defining stance of militant suffrage as that of rebellious daughters, a
stance which affected not only the career decisions of college-educated
women but the picket line strategies of striking garment workers.

By the early teens, suffragism can be judged one of the largest and most
varied democratic movements in the country's history, encompassing a cast
of characters that stretched far beyond the stalwarts of the nineteenth
century. A lavish sense of likeness combined intellectual force with social
eclecticism. Recruits from the socialists, the trade unions, Afro-American
groups, and the immigrant left worked for the vote. Disgruntled high society
ladies mixed with feisty working women: New Women all. The militant
movement which again surged out of New York City took women's rights
into the era of modern electoral politics. Late-Victorian ladies had kept
politics safely indoors, where they protected themselves from exposure to
the smearing public eye. These women took their campaign outdoors in
marvellous grand outdoor parades (participants all dressed in white march-
ing down Fifth Avenue) and coast-to-coast all-female automobile entou-
rages. They tapped the enlivening properties of commercial culture with
suffrage hats, suffrage postcards, suffrage dances, even suffrage movies at a
moment when the nascent film industry was interested in reform dramas.

Glenda Gilmore provides one more enchanting piece to this immensely
appealing moment, a piece that has been truly 'hidden from history'. The
conventional wisdom has been that the suffrage movement was so racist
that the vote was finally won only when the white women in control of the
national organisation drove black suffragists out of suffrage work and thus
secured the support of the Southern states. The judgement is in line with a
profoundly cynical view of the woman's rights tradition and implicitly
involves a dark assessment of black women's powerlessness.[12] Gilmore, to
the contrary, finds that the Nineteenth Amendment actually did open the
door to black women, just like racist opponents said it would. This was not
because white women defended the right of black women to vote (in fact
they were blinded to the effects of Jim Crow on suffrage); it was because
the same middle-class black women, who had been sharpening their political skills in seemingly innocuous uplift work like temperance, used the
Nineteenth Amendment to put African Americans back in the act on
Southern election days. Afro-American women showed up in droves at the
same polls where black men had been systematically excluded and ter-
rorised for over twenty years. When they were turned away, they pressured
the government to intervene. The rudiments of a civil rights movement were
there, put in place by women who identified, stalwartly, with other newly
enfranchised women.

Women as a social group is an inevitably viscous, messy category to use
in doing history. There are no neat boundaries, no group loyalties to be

depended upon in the long run, no hard and fast allegiances. Over here, its members, supposedly adhering to each other, go sliding off into confounding family involvements; over there, they turn against each other because of national enmities; there again, some women squeeze the lives and the labour out of others. They line up with their children rather than each other, they stand by their sons and turn against their daughters. The simple narrative line of sex solidarity, we all know, is only a fiction.

But this is not to say that fictions don't have power in the world. And woman in the nineteenth century was a redolent, even a magnificent fiction. It was an image that carved out a space for mixing, in the interstices of racial conflict, family obligations, and class exploitation, not to mention patriarchal structures – in which women could think and literally move in ways otherwise closed to them. Rather than blocking off or repressing social differences, its universalising tendencies could provoke the consideration of difference and the incorporation of new ideas. It was also a fount of mobility – the identification as Woman pushing women into paths of collaboration, achievement, education, and political activism otherwise denied them. If, as the psychoanalytic theorists tell us, identity is formed from multiform projections and appropriations, then the extravagant sense of likeness of woman in the nineteenth century certainly expanded the repertoire from which women formed their sense of self and other. The pity is that in our present moment, the feminist sense of likeness, far from being extravagant, is so parsed and peaked.

Notes

1. Natalie Zemon Davis, *Woman on the Margins: Three Seventeenth-Century Lives* (Harvard University Press, Cambridge, MA, 1995).

2. The 'Declaration' is reprinted in *Feminism: the Essential Historical Writings*, ed. Miriam Schneir (Random House, New York, 1972), pp. 76–82.

3. See the reproduction in Phillip Lapsansky, 'Graphic Discord: Abolitionist and Antiabolitionist Images', in *The Abolitionist Sisterhood: Women's Political Culture in Antebellum America*, ed. Jean Fagan Yellin and John C. Van Horne (Cornell University Press, Ithaca, 1994), p. 208.

4. Elizabeth Clark, '"The Sacred Rights of the Weak": Pain, Sympathy, and the Culture of Individual Rights in Antebellum America', *Journal of American History*, 82 (1995), pp. 463–93.

5. See Nell Irvin Painter, *Sojourner Truth: A Life, a Symbol* (W. W. Norton, New York, 1996).

6. Stanton to Martha Wright, 12 July 1860, reprinted in *The Selected Papers of Elizabeth Cady Stanton and Susan B. Anthony*, ed. Ann D. Gordon (Rutgers University Press, New Brunswick, 1997), p. 436.

7. Stephen Foster, a supporter, in an 1866 debate in the American Anti-Slavery Society, speech reprinted in *Selected Papers of Elizabeth Cady Stanton and Susan B. Anthony*, pp. 581–2.

8. Amy Dru Stanley, *From Bondage to Contract: Wage Labor, Marriage, and the Market in the Age of Slave Emancipation* (Cambridge University Press, New York, 1998).

9. Evelyn Brooks Higginbotham, *Righteous Discontent: The Women's Movement in the Black Baptist Church, 1880–1920* (Harvard University Press, Cambridge, MA, 1993).

10. Glenda Elizabeth Gilmore, *Gender and Jim Crow: Women and the Politics of White Supremacy in North Carolina, 1896–1920* (University of North Carolina Press, Chapel Hill and London, 1996).

11. Ellen Carol DuBois, *Harriot Stanton Blatch and the Winning of Woman Suffrage* (Yale University Press, New Haven, 1997); Nancy F. Cott, *The Grounding of Modern Feminism* (Yale University Press, New Haven, 1987); Christine Stansell, *American Moderns: New York Bohemia and the Creation of a New Century* (Metropolitan/Holt, New York, 2000).

12. Aileen S. Kraditor, *The Ideas of the Woman Suffrage Movement, 1890–1920* (Columbia University Press, New York, 1965).

2

Silences Broken, Silences Kept: Gender and Sexuality in African-American History

Michele Mitchell

'Even today,' Evelyn Brooks Higginbotham lamented in 1989, 'the black woman's voice goes largely unheard … Afro-American history has failed to address gender issues adequately, while women's history has similarly failed to address questions of race'. African-American women's history was neither compensatory measure nor quaint sub-field according to Higginbotham. Rather, the inclusion of black women in historical analysis facilitated sophisticated theorising on the nexus of gender, power, and oppression; the acknowledgement that gender could not be separated out from race would, Higginbotham maintained, enable historians of US women to break away from what she termed a 'white, middle-class … northeastern bias'. And, as more literature on black women was written, Higginbotham contended, it would become manifestly evident that gender history method-ologies had something dynamic to offer African-American history as well.[1]

When Higginbotham's 'Beyond the Sound of Silence' appeared in the inaugural issue of *Gender & History*, African-American women's history was well on its way to becoming an established field. Deborah Gray White had recently transformed the study of slavery by investigating women's net-works and life cycles along with gendered divisions of labour and domestic relationships. Jacqueline Jones had already produced her magisterial survey of black women's labour and experience while Dolores Janiewski had powerfully analysed class, gender, and race in her study of black women tobacco workers.[2] Pioneering work by Rosalyn Terborg-Penn, Sharon Harley, Andrea Benton Rushing, Paula Giddings, and Dorothy Sterling laid foun-dations for the field by providing analytical frameworks, methodologies, and source materials; landmark essays by Hazel Carby, Elsa Barkley Brown, and Darlene Clark Hine had either appeared or were in the offing.[3] Still, all was not well. What Higginbotham found so unsettling – indeed, vexing – was that African-American women remained marginal to interpretations of US history: US women's historians and African Americanists might have paid black women cursory attention, but other Americanists virtually ignored them. Higginbotham concluded that such oversights impoverished histori-ography, compromised the potential of gender analysis to uncover the

complexities of women's lives, and frustrated attempts to 'explain the contradictory relationship of women and blacks to the American experience'.[4]
Silence, in other words, had its consequences.

Happily, the discomfiting hush surrounding race and gender that
Higginbotham identified has become a full-throated shout a mere decade
later: women are no longer considered auxiliary or irrelevant to the African-
American past. Gender analysis has recast the ways we think about slavery,
the era of Reconstruction, protest, and social movements; it has transformed
our assumptions about political involvement, lynching, migration, urbanisation, and labour. Sexuality, in its own right, has emerged as a critical site
of inquiry.[5] Not only have many African Americanists and Americanists
heeded the call to consider race and gender as integral to the writing of
history, the very attention to gender Higginbotham and others longed for has
led some scholars to explore manhood and masculinity.[6] If, over the past
ten years, gender historians have produced some of the most important
monographs in US history, the same can certainly be said of African-
American history. 'Vibrant' hardly begins to characterise the field – books
keep coming, articles appear with regularity, the production of dissertations
proceeds apace.

However, in 1999, are there other causes for alarm, other reasons to
lament? Whereas it would be useful and perhaps revealing to ask whether
Americanists have met Higginbotham's challenge to analyse race and
gender in tandem, it is more important to ponder whether African Americanists who theorise gender and sexuality have fomented new silences.
Although I am not worried that the push to think of race and gender as
interlocked has resulted in conflation of categories, much in African-
American history remains unsaid or barely articulated. I am, then, somewhat bothered by lurking suspicions that certain subjects are avoided
because they have been deemed either dangerous or damaging. If on
occasion we censor ourselves out of understandable desires not to fuel
racist canards pertaining to alleged black pathologies, I am nonetheless
uneasy about the costs attached to this particular quiet.

Scholars broached difficult topics such as rape, domestic violence, and
sexism before and since Higginbotham's article was published. Still, which
subjects have been largely avoided? Have those of us who work on African-
American history unwittingly limited the interpretative, analytic power of
gender by steering clear of the explosive? Gender analysis has effectively
complicated notions that there ever was a 'monolithic black community',
but have we used it rigorously enough to uncover ways in which black
communities – not to mention households, organisations, and movements
– were fraught with tensions? On a slightly different point, what phenomena
have influential, much-used concepts obscured? To borrow from Elsa Barkley
Brown, just 'what *has* happened here'?[7]

Though Higginbotham would soon publish another critical essay on the
writing of US history after 'Beyond the Sound of Silence', perhaps an earlier

essay was instrumental in starting a veritable revolution within African-Americanist circles.[8] James Horton's breakthrough article on gender conventions among free blacks during the antebellum era was published in 1986 and accomplished something not even Higginbotham called for: it deftly considered both manhood and womanhood as it uncovered how antebellum Afro-American journals typically 'preached the gospel of continued gender oppression even as they supported the struggle for racial freedom'.[9] Horton illuminated how race was inseparable from gender by demonstrating that bondage had a profound effect on black gender roles, that free people's decisions to follow conventions of the larger society were at once liberating and limiting. Not only was he sensitive to power dynamics between African-American men and women, Horton came to incisive conclusions about how the longing of black men to seize the prerogatives of manhood denied them by the larger society could and did stultify black women's own desires. Overall, 'Freedom's Yoke' was a notable departure in the existing literature since most African Americanists at the time focused primarily upon women as did other scholars whose labours established gender history.

Horton's work offered an outstanding analysis that would influence other initial essays in African-Americanist gender history, including Sharon Harley's important article on work and domestic roles in black communities.[10] The deployment of feminist theory evident in Horton would, as the field developed, repeatedly confound notions that there ever was a time when gender politics did not affect black communities or when the interests of black men and women were always in harmony. 'Difference', then, was not only a meaningful concept for women's studies, feminist theory, and US history but could say much about intra-racial dynamics.[11]

Four years after 'Freedom's Yoke' appeared in print, E. Frances White pushed the analysis of gender politics further. With empathetic yet unflinching aplomb, White assessed ways in which African-American nationalist discourse contained sexist and homophobic elements. Black nationalism was a powerful oppositional discourse, but, as White warned, it could also be profoundly conservative when it came to gendered expectations about how members of the collective should interact or with whom they should make love.[12] 'Africa on My Mind' was more than a much-needed history of the fallout between feminists and nationalists during the 1970s: White produced a discursive study that dramatised the impact of ideas on people's daily lives. As Hazel Carby, Barbara Bair, and Elsa Barkley Brown would accomplish in short order, White revealed deep, competing interests between men and women – indeed, between women.[13] And, as Bair's work did two years later, White revealed why ideologies 'against which many … white feminists revolted' could be appealing for some black women.[14]

White's treatment of twentieth-century black nationalist discourse and its complicated deployment of ideas regarding gender and sexuality would

soon be followed by two assessments of racialised gender ideologies a
century earlier. In one of the first extended gender analyses focused upon
black men, Jim Cullen convincingly portrayed the Civil War as a 'water-
shed for black manhood' that altered gender conventions in African-
American communities so that 'they more closely resembled those of
whites'. He traced the usage of muscular rhetoric among African-American
men as he vivified reasons why cultural acknowledgement of black manliness was so important to ex-slaves and freedmen alike. Cullen said little
about the domestic conflict that probably occurred when soldiers returned
from war determined to assert their new-found sense of authority at home,
but 'I's a Man Now' did suggest that the postbellum reorientation of gender
dynamics among black Americans was both marked and profound.
Significantly, Cullen cited Gail Bederman whose work on race, manliness,
and notions of civilisation would yield a major article on the 1892–4 antilynching campaign of Ida B. Wells. Wells was arguably the most effective
crusader against the murderous racial terrorism of her day; she knew how
to seize upon 'the Northern middle class's widespread fears about declining male power' in order to 'convinc[e] nervous whites that lynching
imperiled American manhood'. In print and on the podium, Wells pro-
claimed that black men embodied manhood, that the progress made by
African Americans in less than thirty years of freedom epitomised civilisation. By focusing upon Wells's skilful manipulation of gender and race,
Bederman constructed a breathtaking narrative of how members of an
oppressed people transform dominant discourses into counter-discourses.
Bederman's close attention to the historical context surrounding a notor-
ious system of oppression further enabled her to capture how competing
racialised and classed notions of gender operate simultaneously.[15]

Just as Horton's efforts helped introduce a vital methodology to African-
American history, White offered one of the most striking statements to date,
and gender analysis was pushed in new directions by Cullen and Bederman,
two concepts introduced by Darlene Hine and Evelyn Higginbotham
assisted the maturation of African-Americanist gender history and dominated the field. The notion that African-American women developed a code
of silence around intimate matters as a response to discursive and literal
attacks on black sexuality has influenced studies of turn-of-the-century club
women, reformers, and workers ever since Darlene Clark Hine labelled this
practice the 'culture of dissemblance' in 1989.[16] Hine argued that, after
slavery, routine sexual assault and pervasive stereotypes about black female
sexuality prompted women of African descent to shroud sensual aspects of
their persons from public view. If popular notions about lewd, lascivious
'negroes' justified ritualised rape then black women assumed some control
over a noxious situation by protecting their 'inner lives and selves' through
a selective revelation of the personal that 'created the appearance of …
disclosure'.[17] This strategy not only made employment in white households
tolerable for domestic workers who faced on-the-job harassment, it shaped

most daily interactions and informed the flurry of institution building by activist women.

As a concept deployed by historians of gender and sexuality, the 'culture of dissemblance' has been inordinately useful in explaining the motives of women who migrated out of southern states in order to find various forms of social autonomy. Dissemblance has helped us understand why a signifi-cant cohort of black women who were, in many respects, 'New Women', did not indulge in late nineteenth- and early twentieth-century social emancipations to the same extent as their white peers. It has enriched our understanding of class in African-American communities in that dissem-blance underscores how sexual comportment was integral to the class identities of aspiring-class and elite people. The reality that many black women found it useful to dissemble has provided critical clues about how aspiring-class and elite parents reared their daughters. Moreover, we are now better able to assess how black women and men have consistently engaged practices of dissemblance in order to 'survive in a racialized world not of their own making'.[18]

Embracing the concept of dissemblance even helped Evelyn Higginbotham interpret how black women guarded their sexuality as part of a 'politics of respectability'.[19] Although scholars such as Willard Gatewood, Wilson Jeremiah Moses, and E. Frances White had already written on the signifi-cance of controlled morality to the black elite and to nationalists, it was Higginbotham who provided analytical language that would guide future work.[20] Higginbotham elaborated upon existing literature in that she limned salient connections between desires of post-emancipation African Americans – particularly those in the aspiring and elite classes – to appear 'respectable' and attempts by women activists to bring about collective improvement. Building upon a wealth of existing work on intra-racial reform, Higginbotham's *Righteous Discontent* was part of an ongoing mission to demonstrate how central women and gender were to understanding key aspects of the decades following emancipation.[21]

Beyond matters of sexual behaviour, comportment, dress, and leisure, a sizeable cohort of African Americans during the late nineteenth and early twentieth centuries expected members of the race to maintain upright appearances in households, family matters, seats of learning, and work-places. Higginbotham's analysis of this phenomenon echoed E. Frances White's observation that intra-racial politics could be simultaneously emancipatory and oppressive: if notions about respectability were a politi-cised insistence 'upon [the race's] conformity to the dominant society's norms of manners and morals' and if black women could use this form of personal politics as a 'powerful weapon of resistance to race and gender subordination', those same notions also led reformers to behave in prob-lematic ways towards the working poor on occasion.[22] Certainly, some workers, sharecroppers, and recent migrants to cities welcomed activists' attempts to facilitate racial uplift; other workers, sharecroppers, and migrants, however, undoubtedly felt more like targets and less like agents of reform initiatives.

Historians such as Hazel Carby and Christina Simmons came to similar conclusions about class, sexuality, and African-American reform activism within a year of *Righteous Discontent's* publication.[23] Even scholars who came to different conclusions dealt with the politics of respectability either implicitly or explicitly. In her study of household labourers, Tera Hunter offered compelling evidence that in leisure settings black domestics were not concerned with hiding their sexuality or acting genteel. Victoria Wolcott, on the other hand, demonstrated that respectability held a certain currency for working-class elders concerned about the chastity of daughters, nieces, and granddaughters; she also stressed that meanings and practices of respectability were not the same for all women.[24]

'Respectability', then, resonated with the concentration of scholars working on the late nineteenth and early twentieth centuries. Conceptually, the politics of respectability was not only part of a historiographical turn towards class and intra-racial dynamics, it coincided with greater numbers of African Americanists doing work on the history of sexuality. Historians produced work touching upon or exploring black sexuality before publication of *Righteous Discontent* – Nell Painter examined 'miscegenation, labor, and power' while Eric Garber's article on the Harlem Renaissance was an early foray into African-American gay and lesbian history[25] – but it was not until the early and mid 1990s that scholars started to write on black sexuality in earnest. Arguably, *Righteous Discontent* and essays such as Simmons's 'African Americans and Sexual Victorianism' enabled this shift as did the 1988 publication of D'Emilio and Freedman's *Intimate Matters* and the pointed response it evoked from literary scholar Ann du Cille.[26]

More specifically, African-Americanist work on the history of sexuality has developed rapidly since du Cille charged D'Emilio and Freedman with giving people of colour short shrift in their landmark study of sexuality in the US. Between 1993 and 1997 alone, historians published articles regarding slave children and sexual identity, an erotic relationship between two free women, and white Southerners' anxieties about black male sexuality during Reconstruction. Analyses of inter-racial couplings have emerged as well. For example, Kevin Mumford's monograph on early twentieth-century urban 'interzones' describes how a range of Americans crossed the colour line in search of sundry carnal pleasures as it reveals how black city dwellers broke with convention and flaunted behaviours that social purity reformers considered degenerate.[27] Not only is Mumford's work provocative, he is part of a new cohort of scholars who are furthering our understanding of how time and place shape individual and collective reactions to sexual 'race-mixing'. Given that the US has been a nation obsessed with racial boundaries throughout much if not most of its existence, their contributions to the field are both welcome and needed.[28] Work on other aspects of African Americans' sexuality also have something to offer US historiography, including a forthcoming dissertation on the sexual terrorism enacted upon black women after the Civil War and another on African-American sex workers in the early decades of the twentieth century. Additionally, recent dissertations explore enslaved women's reproductive labour during the seventeenth and eighteenth centuries, discuss African Americans' concepts about racial reproduction during the Progressive Era, and analyse gendered struggle within the Black Panther Party. These dissertations should broaden our knowledge about mob violence and prostitution and expand what we know about slavery, popular eugenics, and sexual dynamics within political movements.[29]

Over the past decade, African Americanist gender history has consistently noted how specific phenomena – subjugation, racist discourse, attempts to realise collective improvement, initiatives for community mobilisation, longings for self-determination, desires to break free from social strictures – spurred black women and men to seize or alter mainstream gender conventions. Attention to gender and sexuality has added considerable nuance to how we analyse the convergence and divergence of African Americans' experiences with and from the experiences of other ethnic groups in the US. We better appreciate the remarkable variety of African Americans' lives and communities over the course of US history because of questions asked by gender scholars.

In terms of what African-Americanist scholarship can yet accomplish, Elsa Barkley Brown made an observation in 1995 that bears repetition now: she has heard few 'people question the notion that lynching … is a masculine experience'. Brown's remark sounds a tocsin as it reminds us that assumptions perpetuate silences. If African Americanists have done little work on the lynching of black women, scholars in the field have also neglected to ask whether decreases in post-emancipation birth rates were in any way connected to changes in males' sexual practices. Much can still be gained, then, by interrogating our own assumptions and conclusions.[30]

This is not to suggest that no one is engaged in the work of reconceptualisation. For example, scholars who consider African Americans alongside other people from non-majority US populations or within the Black Atlantic world are currently reorienting the field. As this trend continues, perhaps historians shall start writing about black men in conjunction with other men of colour; hopefully, this will occur since studies of black men, manhood, and masculinity are few in number. Moreover, what can we discover about social reform by juxtaposing sex reform efforts among African Americans to those among Native Americans? What can be revealed about leisure, urbanisation, and sexual self-presentation if black Americans are discussed together with Afro-Cubans? What can we find out about processes of oppression by analysing gendered forms of violence towards Mexican Americans, Asian Americans, and African Americans in tandem? What more can we reveal about gender, sexuality, and social movements by doing comparative work on African Americans and Afro-Brazilians? These groupings are random but nonetheless suggest the range of work that is possible. The turn towards the Black Atlantic might, for example, lead African Americanists to write more histories of medicine and craft different narratives about gender and religion.

In addition, it remains crucial to consider how analytical frameworks can obscure as well as reveal. In terms of sexuality, concepts regarding dissemblance and respectability have facilitated much important work about reform, institution building, and their relationship to class formation; those same concepts have not, however, generated African-Americanist work on gay and lesbian history. Similarly, no two concepts can generate all the questions that need to be asked about intra-racial relationships, repro- ductive concerns, or the variety of ways sexuality informed, complicated, and enriched African Americans' lives. Since recent work on sexuality is pushing the field in new directions and because more African Americanists are engaged in comparative analyses, the conceptual landscape shall certainly expand over the next ten years.

During the next decade historians might break lingering silences as well. In addition to needing more histories that engage the spectrum of African Americans' sexual identities and more studies on children, further investi- gation into how, why, and when black women and men have been at odds is necessary. In particular, we need to know more about conflicts that occur outside of organised protest. African Americanists have consistently acknow- ledged hierarchies; scholars have made pathbreaking contributions by examining conflicts between women, between men. Still, writing about clashes between black women and men remains somewhat prickly because themes of collective survival, community mobilisation, and institution building are of signal importance to the field. Moreover, examining gen- dered strife is potentially explosive since African Americans are still hounded by notions that gender, domestic, and sexual relationships between black women and men are warped, pathological. That acknowledged, staying quiet will hardly eradicate such notions – silence might actually enable them.

Just as African Americans are now analysing intra-racial class tensions with nuance – and are increasingly doing so with issues surrounding colour – there is little reason why research on intra-racial gender conflicts that occur beyond organisational life can not be conducted in similar fashion. If the eloquence of gender history is its very ability to elaborate upon both expressed and inchoate discourses of power, then why not explore conflict as a means of exploding the sway of racialised discourse? If gender analysis can say volumes about how power operates in quotidian life, then why should we avoid rigorous examination of the power dynamics between black women and men in households, on work-sites, in public spaces? Exploring conflict in all of its aspects might be uncomfortable for many historians working in the field, but certainly no more so than our being plagued by the haunting, redounding echo of an uneasy silence.

Notes

1. Evelyn Brooks Higginbotham, 'Beyond the Sound of Silence: Afro-American Women in History', *Gender & History*, 1 (1989), pp. 50–67, esp. pp. 50, 52, 60.

2. Deborah Gray White, *Ar'n't I A Woman?: Female Slaves in the Plantation South* (W. W. Norton & Company, New York, 1985); Jacqueline Jones, *Labor of Love, Labor of Sorrow: Black Women, Work, and the Family from Slavery to the Present* (Basic Books, Inc., New York, 1985); Dolores Janiewski, *Sisterhood Denied: Race, Gender, and Class in a New South Community* (Temple University Press, Philadelphia, 1986).

3. Rosalyn Terborg-Penn, 'Discontented Black Feminists: Prelude and Postscript to the Passage of the Nineteenth Amendment', in *Decades of Discontent: The Women's Movement*, ed. Lois Sharf and Joan M. Jensen (Greenwood Press, Westport, CT, 1983); Rosalyn Terborg-Penn, Sharon Harley, and Andrea Benton Rushing (eds), *Women in Africa and the African Diaspora* (Howard University Press, Washington, DC, 1987); Paula Giddings, *When and Where I Enter: The Impact of Black Women on Race and Sex in America* (Morrow, New York, 1984); Dorothy Sterling, *We Are Your Sisters: Black Women in the Nineteenth Century* (W. W. Norton & Company, New York, 1984); Hazel V. Carby, '"On the Threshold of Woman's Era": Lynching, Empire, and Sexuality in Black Feminist Theory', *Critical Inquiry*, 12 (1985), pp. 262–77; Hazel V. Carby, '"It Jus Be's Dat Way Sometime": The Sexual Politics of Women's Blues', *Radical America*, 20 (1986), pp. 9–22; Elsa Barkley Brown, 'Womanist Consciousness: Maggie Lena Walker and the Independent Order of Saint Luke', *Signs*, 14 (1989), pp. 610–33; Darlene Clark Hine, 'Rape and the Inner Lives of Black Women in the Middle West: Preliminary Thoughts on the Culture of Dissemblance', *Signs*, 14 (1989), pp. 912–20.

4. Higginbotham, 'Beyond the Sound of Silence', p. 63.

5. Kathleen M. Brown, *Good Wives, Nasty Wenches, and Anxious Patriarchs: Gender, Race, and Power in Colonial Virginia* (University of North Carolina Press, Chapel Hill, 1996); Susan Juster and Lisa MacFarlane (eds), *A Mighty Baptism: Race, Gender, and the Creation of American Protestantism* (Cornell University Press, Ithaca and London, 1996); Amy Dru Stanley, *From Bondage to Contract: Wage Labor, Marriage, and the Market in the Age of Slave Emancipation* (Cambridge University Press, Cambridge, 1998); Leslie A. Schwalm, *A Hard Fight for We: Women's Transition from Slavery to Freedom in South Carolina* (University of Illinois Press, Urbana, 1997); Laura F. Edwards, *Gendered Strife and Confusion: The Political Culture of Reconstruction* (University of Illinois Press, Urbana, 1997); Beryl Satter, 'Marcus Garvey, Father Divine, and the Gender Politics of Race Difference and Race Neutrality', *American Quarterly*, 48 (1996), pp. 43–76; Susan L. Smith, *Sick and Tired of Being Sick and Tired: Black Women's Health Activism in America, 1890–1950* (University of Pennsylvania Press, Philadelphia, 1995); Glenda Elizabeth Gilmore, *Gender & Jim Crow: Women and the Politics of White Supremacy in North Carolina, 1896–1920* (University of North Carolina Press, Chapel Hill, 1996); Gail Bederman, *Manliness and Civilization: A Cultural History of Gender and Race in the United States, 1880–1917* (University of Chicago Press, Chicago and London, 1995); Elsa Barkley Brown, 'Imaging Lynching: African American Women, Communities of Struggle, and Collective Memory', in *African American Women Speak Out on Anita Hill-Clarence Thomas*, ed. Geneva Smitherman (Wayne State University Press, Detroit, 1995), pp. 100–124; Darlene Clark Hine, 'Black Migration to the Urban Midwest: The Gender Dimension, 1915–1945', in *The Great Migration in Historical Perspective: New Dimensions of Race, Class, & Gender* (Indiana University Press, Bloomington, 1991), pp. 127–46; Gretchen Lemke-Santangelo, *Abiding Courage: African American Migrant Women and*

the East Bay Community (University of North Carolina Press, Chapel Hill, 1996); Tera W. Hunter, *To 'Joy My Freedom: Southern Black Women's Lives and Labors after the Civil War* (Harvard University Press, Cambridge and London, 1997); Elizabeth Lapovsky Kennedy and Madeline D. Davis, *Boots of Leather, Slippers of Gold: The History of a Lesbian Community* (Routledge, New York, 1993); Martha Hodes, *White Women, Black Men: Illicit Sex in the Nineteenth Century South* (Yale University Press, New Haven and London, 1997).

See also Martin Anthony Summers, 'Nationalism, Race Consciousness, and the Constructions of Black Middle Class Masculinity During the New Negro Era, 1915–1930' (PhD diss., Rutgers University, 1997); Premilla Nadasen, 'The Welfare Rights Movement in the United States, 1960–1975' (Columbia University, PhD diss., 1999); M. Elaine Roland, 'A Land Where You Can Be Free: Gender, Black Nationalism, and the All-Black Towns of Oklahoma' (PhD diss., University of Michigan, forthcoming).

As testimony to developments in US historiography, not all of the above works deal exclusively with African Americans.

6. See, for example, James Oliver Horton, *Free People of Color: Inside the African American Community* (Smithsonian Institution Press, Washington, DC, 1993); Harry Stecopoulos and Michael Uebel (eds), *Race and the Subject of Masculinities* (Duke University Press, Durham and London, 1997); and Darlene Clark Hine and Earnestine Jenkins (eds), *A Question of Manhood: A Reader in US Black Men's History and Masculinity* (Indiana University Press, Bloomington, 1999).

7. Higginbotham, 'Beyond the Sound of Silence', p. 63; Elsa Barkley Brown, '"What Has Happened Here": The Politics of Difference in Women's History and Feminist Politics', *Feminist Studies*, 18 (1992), pp. 295–312.

8. Evelyn Brooks Higginbotham, 'African-American Women's History and the Metalanguage of Race', *Signs*, 17 (1992), pp. 251–74.

9. James Oliver Horton, 'Freedom's Yoke: Gender Conventions Among Antebellum Free Blacks', *Feminist Studies*, 12 (1986), pp. 51–76, esp. p. 74. A contemporary analysis of African-American manhood is David Leverenz's discussion of Frederick Douglass in Leverenz, *Manhood and the American Renaissance* (Cornell University Press, Ithaca and London, 1989), pp. 108–34.

10. Sharon Harley, 'For the Good of Family and Race: Gender, Work, and Domestic Roles in the Black Community, 1880–1930', *Signs*, 15 (1990), pp. 336–49, esp. p. 337, n. 1.

11. Brown, '"What Has Happened Here"'; Higginbotham, 'African-American Women's History and the Metalanguage of Race'.

12. E. Frances White, 'Africa on My Mind: Gender, Counter Discourse and African-American Nationalism', *Journal of Women's History*, 2 (1990), pp. 73–97, esp. pp. 76–7, 93–4.

13. Hazel V. Carby, 'Policing the Black Woman's Body in an Urban Context', *Critical Inquiry*, 18 (1992), pp. 738–55; Barbara Bair, 'True Women, Real Men: Gender, Ideology, and Social Roles in the Garvey Movement', in *Gendered Domains: Rethinking Public and Private in Women's History*, ed. Dorothy O. Helly and Susan Reverby (Cornell University Press, Ithaca, 1992), pp. 154–66; Elsa Barkley Brown, 'Negotiating and Transforming the Public Sphere: African American Political Life in the Transition from Slavery to Freedom', *Public Culture*, 7 (1994), pp. 107–46.

14. Bair, 'True Women, Real Men', p. 156; White, 'Africa on My Mind', pp. 86–90.

15. Jim Cullen, '"I's a Man Now": Gender and African American Men', in *Divided Houses: Gender and the Civil War*, ed. Catherine Clinton and Nina Silber (Oxford University Press, New York, 1992), pp. 76–91, esp. pp. 77, 90; Gail Bederman,

'"Civilization," the Decline of Middle-Class Manliness, and Ida B. Wells's Antilynching Campaign (1892–94)', *Radical History Review*, 52 (1992), pp. 5–30, esp. pp. 5–6, 11–14, 22.

16. Hine, 'Rape and the Inner Lives of Black Women'.

17. Hine, 'Rape and the Inner Lives of Black Women', pp. 912, 915.

18. Hine, 'Rape and the Inner Lives of Black Women'; Christina Simmons, 'African Americans and Sexual Victorianism in the Social Hygiene Movement, 1910–1940', *Journal of the History of Sexuality*, 4 (1993), pp. 51–75; Deborah Gray White, *Too Heavy a Load: Black Women in Defense of Themselves, 1894–1994* (W. W. Norton & Company, New York and London, 1999), pp. 87–141, esp. 87–8, 124–30; Stephanie Shaw, *What a Woman Ought to Be and to Do: Black Professional Women Workers During the Jim Crow Era* (University of Chicago Press, Chicago and London, 1996), pp. 13–40, esp. pp. 23–4; Kevin K. Gaines, *Uplifting the Race: Black Leadership, Politics, and Culture in the Twentieth Century* (University of North Carolina Press, Chapel Hill, 1996), pp. 5–9, esp. p. 5.

Here, I use 'aspiring class' because I find 'middle class' to be a particularly unsatisfactory term to describe post-Reconstruction era African-Americans. 'Aspiring class' refers to folk – many were self-educated, had a normal school education, or attended college – who worked for a living and were able to save a portion of their earnings and perhaps acquire property. What distinguishes these African Americans from industrial age bourgeoisie is that the socio-economic standing of aspiring-class people was somewhat more tenuous: economic downturn or personal calamity was likely to move an aspiring-class person into poverty, not the working class.

19. Evelyn Brooks Higginbotham, *Righteous Discontent: The Women's Movement in the Black Baptist Church, 1880–1920* (Harvard University Press, Cambridge and London, 1993), pp. 185–229, esp. pp. 193–4.

20. Willard Gatewood, *Aristocrats of Color: The Black Elite, 1880–1920* (Indiana University Press, Bloomington, 1990), pp. 182–209; Wilson Jeremiah Moses, 'Sexual Anxieties of the Black Bourgeoisie in Victorian America: The Cultural Context of W. E. B. Du Bois' First Novel', *Western Journal of Black Studies*, 4 (1982), pp. 202–11; White, 'Africa on My Mind', pp. 76–7.

21. Cynthia Neverdon-Morton, *Afro-American Women of the South and the Advancement of the Race, 1895–1925* (University of Tennessee Press, Knoxville, 1989); Dorothy Salem, *To Better Our World: Black Women in Organized Reform, 1890–1920* (Carlson Publishing, Brooklyn, 1990); Beverly Guy-Sheftall, *Daughters of Sorrow: Attitudes Toward Black Women*, 1880–1920 (Carlson Publishing, Brooklyn, 1990).

22. Higginbotham, *Righteous Discontent*, pp. 187, 198–204, 227. For insightful commentary on uplift politics and its gendered components, see Gaines, *Uplifting the Race*.

23. Carby, 'Policing the Black Woman's Body'; Simmons, 'African Americans and Sexual Victorianism'.

24. Hunter, *To 'Joy My Freedom*, esp. pp. 168–86; Victoria W. Wolcott, '"Bible, Bath and Broom": Nannie Helen Burrough's National Training School and African-American Racial Uplift', *Journal of Women's History*, 9 (1997), pp. 88–110; Victoria W. Wolcott, 'Remaking Respectability: African-American Women and the Politics of Identity in Interwar Detroit' (University of Michigan, PhD diss., 1995). For yet another take on respectability, see Amy Jordan, 'Extending the Organizing Tradition: Welfare Rights and the Politics of Respectability' (University of Michigan, PhD diss., 1999).

25. Nell Irvin Painter, '"Social Equality," Miscegenation, Labor, and Power', in *The Evolution of Southern Culture*, ed. Numan V. Bartley (University of Georgia Press,

Athens, 1988), pp. 47–67; Eric Garber, 'A Spectacle in Color: The Lesbian and Gay Subculture of Jazz Age Harlem', in *Hidden From History: Reclaiming the Gay and Lesbian Past*, ed. Martin Bauml Duberman, Martha Vicinus and George Chauncey, Jr (New American Library, New York, 1989), pp. 318–31.

26. John D'Emilio and Estelle B. Freedman, *Intimate Matters: A History of Sexuality in America* (Harper & Row Publishers, New York, 1988); Ann du Cille, '"Othered" Matters: Reconceptualizing Dominance and Difference in the History of Sexuality in America', *Journal of the History of Sexuality*, 1 (1990), pp. 102–27.

27. Anthony S. Parent, Jr, and Susan Brown Wallace, 'Childhood and Sexual Identity under Slavery', *Journal of the History of Sexuality*, 3 (1993), pp. 363–401; Martha Hodes, 'The Sexualization of Reconstruction Politics: White Women and Black Men in the South after the Civil War', *Journal of the History of Sexuality*, 3 (1993), pp. 402–17; Kevin J. Mumford, *Interzones: Black/White Sex Districts in Chicago and New York in the Early Twentieth Century* (Columbia University Press, New York, 1997).

28. The following articles are representative of new work in the field: Graham Russell Hodges, 'The Pastor and the Prostitute: Sexual Power among African Americans and Germans in Colonial New York', in *Sex, Love, Race: Crossing Boundaries in North American History*, ed. Martha Hodes (New York University Press, New York, 1999); Leslie M. Harris, 'From Abolitionist Amalgamators to "Rulers of the Five Points": The Discourse of Interracial Sex and Reform in Antebellum New York City', *Sex, Love, Race*, pp. 191–212; Daniel R. Mandell, 'The Saga of Sarah Muckamugg: Indian and African American Intermarriage in Colonial New England', *Sex, Love, Race*, pp. 72–90; Jonathan Zimmerman, 'Crossing Oceans, Crossing Colors: Black Peace Corps Volunteers and Interracial Love in Africa, 1961–1971', *Sex, Love, Race*, pp. 514–30.

29. Hannah Rosen is writing a history of postbellum sexual violence (University of Chicago, PhD diss., forthcoming) while Cynthia Blair is writing on black women sex workers in Chicago (Harvard University, PhD diss., forthcoming). The recent dissertations referred to in the text are: Jennifer Lyle Morgan, 'Laboring Women: Enslaved Women, Reproduction, and Slavery in Barbados and South Carolina, 1650–1750' (Duke University, PhD diss., 1995); Michele Mitchell, 'Adjusting the Race: Gender, Sexuality, and the Question of African-American Destiny, 1877–1930' (Northwestern University, PhD diss., 1998); Tracye Ann Matthews, '"No One Ever Asks What a Man's Place in the Revolution Is": Gender and Sexual Politics in the Black Panther Party, 1966–1971' (University of Michigan, PhD diss., 1998).

See also Jennifer L. Morgan, '"Some Could Suckle over Their Shoulder": Male Travelers, Female Bodies, and the Gendering of Racial Ideology, 1500–1770', *William and Mary Quarterly*, 54 (1997), pp. 167–92; Hannah Rosen, '"Not That Sort of Women": Race, Gender, and Sexual Violence during the Memphis Riot of 1866', *Sex, Love, Race*, pp. 267–93.

30. Brown, 'Imaging Lynching', pp. 100–2.

For an example of the promise of such reconceptualisation, see Marilynn S. Johnson, 'Gender, Race, and Rumours: Re-examining the 1943 Race Riots', *Gender & History*, 10 (1998), pp. 252–77.

3

Giving Masculinity a History: Some Contributions from the Historiography of Colonial India

Mrinalini Sinha

Contemporary historiography, especially in North American, European and Australian history, now includes a fairly respectable body of literature on men and masculinity.[1] At its best, this scholarship has gone well beyond the limitations of 'sex-role theory', and the sex-role socialisation of men, to make important and valuable contributions to the recognition of gender as a 'useful category of historical analysis'.[2] Yet the new interest in 'masculinity' and the related development of 'men's studies' and the 'men's movement' has also produced a certain wariness within feminist scholarship, the latter being of course the main inspiration for the critical attention to gendered identities. After having pioneered the call to study constructions of masculinity as much as of femininity, however, many feminist scholars have now become more cautious in response to some trends within the new scholarship, sensing a potential evasion of the central feminist problematic: the gendered organisation of power.[3] It may still be necessary to be reminded of the question that R. W. Connell, whose own pioneering work on gender and masculinity consistently refuses such evasions, asks in connection with a recent collection of essays on masculinity: What, exactly, is involved in writing a history of masculinity?[4] I invoke this double legacy of the scholarship on men and masculinity to reflect on the potential contribution that the historiography of colonial India offers to the study of masculinity.

Until recently, the urgent task for women's history, as well as for gender studies and feminist scholarship more generally, was to make the history of women 'visible'.[5] It soon became apparent, however, that in many ways it is men who have no history. To be sure, almost the entire corpus of historical scholarship that does not specifically allude to 'women' is, and always has been, about the doings of men. Yet, in the sense that Michael Kimmel suggests, these have not been histories of men *as men*.[6] For, according to Kimmel, to write the histories of men as men would require at the least an examination of how the construction and experience of manhood has informed the course and meanings of the activities of men. It would

also require an examination of the ways in which the meanings of manhood and masculinity have differed across different groups and classes and
changed over the course of history, and a critical analysis of the ways in
which the pursuit of an always-elusive ideal of masculinity has animated
some of the central events of history. It is in this sense, then, that he argues
that men and masculinity were until recently barely visible in history.

The emergence of masculinity as a category of historical analysis, however, occupies a somewhat paradoxical position in the gendered mode of
analyses that have gained currency in the contemporary historiography of
colonial India. The scholarship on gender in colonial India has by and large
been about women.[7] Both social histories of gender relations in colonial
India and discursive analyses of the gendered constructions of colonialism
and nationalism have tended to focus on women. Yet this scholarship as a
whole – notwithstanding the variety of its theoretical and methodological
orientations – has also contributed to giving the history of masculinity in
colonial India a certain visibility.[8] On the one hand, therefore, there remains
a relative dearth of scholarship on men and masculinities in colonial India.
On the other hand, however, the existing scholarship on gender has served
to denaturalise the history of men and masculinities in significant ways.
This paradoxical situation, I want to suggest, is not a sign of weakness. Rather,
it holds enormous potential for developing adequately contextualised histories of masculinity in which masculinity itself is understood as constituted
by, as well as constitutive of, a wide set of social relations. Masculinity, seen
thus, traverses multiple axes of race, caste, class, sexuality, religion, and
ethnicity. Masculinity, that is to say, cannot be confined solely within its
supposedly 'proper' domain of male–female relations. The contribution of
the historiography of colonial India, then, is significant precisely as an
example of what would be involved in writing a history of masculinity.

There are several ways, indeed, in which the existing historiography of
colonial India provides fertile ground for further explorations of the history
of masculinity. At the most obvious level, the historiography of colonial
India forces a reconsideration of the seeming embodiments of what Ed
Cohen has referred to as the '"imaginary" mappings' of bodily difference
(i.e. 'masculinity' and 'femininity').[9] In other words, it makes considerations of power central to the assignment of qualitative attributes to bodily
signifiers of difference. The context for this problematising of gendered
categories comes of course from the peculiar investment of colonial power
in India in the cult of manliness and masculinity. Historians of Victorian
and Edwardian Britain have already charted the shifting 'cult of manliness'
in Britain and its particular articulation with British imperialism.[10] This has
meant that the impact of such bastions of male culture as the Victorian
public schools and the 'clubland' and of the ideals of Victorian manliness,
athleticism, and militarism, has featured centrally in studies of British or
Anglo-Indian society in India, especially in accounts of the colonial Indian
bureaucracy and the Indian Army.[11] On the Indian side, moreover, scholars

have explored an equivalent elite male culture among the rajas and maha-rajas of Princely India and in such institutions as Mayo College and Doon School, initially founded under colonial auspices for the socialisation of the sons of the Indian aristocracy in appropriate 'manly' behaviour.[12] Of greater significance, perhaps, have been studies of the ubiquity of the colonialist stereotype of 'effeminacy' and of the development after the revolt of 1857 of an elaborate colonialist ethnography of 'martial' and 'non-martial' races in India for the purposes of reorganising the recruitment of Indians to the Indian Army. The contrasts in imperialist thinking between the so-called 'manly' peoples of the Punjab and the North-West Frontier Provinces and the 'effeminate' peoples of Bengal and the more 'settled' regions of British India, or between virile Muslims and effeminate Hindus, have long been known to scholars of colonial India. At its best, this scholar-ship has shed light on such things as the exercise of bureaucratic control in colonial India through the recruitment of men of different regions, reli-gions, castes and classes into various colonial institutions and the impli-cations of the internalisation of ideas about effeminacy by a certain class of Indians.[13] Although much of this scholarship, like the early accounts of the cult of manliness in metropolitan British society, has not been concerned with gender ideology per se, it has nevertheless served to clear the ground for a more profound troubling of gendered categories. This subsequent scholarship has achieved a fuller articulation of masculinity with relations of power.

In recent years, especially in the wake of Edward Said's pathbreaking work on the discursive constructions of imperial power, the gendering of imperial power has received considerable attention.[14] Although Said himself made only passing references to such things as the eroticisation of the 'Orient' as female and to the feminisation of the colonised male in relation to the colonising male in colonial discourse, he inspired a gener-ation of scholars to explore the specifically gendered implications of colonial discourse. In the particular context of the British in India, moreover, the gendered investments of colonial discourse have been further elaborated and modified to render masculinity in particular more visible. So in *The Rhetoric of English India*, for example, Sara Suleri complicates the familiar trope in colonial discourse of heterosexual rape – the figuration of the colonised country as a woman raped by the coloniser – by way of the more complex dynamics of a 'deferred homosexual decorum'.[15] For Suleri, then, an underlying script of homosocial eroticism – figured in the encounter between hypermasculinised British men and effeminate Indian men – subtended British colonial discourse in India and relegated women, both British and Indian, to the peripheries of an exchange essentially 'between men'.[16] The most influential elaboration of the implications of the hyper-masculinist discourse of British Orientalism in India, however, comes from the pioneering work of Ashis Nandy on the psychology of colonialism. Nandy focuses on what he calls a 'language of homology between the sexual and the political' in colonial culture.[17] Nandy suggests that the rigid dichotomy between the masculine and the feminine that was part of the gender ideologies of the post-Enlightenment West was manifested in the hypermasculinity of British imperial ideology in India, which reshaped the more fluid and diffuse gender identities in Indian tradition. For the masculinised ethos of aggressive-but-gentlemanly competition among the British was accepted by much of the nineteenth-century Indian male elite, according to Nandy, who took the existence of British domination as proof of a masculine superiority that they should emulate. Thus Nandy identifies M. K. Gandhi's profound challenge to British colonialism as lying precisely in his refusal to accept the inherent superiority of a 'masculinity' that was increasingly equated with rationality, materialism, and physical strength.[18] While various aspects of the binary that Nandy constructs between 'Western' and 'traditional' Indian masculinity remain problematic, his work has inspired much of the subsequent literary and historical work on the construction and reconstruction of masculinity in colonial India.[19]

What the scholarship in the wake of Nandy has demonstrated is precisely the centrality of questions of power to any history of masculinity. Much of this scholarship has, not surprisingly, focused on the Bengali Hindu *bhadralok* (elite or respectable class) that, throughout the nineteenth century, was perhaps most noted for its peculiarly symbiotic relationship with the colonial British elite.[20] In the case of Bengal, moreover, there was a particularly physical dimension to the Bengali *bhadralok's* self-perception of effeteness that was manifested in the flowering of the new physical culture of *akharas* (gymnasia) in the nineteenth century and in the later masculinist subculture of secret terrorist societies in the early twentieth century.[21] There was also a certain pointed dimension to the masculine anxieties that plagued the leading nineteenth-century male figures among the Bengali *bhadralok*, who developed elaborate and creative responses to the perceived crisis of masculinity. Bankim Chandra Chatterjee tried in his writings to respond to Bengali effeminacy (the *Bharata Kalanka* or the Indian Stigma) by reconstructing the iconic figure of Krishna, cleansed of his famed qualities of sensuality and playfulness, and thus sublimated into a new representation of masculinity defined by love of action and rational self-control.[22] Ramakrishna Paramhansa defiantly and ambivalently appropriated representations both of the masculine and the feminine in his own self-presentation, a response that prefigured Gandhi's construction of his persona as both father and mother to his disciples.[23] Swami Vivekananda aggressively advocated a masculinised Bengali and Hindu identity that combined Hindu spirituality with the 'Western' emphasis on physical strength to create his own brand of a superior Indian/Hindu spiritual masculinity.[24] This 'redemptive pedagogy of manliness' in Bengal, indeed, is the focus of a new book by Indira Chowdhury in which she examines the creation and re-creation of masculinity in a network of institutions from the *Hindu Mela* of the 1870s to the popular songs of the *Swadeshi* movement of 1905.[25]

This internalisation of effeminacy, as various scholars have shown, was itself part of a new hegemonising project that assured the dominance of a predominantly elite, upper caste, and Hindu masculinity in the process of remasculinisation.[26] The sense of 'effeminacy', of course, has characterised other social groups in varying degrees and for a variety of reasons in different historical periods; so, for example, effeminacy emerged as part of the self-perception of Parsis in post-independent India partly in response to a perceived sense of decline in their status from the colonial period.[27] The larger point, indeed, is that the scholarship on masculinity in the colonial context has helped lay the ground for histories of masculinity that go beyond the mere tracking of changing historical and cultural perceptions of masculinity. It suggests, in fact, that histories of masculinity can be – and, indeed, should be – more fundamentally about relations of power: a network variously criss-crossed by hierarchies of race, class, caste, gender, and sexuality.

At a second level, and following in many ways from the first, the historiography of colonial India also makes visible both the relational construction of masculinity and the anxieties percolating within its norms. This has been an important implication, for example, of much of the scholarship on the gendered construction of national and communal identities in India. Hence Partha Chatterjee, one of the most influential theorists of official nationalism in India, identifies an elaborate gendered dichotomy between an inner/spiritual and outer/material world as crucial to the construction of national identity in India.[28] Given the 'constitutive contradictions' of a belated nationalism under conditions of colonialism, he suggests, Indian nationalists located their own autonomous identity in the inner/spiritual world while conceding superiority to the West in the outer/material world. The discursive strategies of Indian nationalism, having acknowledged its own surrender and impotence in the 'outer' world of men, thus invested the figure of the Indian Woman with the burden of an authentic Indian identity.[29] Henceforth, indeed, the terms for the emancipation and self-emancipation of women were set within the parameters of a new and improved nationalist patriarchy. One implication to be drawn from this gendered analysis of nationalism is that the consequent nationalist investment in the reconstitution of the Indian home and of Indian domesticity was as much about an ambivalence in the construction of masculinity as about a normative construction of femininity.

The context for the relational construction of masculine identities is further expanded in the work of Sumit Sarkar, who looks beyond the binary of coloniser and colonised to illuminate the masculine anxieties of lower-middle-class men in nineteenth-century Bengal. His analysis of the construction of masculinity in the context of the confinement of a majority of the Bengali middle-class males to the slavery of *chakri*, or petty clerical work under the particular conditions of the colonial political economy in Bengal, raises interesting questions about the relationship of masculinity to work and to specific forms of property relations.[30] His study of lower-middle-class men's culture against the background of *chakri*, and against the supposedly debilitating attractions associated with *kanchan* (gold) and *kamini* (women), offers a picture of a colonial middle class that is much more internally divided in terms of status than has been commonly assumed. What these different contexts for the construction of masculinity reveal, however, is precisely the extent to which masculine identities are constructed in relationship to men of other communities no less than to women.

The new interest in masculinity has been most marked, perhaps, in the scholarship on the gendered politics of communalism (religious sectarianism) in colonial as well as contemporary India. One context for this interest is provided by the reconfiguration of gendered politics in the current ascendancy of the Hindu Right in contemporary India.[31] So, for example, the rhetoric that accompanied the demolition by right-wing Hindu communalist groups of the Babri Masjid (mosque) in 1992, on the ostensible ground of reclaiming Ram Janmabhumi (the birthplace of Ram), appealed both to a remasculinised figure of Ram (the hero of the eponymous Indian epic *Ramayana*) as Hindu saviour and to an infantilised Ram *lalla* or 'baby Ram' (evoking women's maternal protection).[32] This marked a broader shift in the image of the Hindu Right in contemporary India from disillusioned young men with 'khaki shorts and saffron flags' to assertive women in saffron robes spouting hate-filled speech.[33] For the militant Hindu organisations of late colonial India, which drew mainly from the ranks of urban teenage boys 'not yet corrupted and made timid by family concerns, university students and lower middle classes such as shopkeepers and clerks', had been associated with a very different kind of hypermasculinist rhetoric in which women's own agency was considered marginal at best.[34] The study of communal riots, both before and during the eventual Partition of the subcontinent in 1947, has demonstrated both the ways in which women's actual bodies were the sites for demarcating and violating the boundaries of communities and the ways in which the men of rival communities were constructed as the rapists and abductors of hapless women.[35] So, also, the examination of the gendered rhetoric of communalism has revealed the significance of such notions as those of male honour and shame, as well as of calls for male revenge and for tests of manhood, in keeping the fires of Hindu, Muslim, and Sikh communalisms burning.[36] The hypermasculinist rhetoric of Hindu communalism, furthermore, reconstructed the 'virility' of the Hindu not just in relation to women and to men of 'other' communities, but also against men who, although defined as part of the same community, were held responsible for its decline and emasculation. Hence, as Gyanendra Pandey notes, ever since the 1940s militant Hindu organisations have periodically raised the question: 'How Mahatma Gandhi with his "feminine" *charkha* (spinning wheel) can possibly be considered the "Father of the Nation"?'[37] What this scholarship amply demonstrates is that masculinity is constructed neither in isolation from the full dynamics of social relations nor on the basis of a self-evident foundation. In this sense, then, it suggests that masculinity cannot be adequately studied in terms of the self-contained history of any particular group.

Finally, and perhaps most importantly, the knowledge about masculinity that emerges from the scholarship on shifting gender relations in colonial India serves as a timely reminder that masculinity needs to be examined not just in the context of cultural representations but also in the context of material and ideological arrangements.[38] Just a few examples must suffice here. The work of Tanika Sarkar on nineteenth-century Bengal is suggestive in positing Hindu domesticity – constructed as a space of love and affection, and of the wife's willing surrender to the husband – as a central site for Hindu male identity in colonial India, given that his access to rights in the colonial public sphere remained limited. Having allowed himself to be colonised and having surrendered his autonomy to the West, the Hindu male now constructed a vision of Hindu domesticity in which the 'chaste body of the Hindu woman' carried the burden of marking the difference of the Hindu from the West. The crucial point for Sarkar, as her analysis of debates over such practices as child marriage and premature sexual intercourse demonstrates, is precisely the particular domestic arrangements that this construction of masculinity sustained.[39] Similarly, when Uma Chakravarti examines the reconstitution of 'Brahmanical patriarchy' in nineteenth-century western India under pressure from the processes of caste contestation, class-formation, and the emergence of nationalism, her interest is in the ideological and material practices that sustain, and are sustained by, issues of gender.[40] Yet another context for masculinity as a material and ideological arrangement is suggested in Padma Anagol-McGinn's study of that peculiar pattern of public sexual harassment of women by men that is today known in both official and popular discourse in India as 'Eve teasing'. The skewed urbanisation of colonial India – which resulted in a preponderance of men in the cities as the result of a pattern of recruiting migrant male labour for mills and industries that necessitated leaving behind females in rural areas – provides the historical context in which Anagol-McGinn locates her study of the phenomenon of Eve-teasing.[41] What this scholarship on gender relations in colonial India strongly suggests is that the project of 'recasting men', like the argument that Kumkum Sangari and Sudesh Vaid make about 'recasting women', cannot be abstracted from an entire range of social arrangements and their cumulative material and ideological effects.[42]

What I have been suggesting so far, then, is that there is much to build upon, despite a relative absence of histories devoted specifically to the exploration of masculinity, from the ways in which masculinity has been made visible in the scholarship on gender in colonial India. From here, indeed, there are several possible directions in which a scholarship explicitly about masculinity may proceed. One direction is best represented in Rosalind O'Hanlon's essay 'Issues of Masculinity in North Indian History: The Bangash Nawabs of Farrukhabad', on the political culture of late pre-colonial India.[43] Here O'Hanlon examines the gendered culture of the 'codes of martial bravery and correct manly behaviour'[44] as they were used to cement alliances between rulers and their clients and between mercenary leaders and their warbands in the politically volatile context of the relative decline of Mughal power in north India and the rise of numerous regional power-holders. O'Hanlon suggests that the norms of military masculinity, once so successfully deployed by the Mughal rulers to recruit elite supporters, gradually declined as rival models of military masculinity emerged to challenge the Mughal model. She establishes the centrality of a Mughal 'imperial masculinity' – a code that was both shared and competed over by rival political elites – in the working of the eighteenth-century political system in north India. The terms of this 'imperial masculinity', as O'Hanlon's analysis of a Mughal military servant's manipulation of its codes suggests, were defined in a variety of contexts: the contrast between the simple and manly world of the soldier, on the one hand, and the 'womanly realm of the harem' and the 'luxurious world of the court', on the other;[45] the ethos of fighting contests between warriors at court; the courtly ethos of recreational hunting and animal fights; and, of course, the experience of the battlefield itself.[46] The codes of 'imperial masculinity', she suggests, defined 'what it meant to be a man [in the political elite] in 18th century north India at the level of individual identity and experience'.[47]

The direction taken by O'Hanlon's richly contextualised study of the gendered culture of eighteenth-century north Indian politics – and, in particular, of masculinity – is one that constructs a scholarship about masculinity around a history of men as gendered beings. O'Hanlon, indeed, defines masculinity as 'that aspect of a man's social being which is gendered: which defines him as a man and links him to other men, and conditions other aspects of his identity, such as of class, occupation, race, and ethnicity'.[48] Working with this definition, her analysis succeeds not only in looking at a familiar aspect of eighteenth-century north Indian politics in a new light – political diplomacy, alliances, and negotiations – but also in reconsidering the nature and implications of the gendered articulation of British colonial power later in the century. This latter consideration, as O'Hanlon herself points out, is the broader implication of her study. First, as she suggests, her study of 'imperial masculinity' in pre-colonial India makes clear that British colonial culture was certainly not the first to deploy masculinity as a form of power and may, indeed, have built on earlier such deployments of masculinity. Her challenge here is directed quite explicitly at Nandy's claim that martial *Kshatriya* traditions were a relatively minor part of pre-colonial culture in India until they were inflated by the hypermasculinist culture of British colonial rule. The supposed break between the fluid gender identities of pre-colonial India and the rigid gender identities introduced under the British may, indeed, be in need of some qualification. Second, since the shared codes of imperial masculinity were defined primarily in an 'outdoor world of the contest, the game, the hunt, and the battlefield' – and explicitly against the 'indoor realms of court, household and harem' – they provided a space that brought men together in 'contests about and in recognition of commonalities of gender that often transcended other forms of cultural difference'.[49] The decline of this world of imperial masculinity – especially its integrative potential for the Hindu or Muslim, Rajput, Maratha or Pathan to compete within a broadly shared code of martial masculinity – had implications for the redrawing of sectional and communal boundaries in India. Finally, with the contraction of opportunities for the expression of this imperial masculinity under British rule, the indoor realm of household and family acquired greater significance in the social world in India. This had important implications both for women and for the nature of the transformation of gender relations under colonial rule.

What O'Hanlon's approach demonstrates, indeed, is precisely what can be achieved by filling out the history of men as gendered beings in late pre-colonial as in colonial India. There remain, indeed, vast areas of scholarship in which the history of men as gendered beings has scarcely begun to be made visible: in working-class culture; in the construction of sexualities; in subaltern politics; in social movements; and in popular culture, to name only a few.[50] Yet, as Judith Allen suggests in a different context, one tendency of such an approach might be to assume, rather than explain, the 'relationship between male bodies (men) and historical forms of masculinity'. Hence manifestations of masculinity (and femininity) can always already be found in the 'home', 'the workplace', 'the neighbourhood', and so on.[51] While providing illustrations of a certain masculinity (and a certain femininity), such an approach may not exhaust the political efficacy or ideological significance of masculinity. It risks assuming an underlying continuity of real women [and real men], above whose constant bodies changing aerial descriptions dance'.[52]

A second direction for explorations of masculinity is represented in my own work *Colonial Masculinity: The 'Manly' Englishman and the 'Effeminate' Bengali in the Late Nineteenth Century.*[53] One aim of this work is to bring together the existing scholarship on masculinity in colonial India with the gender-studies scholarship concerned more explicitly with providing gendered modes of analysis of colonialism and nationalism. In so doing, I bring to an exploration of masculinity many of the traditional concerns of a feminist-inspired scholarship on the implications of the gendered organisation of social relations in colonial Indian society. Another aim of my work is to bring a historical-materialist approach to the analysis of colonial masculinity that posits the entire imperial social formation as the unit of its analysis. The heuristic model of an imperial social formation for the study of colonial masculinity is meant to enable the following: first, to bring together the formation of 'English' masculinity and 'Bengali' effeminacy within the same field of analysis by examining their mutual constitution in the historical contingencies of specific *practices* of colonial rule; and second, to explore the resulting 'colonial masculinity' as the product of the mediations of various contradictions both between coloniser and colonised and within each group arising out of the divisions of gender, caste, class, status, religious and provincial identities. I thus reject the tendency to overlook the ways in which the colonial encounter itself produced *both* the hypermasculinist rhetoric of the colonial British elite *and* its corollary: the distinction, as elaborated and given new meaning by a racialising colonial ethnography, between a 'manly' and 'effeminate' native elite. British hypermasculinity, then, is understood not as constituted within Britain itself and then merely transplanted to India as the basis for distinguishing between 'manly' and 'unmanly' native races. I see British masculinity, no less than native masculinity, as shaped by the contingent practices of colonial rule. In other words, 'masculinity' in my analysis acquires its meaning only in specific practices: it has no a priori context or origin.

The direction represented by *Colonial Masculinity*, then, is one that entails a dislodging of masculinity from its privileged grounding in (the biologically sexed bodies of) 'real men'. For giving priority to this context – even when such an approach acknowledges interconnections with other axes of power – does not render sufficiently problematic the always mediated relationship between male bodies and masculinity. In this sense, the book neither attempts to provide a single definition of colonial masculinity nor seeks to exhaust all the possible terrains for the articulation of colonial masculinity. Rather, the term 'colonial masculinity' here quite specifically encapsulates the overdetermined terrain for the encounters between the colonial British elite and the Bengali Hindu middle class at a specific historical moment in the imperial social formation of the late nineteenth century. The implication of this approach is that the meaning of masculinity itself is derived from the specific power relations that it is deployed to reproduce in particular historical contexts. This second direction for the scholarship on masculinity, then, is based on a more radical problematising of masculinity as such. The meaning of 'masculinity' studied thus is constituted in practices that cover the full range of social relations.

From a certain reading of its contribution, then, the historiography of colonial India holds crucial implications for the broader scholarship on masculinity. For the real contribution of this historiography, to paraphrase Joan Scott in a different context, may well lie in more than just establishing that masculinity was an important issue in history: for it has also laid the foundation for giving masculinity itself a history.[54] One implication of recognising the multiple social relations that were reproduced by the politics of masculinity in colonial India, indeed, is to be compelled to think beyond an easy equation between men and masculinity.[55] This means that there is no domain where masculinity necessarily or naturally belongs, no foundation or anchor that could allow one to trace the progress of a continuous, albeit changing, relation between men and masculinity. Lacking any secure ground for masculinity, then, a history of masculinity still to come may find that the unit of analysis most adequate to its study is the social as defined in the broadest of terms. If masculinity and maleness are delinked, then the domain of 'masculinity' need no longer be confined to histories of men as gendered beings. It can be opened up, instead, to historical analyses of its rhetorical and ideological efficacy in underwriting various arrangements of power. Herein may lie the most radical implication of the historiography of colonial India: the realisation that there may be no proper or predetermined subject for a history of masculinity.

Notes

1. The recent literature on men and masculinity is too numerous to name. For reviews of some of this recent scholarship, see J. Hearn, 'Review: Men and Masculinity or Mostly Boy's Own Papers', *Theory, Culture and Society*, 6 (1987), pp. 665–89; Lisa Cody, 'This Sex Which Seems to Have Won: The Emergence of Masculinity as a Category of Historical Analysis', *Radical History Review*, 61 (1995), pp. 175–83; Michael Roper et al., 'Recent Books on Masculinity', *History Workshop Journal*, 29 (1990), pp. 184–92; David H. Morgan, 'Men Made Manifest: Histories and Masculinities', *Gender and History*, 1 (1989), pp. 87–91; R. W. Connell, 'Book Review', *Signs*, 19 (1993), pp. 280–85; James Eli Adams et al., 'Recent Works on Masculinity: A Forum', *Victorian Studies*, 36 (1993), pp. 207–26; Jeffrey Weeks, 'Telling Stories about Men', *The Sociological Review*, 44 (1996), pp. 746–57; Victoria Thompson, 'Sexuality: Another Useful Category of Analysis in European History', *Journal of Women's History*, 9 (1998), pp. 211–19; James A. Hammerton, 'Forgotten People? Marriage and Masculine Identities in Britain', *Journal of Family History*, 22 (1997), pp. 110–17. See also Judith Allen, 'Discussion: Mundane Men: Historians, Masculinity and Masculinism', *Historical Studies*, 22 (1987), pp. 617–28; John Tosh, 'What Should Historians Do with Masculinity? Reflections on Nineteenth Century Britain', *History Workshop Journal*, 38 (1994), pp. 179–202; and Michael Roper and John Tosh, 'Introduction: Historians and the Politics of Masculinity', in *Manful Assertions: Masculinities in Britain Since 1800*, ed. M. Roper and J. Tosh (Routledge, London, 1991), pp. 1–24.

2. The reference, of course, is to Joan Wallach Scott's pathbreaking essay, 'Gender: A Useful Category of Historical Analysis', *American Historical Review*, 91 (1986), pp. 1053–75; reprinted in *Gender and the Politics of History* (Columbia University Press, New York: 1988), pp. 28–50.

3. For some examples of the issues at stake, see Caroline Ramazanoglu, 'What Can You Do with a Man? Feminism and the Critical Appraisal of Masculinity', *Women's Studies International Forum*, 15 (1992), pp. 339–50; Diane Richardson and Victoria Robinson, 'Theorizing Women's Studies, Gender Studies and Masculinity: The Politics of Naming', *The European Journal of Women's Studies*, 1 (1994), pp. 11–27; Christine Griffin and Joyce E. Canaan, 'The New Men's Studies: Part of the Problem or Part of the Solution?', in *Men, Masculinities and Social Theory*, ed. Jeff Hearn and David Morgan (Unwin Hyman, London, 1990); and Thomas Laqueur, 'The Facts of Fatherhood', and the response by Sara Riddick, 'Thinking about Fathers', in *Conflicts in Feminism*, ed. Marianne Hirsch and Evelyn Fox Keller (Routledge, New York, 1990), pp. 205–21, and pp. 222–33.

4. See Connell, 'Book Review', p. 282. For Connell's own pioneering work in the field, see *Gender and Power: Society, The Person and Sexual Politics* (Polity Press, Cambridge, 1987); and *Masculinities* (University of California Press, Berkeley, 1995). For another reassessment of 'masculinity' studies, see Jeff Hearn, 'Is Masculinity Dead? A Critique of the Concept of Masculinity/Masculinities', in *Understanding Masculinities: Social Relations and Cultural Arenas*, ed. Mairtin Mac An Ghaill (Open University Press, Buckingham, 1996), pp. 202–17.

5. See the title of a book that was an early pioneer in the modern field of women's history, Claudia Koonz and Renate Bridenthal (eds), *Becoming Visible: Women in European History* (Houghton Mifflin and Co., Boston, 1977).

6. Michael Kimmel, 'Invisible Masculinity: Examining Masculinity in Relation to History and the Social Sciences', *Society*, 30 (1993), pp. 28–36.

7. For overviews of the historiography on women and gender in India, see Barbara Ramusack, 'From Symbol to Diversity: The Historical Literature on Women in India', *South Asia Research*, 10 (1990), pp. 139–57; and Tanika Sarkar, 'Women's Histories and Feminist Writings in India: A Review and A Caution', *Plenary Address to the Seventh Berkshire Conference on Women's History*, Chapel Hill, North Carolina, June 1996.

8. For two contrasting theoretical approaches as manifested in the historiography of women and gender relations in India, see Dipesh Chakrabarty, 'The Difference-Deferral of (A) Colonial Modernity: Public Debates on Domesticity in British Bengal', *History Workshop Journal*, 36 (1993), pp. 1–33; and Tanika Sarkar, 'Rhetoric Against Age of Consent: Resisting Colonial Reason and Death of a Child-Wife', *Economic and Political Weekly*, 4 September 1993, pp. 1869–78. For contrasting examples of the contemporary historiographical debate in the study of colonial India, see Partha Chatterjee, *The Nation and its Fragments: Colonial and Postcolonial Histories* (Princeton University Press, Princeton, 1993); and Sumit Sarkar, *Writing Social History* (Oxford University Press, New Delhi, 1997).

9. The phrase is from Ed Cohen in Adams et al., 'Recent Works on Masculinity: A Forum', p. 218.

10. For some examples, see David Newsome, *Godliness and Good Learning: Four Studies on a Victorian Ideal* (John Murray, London, 1961); J. R. de S. Honey, *Tom Brown's Universe: The Development of the English Public School in the Late Nineteenth Century* (Quadrangle/New York Times Book Co., New York, 1977); Norman Vance, *The Sinews of the Spirit: The Ideal of Christian Manliness in Victorian Literature and Religious Thought* (Cambridge University Press, Cambridge, 1985); J. A. Mangan, *Athleticism in the Victorian and Edwardian Public Schools* (Cambridge University Press, Cambridge, 1981); Michael Rosenthal, *The Character Factory: Baden Powell and the Origins of the Boy Scout Movement* (Collins, London, 1986); H. John Field, *Toward a Programme of Imperial Life: The British Empire at the Turn of the Century* (Greenwood Press, New Haven, CT, 1982); and Graham Dawson, *Soldier Heroes: British Adventure, Empire and Imaging of Masculinities* (Routledge, London and New York, 1994).

11. For classic statements of the ethos of such institutions, see Leonard Woolf, *Growing: An Autobiography of the Years 1904–1911* (Hogarth Press, London, 1967); Philip Mason, *A Matter of Honour* (Holt, Rinehart & Winston, New York, 1974); and Philip Woodruff, *The Men Who Ruled India: The Guardians* (Jonathan Cape, London, 1954). For more critical analyses of its implications, see Kenneth Ballhatchet, *Race, Sex and Class Under the Raj: Imperial Attitudes and Policies and Their Critics* (Weidenfeld & Nicolson, London, 1980); Francis G. Hutchins, *The Illusion of Permanence: British Imperialism in India* (Princeton University Press, Princeton, 1967); and Lewis D. Wurgaft,

The Imperial Imagination: Magic and Myth in Kipling's India (Wesleyan University Press, Middletown, CT, 1983).

12. See, for example, J. A. Mangan, 'Eton in India: The Imperial Diffusion of a Victorian Educational Elite', *History of Education*, 7 (1978), pp. 105–18. Also, Mady Martyn, *Martyn Sahib: The Story of John Martyn of Doon School* (Dass Media, New Delhi, 1985).

13. For some examples, see John Rosselli, 'The Self-Image of Effeteness: Physical Education and Nationalism in Nineteenth-Century Bengal', *Past and Present*, 86 (1980), pp. 121–48; David Omissi, '"Martial Races": Ethnicity and Security in Colonial India, 1858–1939', *War and Society*, 9 (1991), pp. 1–27; and his *The Sepoy and the Raj: The Indian Army, 1660–1940* (Macmillan, Houndshill, Hampshire, 1994); and David Arnold, 'Bureaucratic Recruitment and Subordination in Colonial India: The Madras Constabulary, 1859–1947', in *Subaltern Studies 4: Writing on South Asian History and Society*, ed. R. Guha (Oxford University Press, New Delhi, 1985), pp. 1–53.

14. See E. Said, *Orientalism* (Vintage Books, New York, 1978).

15. S. Suleri, *The Rhetoric of English India* (University of Chicago Press, Chicago, 1992).

16. The reference here is to Eve Kosofsky Sedgewick's pioneering book, *Between Men: English Literature and Homosexual Desire* (Columbia University Press, New York, 1985).

17. A. Nandy, *The Intimate Enemy: Loss and Recovery of Self Under Colonialism* (Oxford University Press, New Delhi, 1983).

18. The ambivalence of Gandhi's attitude towards masculinity has, of course, attracted the attention of scholars other than Nandy; see Erik H. Erickson, *Gandhi's Truth* (Norton, New York, 1969); Susanne Rudolph and Lloyd Rudolph, *The Modernity of Tradition* (University of Chicago Press, Chicago, 1967); Sudhir Kakar, *Intimate Relations: Explorations of Indian Sexuality* (University of Chicago Press, Chicago, 1990). For an interesting analysis of Gandhi's attitude towards sexuality in this context, see Joseph S. Alter, 'Celibacy, Sexuality and the Transformation of Gender into Nationalism in North India', *Journal of Asian Studies*, 53 (1994), pp. 45–66, and 'Gandhi's Body, Gandhi's Truth: Nonviolence and the Biomoral Imperialism of Public Health', *Journal of Asian Studies*, 55 (1996), pp. 301–22.

19. For my critique of Nandy's binary of 'Western' and 'traditional' Indian conceptions of masculinity, see Mrinalini Sinha, *Colonial Masculinity: The 'Manly' Englishman and the 'Effeminate' Bengali in the Late Nineteenth Century* (Manchester University Press, Manchester, 1995; reprinted Kali for Women Press, New Delhi, 1998), Introduction.

20. For examples, see, Rosselli, 'The Self-Image of Effeteness'; Sinha, *Colonial Masculinity*; Indira Chowdhury-Sengupta, 'The Effeminate and the Masculine: Nationalism and the Concept of Race in Colonial Bengal', in *The Concept of Race in South Asia*, ed. Peter Robb (Oxford University Press, New Delhi, 1995), pp. 282–303; and *The Frail Hero and Virile History: Gender and the Politics of Culture in Colonial Bengal* (Oxford University Press, New Delhi, 1998). For a discussion of the colonial politics of masculinity outside Bengal, see M. S. S. Pandian, 'Gendered Negotiations: Hunting and Colonialism in the Late 19th Century Nilgiris', in *Social Reform, Sexuality and the State*, ed. Patricia Uberoi (Sage Publications, New Delhi, 1996), pp. 239–64.

21. Rosselli, 'The Self-Image of Effeteness'.

22. See Sudipta Kaviraj, 'The *Krishnacharita*: The Construction of the Figure of Krishna in the Work of Bankimchandra Chattopadhyaya', in *The Unhappy Consciousness: Bankimchandra Chattopadhyay and the Formation of Nationalist Discourse in India* (Oxford University Press, Bombay, 1995). See also Rachel R. Van Meter, 'Bankim

Chandra's View of the Role of Bengal in Indian Civilization', in _Bengal Regional Identity_, ed. D. Kopf (Michigan State University Press, East Lansing, 1969), pp. 61–72; and Partha Chatterjee, _Nationalist Thought and the Colonial World: A Derivative Discourse?_ (Zed, London, 1986), ch. 3.

23. See Sumit Sarkar, '"_Kaliyuga_", "_Chakri_" and "_Bhakti_": Ramakrishna and His Times', _Economic and Political Weekly_, 18 July 1992, pp. 1543–66; and Partha Chatterjee, 'A Religion of Urban Domesticity: Sri Ramakrishna and the Calcutta Middle Class', in _Subaltern Studies 7: Writings on South Asian History and Society_, ed. P. Chatterjee and G. Pandey (Oxford University Press, New Delhi, 1993), pp. 40–68. For an interesting discussion of androgyny in cultural traditions in India, see Wendy Doniger O'Flaherty, _Sexual Metaphors and Animal Symbols in Indian Mythology_ (Motilalbanarsidas, New Delhi, 1980).

24. See Chowdhury, _The Frail Hero and Virile History_, ch. 5.

25. See Chowdhury, _The Frail Hero and Virile History_, p. 21.

26. See Sinha, _Colonial Masculinity_; and Chowdury, _The Frail Hero and Virile History_.

27. See T. M. Luhrman, 'The Good Parsi: The Postcolonial Feminization of a Colonial Elite', _Man_, 29 (1994), pp. 333–57; and _The Good Parsi: The Fate of a Colonial Elite in a Postcolonial Society_ (Harvard University Press, Cambridge, MA, 1996). For an account of the construction of masculinity by a nineteenth-century Parsi in London in the context of social reforms for women, Indian nationalism, and British imperialism, see Antoinette Burton, 'A "Pilgrim Reformer" at the Heart of Empire: Behramji Malabari in Late-Victorian London', _Gender and History_, 8 (1996), pp. 175–96.

28. See Partha Chatterjee, _Nationalist Thought and the Colonial World; The Nation and Its Fragments: Colonial and Postcolonial Histories_ (Princeton University Press, Princeton, 1993); and 'The Nationalist Resolution of the Women's Question', in _Recasting Women: Essays in Colonial History_, ed. Kumkum Sangari and Sudesh Vaid (Kali for Women, New Delhi, 1989), pp. 233–53.

29. I explore the implications of this discourse on the particular construction of the gendered citizen-subject in India in my forthcoming book _Refashioning Mother India: The Advent of a Nationalist 'Indian' Modernity in Late Colonial India_.

30. See Sarkar, '"_Kaliyuga_", "_Chakri_", and "_Bhakti_"'; and in his _Writing Social History_, pp. 282–357.

31. For an interesting discussion of the politics of masculinity in this context, see Rustom Bharucha, 'Dismantling Men? Crisis of Male Identity in "Father, Son and Holy War"', _Economic and Political Weekly_, 1 July 1995, pp. 1610–16.

32. See Anuradha Kapur, 'Deity to Crusader: The Changing Iconography of Ram', in _Hindus and Others: The Question of Identity in India Today_, ed. Gyanendra Pandey (Viking, New Delhi, 1993), pp. 74–107. For a history of the Babri Masjid-Ram Janmabhumi dispute, see S. Gopal (ed.), _Anatomy of a Confrontation: The Babri Masjid-Ram Janmabhumi Issue_ (Viking, New Delhi, 1991).

33. The phrase is from Tapan Basu et al., _Khaki Shorts and Saffron Flags: A Critique of the Hindu Right_ (Orient Longman, New Delhi, 1993). For the new visibility of women, and the invocation of women's agency and gender equality in the politics of the Hindu Right, see Tanika Sarkar, 'The Woman as Communal Subject: Rashtrasevika Samiti and Ram Janmabhoomi Movement', _Economic and Political Weekly_, 31 August 1991, pp. 2057–662; Tanika Sarkar and Urvashi Butalia (eds) _Women and the Hindu Right_ (Kali for Women, New Delhi, 1995); Kumkum Sangari, 'Consent, Agency and the Rhetorics of Incitement', _Economic and Political Weekly_, 1 May 1993, pp. 867–82; Ratna Kapur and Brenda Crossman, 'Communalizing Gender/Engendering Community: Women, Legal Discourse and Saffron Agenda', _Economic and Political Weekly_,

24 April 1993, pp. Ws. 35—Ws. 44; Paula Bacchetta, 'All our Goddesses Are Armed: Religion, Resistance and Revenge in the Life of Hindu Nationalist Women', *Bulletin of Concerned Asian Scholars*, 25 (1993), pp. 38–52; and Sucheta Majumdar, 'Women on the March: Right-Wing Mobilization in Contemporary India', *Feminist Review*, 49 (1995), pp. 1–28.

34. See Basu et al., *Khaki Shorts and Saffron Flags*, p. 24. For the hypermasculinist discourse of militant Hindu organizations in late colonial India, see Gyanendra Pandey, 'Hindus and Others: The Militant Hindu Construction', *Economic and Political Weekly*, 28 December 1991, pp. 2997–3009.

35. See, for example, Papiya Ghosh, 'The Virile and the Chaste in Community and Nation Making: Bihar 1920s to 1940s', *Social Scientist*, 22 (1994), pp. 80–89.

36. The ideas of 'male honour', as Ritu Menon and Kamla Bhasin have argued, were also evident in the paternalist attitude of secular nationalism; see R. Menon and K. Bhasisn, 'Abducted Women, the State and Questions of Honour: Three Perspectives on the Recovery Operation in Post Partition India', in *Embodied Violence: Communalizing Women's Sexuality in South Asia*, ed. Kumari Jayawardena and Malthi de Alwis (Zed, London, 1996), pp. 1–31. For a discussion of the image of the raped woman in fuelling masculinist revenge in communalist violence, also see Veena Das, *Mirrors of Violence: Communities, Riots and Survivors* (Oxford University Press, New Delhi, 1990), pp. 1–36.

37. G. Pandey, 'Hindus and Others', p. 3005.

38. I am drawing here from Uma Chakravarti's critique of gender analyses that reduce gender to a representational phenomenon rather than examine gender as a material and ideological arrangement; see Uma Chakravarti, *Rewriting History: The Life and Times of Pandita Ramabai* (Kali for Women, New Delhi, 1998).

39. See Tanika Sarkar, 'The Hindu Wife and the Hindu Nation: Domesticity and Nationalism in Nineteenth Century Bengal', *Studies in History*, 8 (1992), pp. 213–35; 'Rhetoric Against Age of Consent'; and also 'Talking About Scandals: Religion, Law and Love in Late Nineteenth Century Bengal', *Studies in History*, 13 (1997), pp. 63–95.

40. Chakravarti, *Rewriting History*. For the concept of 'brahmanical patriarchy', see also her 'Conceptualizing Brahmanical Patriarchy in Early India: Gender, Caste, Class, and State', *Economic and Political Weekly*, 3 April 1993, pp. 579–85.

41. See Padma Anagol-McGinn, 'Sexual Harassment in India: A Case Study of Eve-Teasing in Historical Perspective', in *Rethinking Sexual Harassment*, ed. Clare Brant and Yun Lee Too (Pluto Press, London, 1994), pp. 220–34. For an account of the contemporary menace of Eve-teasing, see Deepti Priya, 'Challenging a Masculinist Culture: Women's Protest in St Stephen's College', *Manushi*, 28 (1985), pp. 32–5. For an example of the gendered imbalance created by the pattern of labour recruitment in the jute industry in colonial India, see Dipesh Chakrabarty, *Rethinking Working Class History, Bengal, 1890–1940* (Oxford University Press, New Delhi, 1989).

42. See Kumkum Sangari and Sudesh Vaid, 'Recasting Women: An Introduction', in *Recasting Women*, ed. Sangari and Vaid, pp. 1–26.

43. *Indian Journal of Gender Studies*, 4 (1997), pp. 1–19. Of note also is her forthcoming book, cited in the above essay, *Masculinity Between Empires: Gender and Power in North India, c. 1750–1850*.

44. O'Hanlon, 'Issues of Masculinity', p. 5.

45. O'Hanlon, 'Issues of Masculinity', p. 11.

46. O'Hanlon, 'Issues of Masculinity', p. 10.

47. O'Hanlon, 'Issues of Masculinity', p. 7.

48. O'Hanlon, 'Issues of Masculinity', p. 3.

49. O'Hanlon, 'Issues of Masculinity', pp. 16–17.

50. For some examples, see Joseph Alter, 'Somatic Nationalism: Indian Wrestling and Militant Hinduism', *Modern Asian Studies*, 28 (1994), pp. 557–88; David Hardiman, 'Community, Patriarchy, Honour: Raghu Bhanagre's Revolt', *Journal of Peasant Studies*, 23 (1995), pp. 88–130; Poonam Arora, 'Devdas: Indian Cinema's Emasculated Hero, Sado-Masochism and Colonialism', *Journal of South Asian Literature*, 30 (1995), pp. 261–70; and Ashwini Sharma, 'Blood Sweat and Tears: Amitabh Bachchan; Urban Demi-God', in *You Tarzan: Masculinity, Movies and Men*, ed. Pat Kirkham and J. Thumim (St Martin's Press, New York, 1993), pp. 167–80.

51. See J. Allen, 'Discussion: Mundane Men'. I find the distinction that Allen makes here useful; I read her against the grain, however, in not subscribing to an 'analytics of origin: sex, sexual distinctions, and sexual politics in history' for studies of masculinity.

52. Denise Riley, *'Am I That Name?' Feminism and the Category of 'Women' in History* (University of Minnesota Press, Minneapolis, 1988), p. 7. See also Judith Butler, *Gender and Trouble: Feminism and the Subversion of Identity* (Routledge, New York, 1990).

53. Sinha, *Colonial Masculinity*.

54. See J. Scott, 'Book Review', *American Historical Review*, 99 (1994), pp. 1329–30.

55. For one example of the theoretical challenge to the 'naturalised' relation between men and masculinity, see Judith Halberstam, *Female Masculinity* (Duke University, Durham, 1998); and 'Annamarie Jagose Interviews Judith Halberstam, "Masculinity without Men"', *Genders*, 29 (1999).

4

The Gender of Militancy: Notes on the Possibilities of a Different History of Political Action

Marco Aurélio Garcia

Is a history of the left possible without a history of political militancy? The answer to this question initially involves considering the directions (whether right or wrong) taken by contemporary historiography when analysing revolutionary phenomena.

Just before his death, Georges Haupt attacked a type of political history which

> ignores the past of the working-class movement in favour of congresses, good or bad leaders, right or wrong decisions, reformist or revolutionary parties or concurrent ideologies.[1]

In what was to become his historiographic will, Haupt explicitly denounced the existence of an ideological burden on the historiography of the working-class and the left-wing parties. At the same time, using theory and methodology, he proposed alternative approaches, excellently illustrated in the essays of his posthumous book. His work criticised the theoretical conservatism with which revolutions and revolutionary organisations were handled, both on the right and on the left. He considered that these were misrepresented by a historiography which replaced major military battles with political-ideological confrontations or kings and generals with party bureaucrats.

Other texts contained further references to the reconstruction of the historiography of the left, at the same time as specific studies emerged which clarified this new approach.[2] From the 1960s, particularly 1968, the debate on both politics and humanities began to provide new ideas about the relationships between the public and private spheres. This would have an impact on historiography, including that of the parties.

Clearly, this reconsideration of the public/private links often risked producing a pan-political approach, given that the invasion of the private sphere by the public sphere (wrongly restricted to the *political* sphere) ended up giving everything a political meaning.

On the other hand, there were those who retrospectively saw in the *Pensée 68* the foundations for the 'hedonistic egoism' responsible for the increasing confinement of men and women to the private sphere,[3] anticipating the idea of the 'end of politics'. Everything seems as if apolitical individualism, which many point to as a present-day characteristic of postmodernity, had its origins in the major social, political and cultural explosion of 1968 when, however, the construction of collective identities and the joint actions were dominant elements.

From this perspective, the history of militancy may at first sight seem to be 'apolitical' and a dangerous area where the borders between the objective and the subjective are weakened to such an extent that they cloud one's capacity for reasoning and understanding the political phenomena to be scrutinised in recreating individual or collective paths.

The suggestions of Haupt and Anderson on the political history of the left, combined with the contributions from contemporary social history, simply confirm the need to provide a specific space for the analysis of the phenomenon of militancy. A party (and political action) cannot be understood, as this historiography may well suggest, without an analysis of its plans, the national and international historical context in which it moved, the cultural traditions which it embodies and the changes in its social bases. However, in order to be comprehensive, the study of parties cannot be separated from the analysis of its militancy, its leading group, its procedures and even its internal 'rituals'.

This militancy, however disciplined it may be – and there is no doubt of the importance of this aspect – is not the result of the action of robots, of isolated individuals who act mechanically according to their 'class conscience', or of the political guidelines which emanate from the party, all within a given national and international political context. Militants are specific people, men and women, bearers of ethical values, political convictions and religious influences who reflect, in their daily life, their cultural education, their family background and a set of 'orders' which affect the way in which they will 'apply' the party 'line' in society, whether through a speech, pamphlet, other methods of 'agitprop' or violent armed action.

> In order to understand political militancy, the idea is valid that the human condition consists of rather more than the conditions which were imposed on man. Men are conditioned beings because everything that they come in contact with turns immediately into a condition of their existence. The world in which the *vita activa* spends itself consists of things produced by human activities; but the things that owe their existence exclusively to men nevertheless constantly condition their human makers ... men constantly create their own self-made conditions, which, their human origin and their variability notwithstanding, possess the same conditioning power as natural things. [But the] ... objectivity of the world – its object- or thing-character – and the human condition supplement each other; because human existence is conditioned existence, it would be impossible without things, and things would be a heap

of unrelated articles, a non-world, if they were not the conditioners of human existence.[4]

The world of militancy has been likened to a microcosm subject to specific rules and codes which may suggest the idea that the party is a 'counter-society'.[5] While this allusion may be used to understand Communist parties, like the French one, which, despite the political and ideological confinement to which they were subject for decades, had a legal existence for much of the time, it has a much greater explanatory force in respect of revolutionary organisations which made armed struggle the centre of their activity, having to survive for most of the time in clandestinity. The conditions of clandestinity, resulting from the choice of revolution, accentuated the closed nature of groups and therefore brought closer and linked the public and private spheres, providing a privileged view of this complex relationship.

As soon as the history of private life stopped being theoretically opposite to the history of the public sphere,[6] it was possible to identify a series of elements previously relegated to factual historiography, chronicles, journalism, biography or other types of historiography regarded as being 'lesser'. It is interesting to observe how this historiographical inflexion contributed to the construction of a history of women. Previously assigned to a nebulous area of history – the private sphere – women started to become an object of historical consideration.

The opening up or reconstruction of this historiographical area led not only to the establishment of a field of research – with specific theoretical and methodological implications – but in particular allowed, due to this specificity, the public/private relationships to be reconsidered, thereby giving a greater complexity to political historiography, including that centred on the analysis of revolutionary processes and organisations.

The aim of these notes is to consider some of the implications of this historiographical development by using three texts devoted to the reconstruction of women's militancy during the recent military dictatorships in Brazil and Argentina. The aim is not simply to recount these texts but to use some of the problems raised by them, or underlying them, in order to discuss the issue of the gender of militancy and the implications which this type of problem has for the construction of a different history of political action.

The texts on Brazil come from academia: *Mulheres, Militância e Memória – histórias de vida e histórias de sobrevivência* (Women, Militancy and Memory – stories of life and survival), by Elizabeth F. Xavier Ferreira[7] and *A Resistência da Mulher à Ditadura Militar no Brasil* (The Resistance of Women to the Military Dictatorship in Brazil), by Ana Maria Colling.[8] The text on Argentina is the work of the journalist Marta Diana, *Mujeres Guerrilleras – la militancia de los setenta en el testimonio de sus protagonistas femeninas* (Guerrilla Women – the militancy of the seventies according to its female protagonists).[9]

Prior to these, the biography of Iara Iavelberg offered extensive material for considering the possibilities of an alternative political historiography centred on militancy, due to both the research carried out and its approach.[10] Memoirs from the '*anos de chumbo*' (the years of violent military dictatorship) dealing with clandestinity, prison and exile have also provided suggestions for this approach.[11]

Finally, the works of Elisabeth Sousa Lobo,[12] although not centred on recent history, offer an analytical framework which is completely relevant to the issue in question.

Women's militancy in revolutionary organisations during the 1960s and 1970s is regarded implicitly or explicitly by all three authors as a dual transgression. This is firstly because enlistment in these organisations, most of which were devoted to carrying out armed actions against the government, meant placing oneself 'outside the law' (a discussion of how illegal or illegitimate this may have been is not appropriate here). The high price paid by female militants – death, torture, prison, exile[13] – and the effects on their private life – family, emotional and professional – clearly demonstrate this. The second transgression was that 'the conduct of female militants also challenged the gender code of their time',[14] which is a rather fancy way of saying that the participation of women in politics was not socially acceptable.

Mainly written using accounts collected in the 1990s, the three texts cover the two stages which occurred within the space of roughly twenty years: (1) the immersion in clandestinity, with all the consequences arising from the repression, and (2) the reintegration into 'law-abiding life'. Apart from the common aspects which may be apparent, the processes by which these women entered into politics differed. For some, politics was in the family background and it is suggested that this can be used in many of the life histories to explain or put into context the enlistment of women.

In almost all the cases, clandestinity was preceded by legal activity – in the student movement, at times in the trade unions – and the passage from one type of militancy to the other is more a result of circumstances – the political 'closure' of the regime or the choices of the organisation – than of a deliberate personal choice. This first step immersed young people – this is a common theme among the interviewees – in restricted situations. Firstly, there were the dangers of clandestine life: from the high tension of armed actions to the permanent tension of life in the 'hide-outs', constantly under the threat of repression.

Then there were the risks of death and torture. In the case of women, the testimonies agree on one crucial point. Besides the physical pain and moral degradation which torture produces (or tries to produce), women are subject to an additional dimension of suffering resulting from sexual violence (rape, sometimes followed by pregnancy) or the rituals of humiliation to which they are subject because they are female. Consequently, prison was seen by many women – as also by men – as a relatively tranquil time, when compared to the period of torture. Finally there was the *reintegration* into what they call 'law-abiding life', with exile sometimes coming in between.

All these extreme situations had a significant impact on private life, particularly because, under the conditions of clandestinity, prison and even, in the closed circles of exile, the rarefaction of political life invades the private space in a suffocating manner. This explains why the love life of militants could be subject to written rules – like those of the Argentinian PRT-ERP[15] – and why the issue of whether or not to have children could become a political problem and, finally, why the fact of a male militant not having resisted torture and betrayal, in addition to imposing a political distance in relation to his party, could be the reason for his wife losing her 'love and respect' for him.[16]

Political enlistment under conditions of clandestinity also represented a sudden and profound change from the personal point of view.

> Those two years – said the militant identified as Hercília – seemed like centuries in our lifetime! I entered the faculty in 1967 and in 1970 I was already a prisoner, had broken off contact with my family and left home and had lost my virginity. Everything happened so quickly.[17]

Clandestinity also causes a crisis of identity. Not only because female militants must assume a false identity – false names and professions and an invented life history – but also because they must break off the many ties which bind them to their former lives, whether these are family, emotional or even amorous ties.

The very fact that amorous relationships occurred in an almost circular manner among militants in the organisation, an obvious consequence of forced intimacy and the security requirements, illustrates this interpenetration of political life and private life.

The testimonies vary in terms of the place of women in militancy. The majority acknowledge that clandestine militancy was a basically masculine world which women entered at a disadvantage. However, their satisfactory performance, particularly in military tasks, can end up acting as an instrument of emancipation.

Luis Mattini, former head of the PRT-ERP, estimates that women made up 40 per cent of his party and had a significant presence in armed actions, including at command levels, although not in the highest positions.[18] He points out the problems which affected couples where the men – invariably with greater responsibility – ended up involving their partners in the tasks which they took on. At times, says Mattini, the high militant qualification of a woman was obscured by the fact that her partner was a leader. The previously mentioned case of Liliana Delfino is explicitly cited. Mattini handles in a balanced manner highly problematic situations in the history of repression in Argentina, such as that of militants who, besides being betrayed, went to live maritally with their torturers. He considers that the 'degradation' occurred in both men and women and that the female cases do not particularly stand out. Finally, his testimony points to particular aspects of the female presence in the political struggle, such as the unintentional temptation which many female militants posed to the rank and file which ended up creating situations of conflict with their wives.

Roberto Perdía talks of the female guerrilla fighters and particularly illustrates the relationship between private life and political life in the years of clandestinity.[19] 'Our house', he says, 'was our base. This inevitably imposed a state of permanent readiness on everyone who lived with us.'[20] He recounts the situation of the 'hide-outs' where weapons and children lived side by side and where more than once the children of militants had to be hidden in cellars or under mattresses during searches of the houses by the army and police in order to escape the firing squads.

The process of reintegration – the second stage involved in the return to law-abiding life – was a long and difficult road. Many of the testi-monies agree that political enlistment in youth – even if at times marked by a lack of thought about the possible consequences – was valid. There is no reason to regret this. However deep the marks made on these sur-vivors – and the horror of the majority of their experiences leaves no doubts in this respect – almost all regard this moment of their lives as full and significant.

However, this was an experience of defeat. Both the Brazilian and Argen-tinian left wings were annihilated, militarily and politically. The fact that almost all the female militants interviewed remain faithful to the ideals which led them to become politically involved in the past, with some now belonging to left-wing parties or movements defending human rights, for example, does not obscure the fact that the projects instigated in that period of their lives failed.

In this respect, we can talk of *disenchantment*, the feeling that antici-pates and prepares for the second stage which these women undertook after their years of clandestinity, torture, prison or exile, when they sought to reintegrate themselves into 'normal life'. This return to 'normal life' specifically involves the recovery of privacy, the discovery of the sub-jectivity obscured by the requirements which clandestine life imposed in the *anos de chumbo*,[21] the need to reconsider the relationships between the public and private spheres and, in particular, the female condition.

It is interesting to note that women's militancy in an eminently 'mascu-line' project (due to its rules, codes and commands) served to emancipate many of the women who participated in this, although this emancipation often only occurred when the women 'behaved like men …', to use a phrase often cited by leaders of the time. But it is also relevant to point out that the emergence of feminism as a strong movement of ideas on the left at the end of the seventies was a product of the failure of these experiences of revolutionary militancy in which women invested so much and from which many learnt their lessons.

The second stage for female militants – their reintegration or return journey to 'normal life' – generally involved processes of self-examination which, as demonstrated by all three books, are full of references to psychoanalysis and feminism. Many former female militants underwent analysis or submitted to therapies and some took up psychoanalysis or psychology as a profession. Others – and sometimes the same ones – joined various women's organisations.

It frequently seems to be the case that some of the groups which contributed most to the development and dissemination of feminist thinking in the 1970s and 1980s in Brazil – *Nós Mulheres, Brasil Mulher* or the *Coletivo Feminista de Paris* – contained a large number of (former) militants from left-wing organisations.

This feminism was constructed through a (self-)critical dialogue in which the left had indulged during the 1960s and 1970s and helped to provide answers to their crises even before the first cracks appeared in the Berlin wall. In other countries where the left were experiencing similar situations to those in Argentina and Brazil – in Chile and Uruguay, for example, or even in countries such as Italy where the political experiences did not have the same radical nature – similar processes occurred.[22]

The first testimony obtained by Marta Diana, from a former militant who asked to be called Adriana, shows how, through feminism, discovered during her exile in Sweden, it was possible for her to perceive 'things from inside me as a woman, for so long pushed aside and subject to the requirement of political militancy'. The most significant moment in her thoughts, however, is when she states that the

> feminists said that no political party took into account the particular problems experienced by female militants. Looking back at my life, I was totally in agreement. Today I could add that no political party has ever considered the problems of its militants (male and female) as people. But this thought came many years later.[23]

The restricted situation of women in revolutionary organisations, subject to the specific conditions of clandestinity, opened the way to establishing a field of debate concerning the specificity of *militancy*, this complex phenomenon in which the public and private spheres are linked. The history of the private life of the left, regarded as the presence of politics in the private sphere – the politicisation of daily life – thus gains its relevance and object.

Both the work on feminine militancy in Argentina and the two texts on Brazil are mainly written on the basis of testimonies. Although Colling tried to research the archives of the DOPS[24] in Rio Grande do Sul, her text does not significantly indicate to what extent these sources helped to shed light on her problems. The opening of the archives of the *Delegacias de Ordem Política e Social* in Rio, São Paulo and other places may mean in the future an increase in the range of research possibilities. In the same way, the monumental work *Brasil Nunca Mais*, now stored in the Edgard Leuenroth archive at Unicamp offers possibilities, surely little explored to date, for new historiographic research about the left.

The choice of oral history to reconstruct the history of the present time has almost always been made as a result of the difficulties arising with other types of source. However, the choice of oral history is also vindicated in view of the suitability of this method in respect of some of the aims pursued, in that autobiographical testimonies allow the subjective dimension of historical processes to be reconstructed in a more consistent manner and this therefore allows *concrete historical subjects to be established* which were previously engulfed by the broad explanatory mechanisms specific to a political historiography in which the militants only appear as participants in an impersonal system.[25]

Various problems arise with this type of source. The autobiographical accounts must be relevant to the research. Colling worked with six interviewees, Ferreira with thirteen, whereas Diana has produced a wider and more complex work, interviewing former (and current) female prisoners and also collecting, orally or in writing, testimonies about women who have died and 'disappeared', from parents, friends or fellow militants. The problem is not so much the number of interviews but the characteristics of the interviewees. The social world of the latter in the three books is more or less the same. Most are young people from the middle classes, students, with only a few of working-class origin.

Judging from the sociological surveys carried out in the Brazilian case,[26] there is a correspondence between the social composition of the left in general and that of the female militants who served as the basis for the research. Empathy between the researchers and the object of their research also exists and does not seem to hinder their analytical capacity. Ferreira and Diana even belong to the same generation as their interviewees. In the Argentinian case, the research is allegedly prompted by the search for a lost friend.[27]

Finally there is the problem of how to connect the life histories, which are full of subjective references, to the context within which these people moved. As explained by Passerini:

> One of the main problems for any autobiographical narrative still remains that of how to combine subjective and objective, or rather, how to move between psychology and history.[28]

This connection can be made as the private sphere, as recreated by the oral history, can establish the paths of individuals within the wider social, political and cultural context of the period analysed. But this context cannot be just a scenario within which the characters move.

In order for these characters to have historicity, it is necessary to examine how this context/scenario is internalised by the militants (male or female) and how this process of internalisation ends up affecting the construction of what is called the microcosm of militancy. As previously explained by Arendt,[29] this involves linking *the objectivity of the world and the human condition*, both regarded as interdependent spheres. This interdependence leads Ferreira to cite Pollak in order to describe the testimonies, and specifically the autobiographical text, as the incarnation of 'a collective destiny', although 'representative of a common social matrix'.[30]

The testimonies obtained using oral history procedures contribute to the more general problem of constructing the memory, either in its specifically individual dimension or in terms of the collective elements present in the autobiographical account. This construction of the memory of (former) female militants, although linked to the past, involves a process significantly affected by political and ideological problems.

The past is not an 'event' or 'fact' to be simply recreated as one would excavate an archaeological fossil, trying to objectively recover something lost at some point of a linearly conceived time. The recreation of this past suffers from a dual political and ideological interference. The 'events' which give this past consistency when being recreated are surrounded by one or more meanings which were previously attributed to them. However, in turn, the reconstruction of the past by the memory also suffers from the influence of the dominant values at the moment when this process is started.

A specific example, but one which is significant in terms of this second aspect, is the reaction which the memoirs of Fernando Gabeira, *O que é isso, companheiro?*, caused for many militants who had intense experiences of the events described by the author, particularly those relating to the kidnapping of the North American ambassador in Brazil.

Many people criticise in the memoirs of Gabeira – which served as the basis for the film by Bruno Barreto – the attempt by the author to attribute to the past a lucidity which he was only to have in later years, including that gained as a result of a process of collective reflection by the left.[31] This particular episode simply points to the more general problems involved in appropriating and reconstructing the past. In the case of the lives of female militants, the depth of the problems of gender has started to attribute meanings to events regarded as devoid of history. But this does not amount to the existence of feminism being recorded before the term existed, projected retrospectively on the past.

The illumination of this side of the past, hitherto hidden, gives historicity to the lives of subjects supposedly without history. But this perspective, which militants (male or female) today possess in order to reappropriate their past life, can only be developed where experience has allowed a different history to be reconstructed. This different history was (is) also composed of fragments of the private sphere, the hidden face of the political event, which gained all its meaning, however, as the private sphere started to internalise and reflect the public sphere and was turned into a decisive element for understanding reality in a more far-reaching sense. This aspect provides a better understanding of the role of oral history in creating a history of women, particularly female militancy.

The use of testimonies is more than a technical resource from which the researcher starts in the absence of other sources. There is a relationship of functionality between these testimonies and the researched object in that the testimonies can recreate, due to their form and the contents which they bring to light, aspects of human action disregarded because, until that point, they were regarded as lacking historicity and political meaning. The historicisation/politicisation of daily life gives meaning to 'marginal' problems confined to private life, and restores the female account of events, frequently discarded due to its 'confessional tone' when not due to its 'psychologism'. This is not a question of epistemological (politically correct) tolerance in view of the accounts of women, but of understanding that it is through this type of account that problems can be illuminated which have until then been disregarded in the world of political action – as in that of militancy – which is an area where the major strategic formulations intervene and collide with the hard requirements of reality.

In the first stage – the entry into clandestine militancy – women adopted the words and requirements of political action specific to the 'world of men'. The 'success' which they had in this process – and the history of the left is full of examples in this respect – became a unique instrument of emancipation in that equality with men was recognised, at least rhetorically.

In the second stage – the almost always difficult exit from clandestinity – equality is no longer sought by mimicking the masculine world. On the contrary, this involves celebrating the differences, which is compatible with aspirations to formal and substantive equality. This second stage occurs through other words, with a basically confessional structure, from which the political aspect is not excluded, but which involves understanding this political side from the experience gained. It is in this way that the public and private are linked and are (inter)determined. It was the reciprocal illumination of these two spheres of the human condition which provided the opportunity to construct a different history of political action.

But this different history must avoid the pitfall of assigning the public space to men while the private space, although 'politicised', is reserved for women, because it is wrong to totally 'masculinise' the public sphere, in the same way as it is wrong to totally 'feminise' the private sphere.[32]

While it is true that the words of women allow a different history of political militancy to be constructed, it is wrong for this history to be just a history of women. It is easy, from the open or veiled misogyny of certain historiographic texts, to succumb to a temptation to create a history of women as a separate area. The Colling text, although it does not fall into this trap, flirts rhetorically with this perspective.

The traditional division of tasks and roles mainly reserved the private spaces for women. Because women were for most of the time denied political rights and were absent from the decision-making centres, they were almost always 'reduced to submitting passively to the events of public life, the "historical" events'. But there are exceptional situations, where the events were

> produced and not passively lived by the women: this involves in most cases a protest, a resistance, a demand, an insurrection, in short a more or less violent form of revolt.[33]

It has already been observed that the study of history using the masculine and feminine perspective identified the themes of public and private space, domestic and social power and public power. But it would be useful to ask

> if the success of these approaches does not end up making it impossible to extend the research to the political field and to work on male/female relationships within the overall social and political system.[34]

The persistence of the impasse, even though it reserves an area for the history of women, ends up denying this history as it is relegated to a marginal space. The price to be paid in order to draw women from this nebulous area of history cannot be the creation of a historiographic ghetto. If this were to occur, the emergence of the problems of gender in humanities, particularly in historiography, would appear as a concession, the result of a kind of 'affirmative action' in the realm of the theoretical.

> Therefore, Farge is right when she proposes establishing a history of the tensions between masculine and feminine roles and creating a link between their conflicts and their complementary aspects which would encompass the whole historical account.[35]

It is possible for the militancy of women and men during the *anos de chumbo* in Argentina, Brazil and other countries to be depicted as one of those situations in which historiography can, using the analysis of the tensions, conflicts and complementary aspects of roles, try to build an alternative and comprehensive analysis.

This complex reflection rightly benefits from the way in which the issues of the public and private spheres in the rarefied spaces of clandestine militancy of the period in question are linked and interpenetrate.

Michelle Perrot, criticising the idea of 'creating a new area which would be the history of women, a tranquil concession where they would move comfortably, protected from any contradiction', insists that this involves 'changing the direction of the historical perspective, making the issue of relationships between the sexes into a central issue'.[36] This change in historical perspective of examining the issues of gender in the world of militancy, and therefore re-linking the public and private spheres, opens up unexpected prospects for political historiography, particularly for that centred on political action and the path of left-wing organisations.

Notes

This chapter first appeared in *Cadernos Pagu*, 8 (1997), pp. 319–42. We are grateful to both the author and the journal for permission to publish this translation.

1. Georges Haupt, *L'Historien et le mouvement social* (François Maspero, Paris, 1980), p. 12.

2. Perry Anderson, 'Communist Party History', in *People's History and Socialist Theory*, ed. Raphael Samuel (Routledge & Kegan Paul, London, 1981), pp. 145–56; E. J. Hobsbawm, *Revolutionaries. Contemporary Essays* (Weidenfeld & Nicolson, London, 1973); and the monumental *História do Marxismo*, in 12 volumes, coordinated by Hobsbawm (Paz e Terra, São Paulo, 1983–9).

3. This interpretation of the events of 1968 is, according to Castoriadis, given by Luc Ferry and Alain Renaut, *O Pensamento 68, ensaio sobre o anti-humanismo contemporâneo* (Editoria Ensaio, São Paulo, 1988) and by Gilles Lipovetsky, *L'Ere du vide, Essai sur l'individualisme contemporain* (Gallimard, Paris, 1983). For Castoriadis's own argument, Cornelius Castoriadis, *Les Carrefours du Labyrinthe IV – La Montée de l'Insignificance* (Seuil, Paris, 1996), pp. 27–8.

4. Hannah Arendt, *The Human Condition* (Doubleday Anchor, New York, 1959), p. 11.

5. The likening of Communist parties to a counter-society is used by Annie Kriegel, *Les Communistes Français, essai d'ethnographie politique* (Editions du Seuil, Paris, 1968). The same theoretical framework inspires the work of Philippe Robrieux, *Maurice Thorez, vie secrète et vie publique* (Fayard, Paris, 1975); *Histoire Intérieure du Parti Communiste Français*, 4 vols (Fayard, Paris, 1980–84); La Secte (Stock, Paris, 1985).

6. 'More than just being anecdotal, the history of private life is also the political history of daily life.' See Michelle Perrot and Georges Duby, *Histoire des femmes en Occident*, vol. 4, *Le XIXème siècle* (Plon, Paris, 1991), p. 13.

7. Editora da Fundação Getúlio Vargas, Rio de Janeiro, 1996.

8. Editora Rosa dos Ventos, Rio de Janeiro, 1997.

9. Planeta, Buenos Aires, 1996.

10. Cf. Judith Patarra, *Iara* (Rosa dos Ventos, Rio de Janeiro, 1992). See also Marco Aurélio Garcia, 'Iara, história e cotidiano', *Estudos Feministas*, 1 (1993), pp. 210–12, in which I try to identify the historiographical contribution of the Patarra book.

11. The Brazilian literature, like the Latin American, is immense. It includes not only memoirs and collective works of oral history, but also fictional works. Recently even cinema targeted this period. The controversies created by films such as *Lamarca* by Sergio Rezende and *O que é isso companheiro?* by Bruno Barreto are signs that the subject of the memory of the *anos de chumbo* is interesting to more than experts or 'ex-fighters'. On the Barreto film, see Daniel Aarão Reis Filho et al., *Versões e ficções: o seqüestro da história* (Fundação Perseu Abramo, São Paulo, 1997). With regard to the memoirs, one in particular stands out, by Albertina de Oliveira Costa, et al., *Memórias (das mulheres) do exílio* (Paz e Terra, Rio de Janeiro, 1980). This is a pioneering text whose writing was to a large extent influenced by the formation of feminist collectives in the Brazilian diaspora in Europe.

12. *Emma Goldman, a vida como revolução* (Brasiliense, São Paulo, 1983) and 'Emma Goldman – Revolução e desencanto: do público ao privado', *Revista Brasileira de História* (São Paulo), 8 (1989).

13. The books of Ferreira and Colling, two excellent works, are written using the testimonies of survivors, whereas that of Diana combines the testimony of survivors with the recreation of the path of women who died and 'disappeared'.

14. Cf. Ferreira, *Mulheres, Militância e Memória*, p. 15.

15. *Partido Revolucionário dos Trabalhadores – Exército Revolucionário do Povo* (Workers' Revolutionary Party – Revolutionary Army of the Poor).

16. The painful testimony of Luis Ortoloni about his wife, Liliana Delfino, is in Diana, *Mujeres Guerrilleras*, pp. 359–66. Liliana, just after being released from prison, where she was informed of the behaviour of her husband, separated from Luis and went to live with the most senior leader of the PRT-ERP, Mário Roberto Santucho. The former wife of Santucho, Ana Maria Villarcal, had died shortly before the 'Trelew operation' when he succeeded in escaping from prison. Later on, Liliana and Santucho were killed together when the 'hide-out' of the PRT leader was located by the police.

17. Cf. Ferreira, *Mulheres, Militância e Memória*, p. 126.

18. Cf. Diana, *Mujeres Guerrilleras*, pp. 370–74. See also Luis Mattini, *Hombres y mujeres del PRT-ERP (La pasión militante)* (Editorial de la Campana, La Plata, 1995).

19. Cf. Diana, *Mujeres Guerrilleras*, pp. 375–80.

20. Diana, *Mujeres Guerrilleras*, p. 375.

21. 'The political project in which [the former prisoners interviewed] became involved contrasts, due to its comprehensive and all-encompassing nature, with social reality and the field to which these young people were attracted, with this contrast constituting – for the purposes of interpretation – one of the most intriguing aspects of their experiences and the most difficult to understand. Therefore, the research on the effects of this passage from cultural pluralism as in the 1960s (particularly in 1968) to the centralising monism of Communism, which required complete adherence and eradication of internal differences, is relevant' (Ferreira, *Mulheres, Militância e Memória*, p. 66).

22. The novel by Marcela Serrano, *Nosotras, que nos amábamos tanto*, depicting the lives of a group of female friends in Pinochet's Chile, provides suggestions for examining this journey made by women. It is well known in Italy that the emergence of feminism had a strong impact both on the parliamentary left and on the extra-parliamentary left. It was the crisis with the women of Lotta Continua, perhaps the most important extra-parliamentary organisation in Italy in the 1970s, which caused this group to collapse during its Second Congress. Even the Italian Communist Party was shaken by the feminist response. The literature on this period is vast. See, among others, Rossana Rossanda, *Anche per me – Donna, persona, memoria dal 1973 al 1986* (Feltrinelli, Milano, 1987).

23. Cf. Diana, *Mujeres Guerrilleras*, p. 41.

24. *Delegacias de Ordem Política e Social* (Offices for Political and Social Order).

25. 'The women's movements were particularly responsible for making the personal narrative a political practice. However, the attempt to create a historical subject on the basis of specific daily conditions, moving from subjection to subjectivity and confirming a dual right to be in history and to have a history, must also be attributed to other movements, particularly the students' movement of 1968.' Cf. Luisa Passerini, *Storia e Soggettività* (La Nuova Italia, Firenze, 1988).

26. Cf. Marcelo Ridenti, *O Fantasma da Revolução Brasileira* (UNESP, São Paulo, 1993), pp. 68–72.

27. This is Adriana Lesgart, code-named Patricia, a guerrilla militant who disappeared with several of her brothers-in-arms. Adriana was at college with Marta Diana and formed a frequent point of reference in the biography of the journalist.

28. Passerini, *Storia e Soggettività*, p. 9.

29. See above, n. 4.

30. Ferreira, *Mulheres, Militância e Memória*, p. 85.

31. Cf. Fernando Gabeira, *O que é isso, companheiro?* (Codecri, Rio de Janeiro, 1980); and also *O crepúsculo do macho* (Codecri, Rio de Janeiro, 1980). The criticism of Gabeira is in Daniel Aarão Reis Filho, 'Versões e ficções: a luta pela apropriação da memória' and Alípio Freire, 'Pela porta dos fundos', in *Versões e ficções*, ed. Aarão Reis Filho.

32. Cf. Michelle Perrot, 'Les femmes, le pouvoir, l'histoire', in *Une Histoire des femmes est-elle possible?*, ed. Michelle Perrot (Rivages, Paris-Marseilles, 1984).

33. Cf. Yvonne Knibiehler, 'Chronologie et histoire des femmes', in *Une Histoire des femmes*, ed. Perrot, p. 51.

34. Arlette Farge, 'Pratique et effets de l'histoire des femmes', in *Une Histoire des femmes*, ed. Perrot, p. 33.

35. Farge, 'Pratique et effets de l'histoire des femmes', p. 33.

36. Cf. Michelle Perrot, Preface to *Une Histoire des femmes*, p. 15.

5

Women and the Public Sphere

Jane Rendall

It is evident that the pervasive and gendered rhetorical contrast between public and private worlds was put to many different purposes in eighteenth-century Britain, as it was in the following century. I want to say immediately that this is of course not an entirely British issue; it is one which in different and specific ways characterised the literature of most Western societies. However, I shall concentrate mainly on Britain and hope that this will stimulate comparative discussion.

The contrasts can be illustrated. To the patriot Reverend Richard Brewster in 1759, 'a Race of Men, who prefer the public Good before any narrow or selfish Views – who choose Dangers in Defence of their Country before an inglorious safety, [and] an honourable Death' was to be contrasted with 'the unmanly pleasures of a useless and effeminate life'.[1] To Gilbert Stuart writing from Scotland, public power for women testified to the qualities of a past golden age: 'what evinces their consideration beyond the possibility of a doubt, is the attention they bestowed on business and affairs. They felt, as well as the noble and the warrior, the cares of the community … They went to the public councils or assemblies of their nations, heard the debates of the statesmen, and were called upon to deliver their sentiments.'[2] The historian of women, William Alexander, writing in 1779, contrasted the absence of women from all forms of public employment with the private influence they might exercise:

> In Britain, we allow a woman to sway our sceptre, but by law and custom we debar her from every other government but that of her own family, as if there were not a public employment between that of superintending the kingdom, and the affairs of her own kitchen, which could be managed by the genius and capacity of woman. We neither allow women to officiate at our altars, to debate in our councils, nor to fight for us in the field; we suffer them not to be members of our senate, to practise any of the learned professions, nor to concern themselves much with our trades and occupations.[3]

But David Davies, writing in 1795, was making a very different point: 'If constant employment were found for the wives and children of labouring men ... the benefit public and private thence resulting would be great'.[4] Adam Smith had famously contrasted the fruitless pursuit of the public good with the miraculous uses of private interest. In that spirit he wrote that

> There are no publick institutions for the education of women, and there is accordingly nothing useless, absurd, or fantastical in the common course of their education. They are taught what their parents or guardians judge it necessary or useful for them to learn; and they are taught nothing else.[5]

Exceptionally, Smith did however advocate national schools for the boys of the labouring poor. Mary Wollstonecraft reversed his argument in her *Vindication* in advocating public national schools for girls as well as boys, asserting that

> To render women truly useful members of society, I argue that they should be led, by having their undertakings cultivated on a large scale, to acquire a rational affection for their country, founded on knowledge, because it is obvious that we are little interested about what we do not understand. And to render this general knowledge of due importance, I have endeavoured to shew that private duties are never properly fulfilled unless the understanding enlarges the heart; and that public virtue is only an aggregate of private.[6]

To anyone who has even sampled British prescriptive literature in the eighteenth and nineteenth centuries, the contrast between private and public worlds, and what I shall here treat as one particular version of it, the language of separate spheres, assigned to women and men, is immediately familiar. So, in the Britain of the 1830s and 1840s, the metaphor of women's sphere pervades the literature of Sarah Stickney Ellis:

> Can it be a subject of regret to any kind and feeling woman, that her sphere of action is one adapted to the exercise of the affections, where she may love, and trust, and hope, and serve, to the utmost of her wishes? Can it be a subject of regret that she is not called upon, so much as man, to calculate, to compete, to struggle, but rather to occupy a sphere in which the elements of discord cannot with propriety be admitted – in which beauty and order are expected to denote her presence, and where the exercise of benevolence is the duty she is most frequently called upon to perform.[7]

Marion Reid, writing *A Plea for Woman* in 1841, quoted extensively from the literature of 'woman's sphere', fallacious, cramped and confining as she saw it, and began with a comparison of the two spheres, here defined as domestic and business duties:

> Having thus attempted to point out to the attention of our readers the most obvious of those fallacies, by the assumption of which, as truths, the forcible cramping and confining of woman's sphere is attempted to be justified, we think it would very much assist us in this investigation, were we now to

institute a comparison between domestic and business duties these appearing to be the broad and distinct divisions into which the peculiar duties of the sexes separate – that we may see whether there is any truth in the very general impression, that woman's sphere is a mean one in comparison with man's ...[8]

Barbara Bodichon opposed the public good to 'narrow private ends':

And among all the reasons for giving women votes, the one which appears to me the strongest is that of the influence it might be expected to have in increasing public spirit. Patriotism, a healthy, lively, intelligent interest in everything which concerns the nation to which we belong, and an unselfish devotedness to the public service, – these are the qualities which make a people great and happy; these are the virtues which ought to be most sedulously cultivated in all classes of the community. And I know no better means at this present time, of counteracting the tendency to prefer narrow private ends to the public good, than this of giving to all women, duly qualified, a direct and conscious participation in political affairs.[9]

Yet to Harriet Martineau, writing of the range of women's labour in 1859, the national interest was identical with that of the private industry of women:

Old obstructions must be removed; and the aim must be set before us, as a nation as well as in private life, to provide for the free development and full use of the powers of every member of the community ... This will secure our welfare, nationally and in our homes, to which few elements can contribute more vitally and more richly than the independent industry of our country-women.[10]

Such a selection of extracts has, of course, a certain arbitrariness to it: many would not agree with my choice of illustrations here. But they are chosen simply to show something of the diversity of uses of this powerful opposition in the eighteenth and nineteenth centuries.

The contrast has been, at the same time, central to much of the writing on women's history in Britain and North America from the early 1970s. The focus on the language of separate spheres and the dichotomies between private and public was fundamental to charting the limitations and oppression of women's lives. Though these contrasts had far older roots, in both Greek and Roman usages, this formulation appeared to be a particular characteristic of Western capitalist societies, from the seventeenth century onwards. Women appeared invisible in representations of both the political economies and modernising states of the nineteenth-century West.

In British history, the work of Leonore Davidoff and Catherine Hall in *Family Fortunes* in 1987 placed gender relations at the heart of class formation.[11] The attention they gave to the language of separate spheres attracted considerable controversy, in comments which did not always acknowledge the extent to which they had traced the integral relations between public and private worlds. Joyce Thomas and Amanda Vickery questioned what they saw as a 'grand narrative' of gender relations in Britain, which identified the language of separate spheres, and the strengthening of the public/private dichotomy, with modernisation and the growth of capitalism. Linda Colley, in examining women's involvement in patriotic activities during the Napoleonic War, suggested that a renewed emphasis on separate spheres could potentially reflect increasing rather than diminishing participation by women in public life.[12]

For the time being I do not want to address these debates directly, but to suggest some different questions. As my hurried sample suggests, the contrast between public and private worlds throughout the eighteenth and nineteenth centuries drew not on one, but on multiple contrasts. But recognising such variations does not necessarily provide us with new analytical tools. I'd like to turn to the ways in which twentieth-century commentators have attempted to categorise these contrasts. I draw on a recent essay by Jeff Weintraub to illustrate them.[13] He reminds us that the public does not necessarily imply the political, suggesting that there are two distinct and underlying kinds of imagery in this contrast: what is open and accessible versus the concealed and hidden; and what is collective, and what relates only to the individual. He also notes four main usages. First, the difference between what is public and what is private may refer to the contrast between state administration and public policy, and the market economy. Secondly, it may relate to that between the political community more broadly conceived, the republic or community of citizens, distinct from both the market and the administrative state. In both these cases, 'public' means the sphere of the political, though in rather different ways; he notes the confusing origins of this difference in the republic of the Greek polis, and notion of sovereignty within Roman law. Thirdly, it may contrast the private and intimate world of the family with that of different forms of public sociability and public space. Fourthly, there is that contrast between public and private worlds which, as Carole Pateman suggested in a much quoted early essay in 1983, was central to the feminist struggle, 'ultimately what the feminist movement is about'.[14] In such work – though it is very diverse – the domestic or private sphere was contrasted with the 'public', the extensive, residual but gendered category incorporating the market, civil society, and the state.

Gender difference defined the latter contrast. Yet, as Weintraub notes, the simplicity of the contrast between the private and the world outside it could obscure the multiple uses of the public. Others of course were there before him. In her fine article of 1995 on 'Some Old Husbands' Tales', Leonore Davidoff traced the growth of multiple publics, including the economic, the social and the political spheres, each clearly an artefact, partly through the conceptual frameworks of evolving nineteenth-century disciplines, increasingly professionalised, though she also reminded us of the untidy nature of men's and women's lives, not marked out in segmented pie charts.[15] And recent work on the social has marked out what Denise Riley has called 'the blurred ground between the old public and private'.[16] I would not necessarily agree with her that such ground brought with it 'the dislocation of the political', but would argue rather that such formulations could coexist, as claims to citizenship continued to draw upon a sense of public good and public spirit.

Leonore Davidoff has enjoined us to maintain continuing historical precision in the analysis of context and meaning as we analyse such terms. We need of course also such precision for the private, but that is another story. Here, I wish to speculate on what may be the advantages and the disadvantages for feminist historians and historians of women, of a different definition of the 'public sphere', one which is not inclusive and residual but has a very specific meaning given to that term by Jürgen Habermas. In doing so I will refer briefly to collaborative work with Catherine Hall and Keith McClelland on the British Reform Act of 1867, where we consider, from our different perspectives, a moment of political conflict which defined the qualifications for one form of citizenship, the right to vote.[17] My own particular interest is in the relationship of the women's suffrage movement to that debate.

In his major work *The Structural Transformation of the Public Sphere*, first published in the early 1960s, Habermas distinguished what he called the bourgeois public sphere both from the institutions of the state and from those of the market-place.[18] This public sphere is one 'which mediates between society and the state, in which the public organises itself as the bearer of public opinion'. It presupposes a range of sociocultural and economic changes, the growth of urban culture and a reading public. It is paradoxically positioned in relation to public/private contrasts in that he conceived it as 'a sphere of private people who have come together as a public'. It emerges from the intimacy of private reading, letters, salons into the political associations and voluntary societies, the periodicals and the press, from which he constructs what is as much ideal as history, a liberal ideal of a reasoning public. It is relevant and important that his model case is Britain, whose bourgeois public sphere is identifiable by the beginning of the eighteenth century.

It has been largely since its translation in 1989 that feminist political scientists and women's historians have responded extensively to Habermas. They have mounted fundamental criticisms of his model, notably the absence of a specifically gendered construction, his reliance on abstract rationality, and his discussion of the family as the source of a new subjectivity. One feminist historian, Joan Landes, writing on the French Revolution, argued that the creation of such a bourgeois public sphere was from its inception intrinsically masculinist, its legacy still embedded in Western democratic society today.[19]

Alternatively, in their very different work on the eighteenth-century Enlightenment, and on the politics of nineteenth-century cities in the United

States, Margaret Jacob and Mary Ryan both argued that such a public sphere permitted women a small but increasing share in participating and shaping public opinion, whether in their participation in the enlightened masonic lodge, or in their role in the ceremonial parade characteristic of city politics.[20] In *Family Fortunes,* Davidoff and Hall too traced the formation of the sphere of public opinion in early nineteenth-century English middle-class provincial life, illustrating both the scope of men's voluntary activity, and the varying and inconsistent ways in which a minority of women might participate within such a public opinion.

I'd like to suggest that there remain some advantages to feminist historians, historians of feminism, and historians of women in public, in looking harder at Habermas's concept of public opinion, part history, part ideal of reasoned communication, and at the institutions of such a bourgeois public sphere in the eighteenth and nineteenth centuries – though we may not put them to the same use. Critics of Habermas like Landes and Nancy Fraser[21] have charged him with erecting an abstract and masculinist ideal of rational-critical discourse. One defender, Keith Baker, suggested that even within discussion of the French Revolution, opposing notions of the public were to be found within Habermas's work.[22] Landes's erection of a Rousseauist notion of the bourgeois republic rooted in the dichotomy between reason and nature is historically unconvincing. It does not allow us to recover the significance of Enlightenment discourses of rational social progress, discourses which, though often unidentified in British political history, were immensely powerful. The vocabularies of civilisation, of progressive historical improvement through the polish of commerce and spread of learning, the political history of liberty, were ones which Mary Wollstonecraft shared with Adam Smith, Harriet Martineau with John Stuart Mill. The complexity of the language of the modernising and the rational Enlightenment has not received full justice in histories of British feminism, though Kathryn Dodd's essay on Ray Strachey has shown us its longevity within the liberal tradition.[23] More precise work on the vocabularies of eighteenth- and nineteenth-century feminism, vocabularies which have to be sited within a complex context which is partly that of the bourgeois public sphere, is only just beginning.

It is important, too, that oppositional frameworks, the assumption of absolute barriers, do not obscure that history. For instance, we know extraordinarily little about the history of middle-class girls' education from *c.* 1750 to 1850, though in an excellent collection of essays on *Gender in Eighteenth-Century England,* one local study has indicated the growth of women's private enterprise and employment, linked to expanding publication.[24] Women's attendance at public lectures or even debating clubs, their participation in subscription libraries, their reading practices might all develop such themes, cutting across imposed public–private distinctions. Stephen Howard, examining periodical and newspaper biographies of women in the eighteenth century, found extensive and expanding coverage, calling into question any narrowing of activities, despite a rhetorical focus on private virtue.[25]

That takes me to another and even more powerful theme. The same volume contains a discussion by Hannah Barker of the significant role of tradeswomen printers, actively participating in the expansion of newspaper and book production.[26] For the expansion of print culture and its many consequences remains one of the most fertile and exciting areas of work for the study of women in public. In 1989, Nancy Armstrong suggested in *Desire and Domestic Fictions* the possibilities of shifting the boundaries between fiction, prescription and politics, through the intervention of middle-class women writers.[27] Though Habermas merely hints at what worlds of scholarship are beginning to explore, there remains much to do, in identifying the obscure as well as the well known, the locally published, the links of patronage and subscription that could extend to the working woman as well as the best-selling novelist. This is fertile but challenging ground for interdisciplinarity. We still need to explore the gendering of genres. Though we may assume such possibilities were present for only a small minority of women, work by Donna Landry, Roger Lonsdale and others has uncovered the working-woman poet.[28] Though there is little space below to explore such themes, they are entirely relevant to my history of politics in the 1860s. It is very clear that the Langham Place feminists shared their commitments through poetry, prose, fiction, and history. Among women suffragists, Anne Isabella Robertson of Dublin chose first to write in fictional form, whether on women's employment, or on the politics of landownership and religion in Ireland.[29]

What I am suggesting is that reading Habermas forces one to consider the historically specific forms of the bourgeois public sphere which he addresses, in ways which do blur public and private distinctions. But I want to turn also to the disadvantages of his model, and my comments on these largely follow those by Davidoff and Geoff Eley.[30]

First, a single focus on the liberal model of the public sphere ignores all counter-publics, for instance, and most notably the gendered plebeian public of which Anna Clark has given us such a fine portrait.[31] And it is important to incorporate the conflict and the interaction between different publics. Such conflicts and negotiations may be immensely valuable to historians of women and feminism. Kathryn Gleadle, for instance, has fruitfully demonstrated the relationship of radical Unitarian, Owenite and Chartist politics, while in my own work I have explored how the links forged between radical-liberal political men and the leaders of the reforming movement of the 1860s facilitated the emergence of the women's suffrage movement.[32] Secondly, the liberal public world was shaped not only by rational ideals but by battles and conflicts over inclusion and exclusion, who was in and who was out, battles which were partly but not entirely determined on the basis of gender. In *Defining the Victorian Nation*, we look at 1867 as a point in the making of a nation, a moment of political history which incorporated a complex pattern of exclusions and inclusions, in which gender was one, but not the only or always the determining criterion.

Now a model of the public sphere which is rooted in a rational politics does not offer us the means of understanding the complex constitution of identities, which are not framed in terms of the public/private dichotomy alone. As Geoff Eley has pointed out, this bourgeois public sphere ignores the history of nationalism and national identities, and indeed largely ignores nineteenth-century politics and political movements altogether. How are we to relate women in public to the history of the nation? Part of that answer may of course lie in the themes which Colley has drawn to our attention. But the issues are surely more fundamental even than demonstrable patriotism at moments of national threat. In the imaginative literature, prose and poetry written by women and men, and read by women as by men from the late eighteenth century onwards, aspects of the national past and present were explored. There are issues here which raise questions both of cultural identity and political practice.

One obvious question here with reference to Britain might be: how far did women, like men, identify with the different nations or publics of the United Kingdom, and what alternative visions of national futures were addressed? In the later nineteenth century the journals of the women's movement took up with some delight the evidence of the power of women in the past, though their accounts are dominated by a feminist version of the Norman Yoke theory of the glories of Anglo-Saxonism, and by powerful medieval women. As I looked at the politics of women's suffrage around 1870, I read the *Englishwoman's Review* and the *Women's Suffrage Journal*. Both offered a detailed guide not only to meetings held in London, Birmingham, Manchester and Bristol but also to meetings held in Dublin, Belfast, Aberdeen and the Shetland Islands. Twentieth-century perspectives have obscured these relationships.

The bourgeois public sphere was itself constructed in a variety of excluding and changing ways. The skilled working man might qualify, the educated single woman householder achieve a local if not a national vote. But they could also draw upon metaphorical structures based upon anthropological histories of civilisation which ultimately looked back to the Enlightenment and upon a sense of modernity and advance which defined itself by contrasts, against the more primitive and less advanced, taking the condition of women as a guide to the level of civilisation attained. That phrase can be found, among those mentioned here, in the writing of William Alexander, Mary Wollstonecraft, Harriet Martineau, and Millicent Fawcett, as also John Stuart Mill and Friedrich Engels. Such structures are relevant also to the intentions of legislators as to the media of the public, its periodicals and literature, its clubs and associations.

My point is that a single version of the public sphere is insufficient to allow us to understand the complicated variety of ways in which women might identify with communities which stretched far beyond the borders – whatever those were – of home and family. Habermas's highly secularised version of the public sphere, for instance, pays very little attention to the understanding of religious identities, not simply to be subsumed as voluntary associations or even as ideologies. How are we to interpret, for instance, the travelling ministries of nineteenth-century middle-class Quaker women preachers? as public or private? Equally, one late nineteenth-century feminist, Josephine Butler, understood those issues of identity perfectly. In 1887, in her pamphlet *Our Christianity Tested by the Irish Question*, she wrote of the internal struggle which was certainly hers, to do justice to a Catholic country. Interpreting the history of Ireland, she wrote of it as 'at its happiest, and freest when most independent of Papal government and influence', and of:

> good people in England, strong in their Protestantism, who are urging against Home Rule, their dread of the future ascendancy of the Pope in the sister island.[33]

Yet for Butler the law of Christ had to overcome her unwillingness, and led her to support Home Rule. Nevertheless, the power of overwhelmingly Protestant or progressively secular identification in response to Papal power was a striking theme for male and female radical liberals.

My case here then is that we need to do justice to Davidoff's view that 'key questions about the creation of identity have to be extended beyond family, home and childhood'.[34] No precise boundaries between public and private worlds can do justice to those many sites. I took Habermas's work simply to illustrate our difficulties. Recent discussions most effectively place his concept of the public sphere as a product of its time, of the early 1960s, in its critique of the mass culture in a prosperous Christian Democratic Germany, and in its attempt to retrieve some aspects of the progressive aspects of an Enlightenment ideal of rational communication, an ideal whose later history was that of degeneration.

As with the questions posed by Habermas, other questions are also prompted. And there have been many signs that simple models of the public sphere, or of the public/private contrast are now limiting our understanding of the vocabulary and practices of eighteenth- or nineteenth-century women. Criticisms of the language of 'separate spheres' came earlier and more forcibly from the US than from Britain. They have clearly drawn theoretically upon approaches to gender shaped by postmodernism. More specifically, both Linda Kerber and Nancy Hewitt indicated the danger of generalisations about 'women' which rested on class-specific languages, in the United States rooted in the lives of white middling-class women of the northern and central states. Their concerns are mirrored in the three editions of the reader in multicultural women's history *Unequal Sisters*. Kerber called for 'separate spheres' to be recognised as a metaphorical device, a powerful trope, by which women and men made sense of their experience and helped to structure it.[35]

British histories, as I have suggested already, have begun to take into account the consequences of that challenge but there is still some way to go in understanding the shaping of eighteenth- and nineteenth-century British feminism and its ambivalent relationship to liberal public spheres, the histories of which, especially those from within British political history, have until very recently been particularly impervious to gendered approaches. To say that is not to underestimate the strength of the work undertaken on working-class women's lives and activism, but rather to emphasise the extent to which they represent an Other and different experience, still posed against a dominant paradigm. At the same time it may be helpful to reflect on the ways in which our own understanding of nineteenth-century women's language is shaped by our inherited perceptions of the meanings of public and private lives in late twentieth-century Britain. So for instance – and here I'm being quite speculative – how far does the concept of being 'economically active' or inactive, the contrast between employment and unemployment, our knowledge of the constrained labour market and bars to the employment of married women in the early twentieth century, shape our approaches to the forms of employment open to eighteenth- and nineteenth-century women? Similarly, as I think about a book I published in 1985, *Origins of Modern Feminism*, I have become increasingly aware of its Whiggishness, its history of modernisation, and its debts to its predecessors, both academic and feminist.[36] Past histories of progress, of the advance from private to public worlds, are very difficult to disavow.

Our perceptions may indeed have unduly limited the range of questions we could be asking. In her study *Private Lives, Public Spirit*, Jose Harris wrote challengingly of the local nature of late nineteenth-century Britain as 'a large, ramshackle and profoundly custom-based society'.[37] She wrote with respect to the forms of family life, but I would suggest, speculatively, that the consequences of such continuity for all forms of women's activism remain to be explored, although there are certainly signs of moves towards a new political history for women, by Elaine Chalus, Amanda Foreman, Sarah Richardson, Matthew Cragoe and others.[38]

I illustrate the problem from one example. In the course of writing about the complexities of the Reform Act of 1867 and the first years of the women's suffrage movement, I came to realise how little, empirically, we know about some fundamental issues, such as the role of women in different forms of eighteenth- and nineteenth-century local government. Before the Municipal Corporations Act of 1835, single or widowed women might legally exercise the municipal franchise, depending on local custom; some authorities suggest they did so. After that Act, they could still vote in unincorporated towns. We do not know how far they did so, or how far they were active at parish level. When, in 1869, some women were given the municipal vote, legislators could view this as a conservative move. The anomaly by which incorporation meant exclusion was recognised. Excluded Manchester female ratepayers compared the right to vote of women in the unincorporated suburbs with their own position.[39] They indicated that women were also, depending on local custom, eligible to vote for Boards of Health and

Improvement Commissions.[40] In May 1869, Jacob Bright of Manchester and John Hibbert of Oldham, both longstanding supporters of the women's cause, rose to amend the Municipal Franchise Bill for England and Wales in its committee stage. Bright argued that the previous Act of 1835 had been innovatory in its exclusion of women, invading their established rights. The recent incorporation of Darlington and Southport had disfranchised women, a quarter of Southport's 2,085 qualified voters. Bright also suggested (and further research is needed here) that in boroughs where such provision existed, women exercised it in the same proportion as men. Henry Austin Bruce, Gladstone's Home Secretary, who had already shown himself a sympathiser with the cause, rose to say that:

> the hon. member had shown conclusively that this proposition was no novelty and that in every form of local government, except under the Municipal Corporations Act, females were allowed to vote. The clause introduced no anomaly, and he should give it his cordial support.[41]

In Scotland, however, women had to wait until 1882 for such municipal enfranchisement, in Ireland until 1898 (although in 1887 it was sneaked into a local Act for Belfast). I highlight here one brief episode; I do not know the answer as to whether women exercised such customary privileges, and I am still working on the motives of Henry Austin Bruce. But a rigid opposition between public and private worlds may have helped to obscure such questions.

Anna Clark has written of the extent to which the masculinity of citizenship was both rewritten and strengthened in the course of the nineteenth century.[42] I agree with that strengthening. My point relates to questions of degree and the significance of alternative frameworks. Our discussion of the politics of the Reform Act suggests that gender cannot be taken as an absolutely defining category in relation to the complexities of citizenship, even though it determined the exclusion of the majority of women. The male electorate after 1867 remained limited to 33 per cent of adult males in 1871, inheriting many archaic local characteristics, varying significantly across the constituent parts of the United Kingdom, and depending for registration largely on the intermittent zeal of local party workers.[43] And, as Catherine Hall has shown, definitions of citizenship were undertaken contemporaneously not only with reference to the four nations of the UK but also with reference to the very diverse situations of the different territories subject to the sovereignty of the UK, white colonies of settlement, the Indian Empire, the West Indies and many more.[44]

I return then to the question of public and private worlds and their different dichotomous meanings. The popularity of Habermas's view of the bourgeois public sphere can serve to remind us of the significance of the contrast between the open and the secret, the public and inaccessible. It may also remind us of the importance of the relationship between the growth of feminism and the liberal public. But he cannot help us very much in that other possible set of meanings to the private and public contrast, those which contrast the individual and different kinds of collectivities. I've suggested some alternative identities which interact with the inclusions and exclusions suggested here: of custom and community, as well as of class, of the power of religious life and loyalty, of nationhood, race, and that sense of progressive civilisation which powerfully characterised so many of the forms of Western feminism.

Notes

1. Richard Brewster, *A Sermon Preached on the Thanksgiving Day* (Newcastle, 1759), quoted in Kathleen Wilson, *The Sense of the People: Politics, Culture and Imperialism in England, 1715–1785* (Cambridge University Press, Cambridge, 1995), p. 137.

2. Gilbert Stuart, *A View of Society in Europe, in its Progress from Rudeness to Refinement: or, Inquiries Concerning the History of Law, Government and Manners* (1778; 2nd edn, 1792; repr. Thoemmes Press, Bristol, 1995), p. 15.

3. William Alexander, *The History of Women from the Earliest Antiquity to the Present Time, Giving Some Account of Almost Every Interesting Particular Concerning That Sex, Among All Nations, Ancient or Modern* (2 vols, 1779; 3rd edn 1781; repr. Thoemmes Press, Bristol, 1995), vol. II, p. 505.

4. David Davies, *The Case of Labourers in Husbandry* (1795), p. 61, quoted in Bridget Hill, *Eighteenth Century Women. An Anthology* (Allen and Unwin, London, 1984), p. 226.

5. Adam Smith, *The Wealth of Nations*, 2 vols (1776; Oxford University Press, Oxford, 1976), vol. II, p. 781.

6. Mary Wollstonecraft, *Vindication of the Rights of Woman* (1792) in *Collected Works of Mary Wollstonecraft*, ed. Janet Todd and Marilyn Butler (William Pickering, London, 1989), vol. 5, p. 264.

7. Mrs Ellis, *The Daughters of England* (Fisher Son & Co, London, 1842), p. 11.

8. Marion Reid, *A Plea for Woman* (1843; repr. Polygon, London, 1988), p. 17.

9. Barbara Bodichon, *Reasons for and against the Enfranchisement of Women* (London 1869), pp. 5–6.

10. Harriet Martineau, 'Female Industry', *Edinburgh Review*, 222 (April 1859), p. 336.

11. Leonore Davidoff and Catherine Hall, *Family Fortunes: Men and Women of the English Middle Class*, (Hutchinson, London, 1987).

12. Joyce Thomas, 'Women and Capitalism: Oppression or Emancipation? A Review Article', *Comparative Studies in Society and History*, 30 (1988), pp. 534–49; Amanda Vickery, 'Historiographical Review: Golden Age to Separate Spheres? A Review of the Categories and Chronology of English Women's History', *Historical Journal*, 36 (1993), pp. 383–414; Linda Colley, *Britons: Forging the Nation 1707–1837* (Yale University Press, New Haven, 1992), p. 281.

13. Jeff Weintraub, 'The Theory and Politics of the Public/Private Distinction', in Jeff Weintraub and Krishan Kumar (eds), *Public and Private in Theory and Practice* (University of Chicago Press, Chicago, 1997).

14. Carole Pateman, 'Feminist Critiques of the Public/Private Dichotomy', in *The Disorder of Women: Democracy, Feminism and Political Theory* (Polity Press, Cambridge, 1989), p. 119. The essay was first published in S. I. Benn and G. G. Gaus (eds), *Public and Private in Social Life* (Croom Helm, London, 1983).

15. Leonore Davidoff, 'Regarding Some "Old Husbands' Tales": Public and Private in Feminist History', in *Worlds Between: Historical Perspectives On Gender and Class* (Polity Press, Oxford, 1995), pp. 227–76.

16. Denise Riley, *'Am I That Name?' Feminism and the Category of Women in History* (Macmillan, Basingstoke, 1989), pp. 49–51.

17. Catherine Hall, Keith McClelland and Jane Rendall, *Defining the Victorian Nation: Class, Race, Gender and the British Reform Act of 1867* (Cambridge University Press, Cambridge, 2000).

18. Jurgen Habermas, *The Structural Transformation of the Public Sphere: An Inquiry into a Category of Bourgeois Society*, trans. Thomas Burger with Frederick Lawrence and with an introduction by Thomas McCarthy (1st pub. in German 1962; The MIT Press, Cambridge, MA, 1989).

19. Joan Landes, *Women and the Public Sphere in the Age of the French Revolution* (Cornell University Press, Ithaca, 1988). Feminist theorists and historians have also criticised Habermas on a number of counts. See the essays in Joanna Meehan (ed.), *Feminists Read Habermas: Gendering the Subject of Discourse* (Routledge, New York and London, 1995).

20. Mary Ryan, *Women in Public. Between Banners and Ballots 1825–1880* (Johns Hopkins University Press, Baltimore and London, 1990); Margaret Jacob, 'The Mental Landscape of the Public Sphere', *Eighteenth Century Studies*, 28 (1994), pp. 95–113.

21. Nancy Fraser, 'Rethinking the Public Sphere: A Contribution to the Critique of Actually Existing Democracy', in *Habermas and the Public Sphere*, ed. Craig Calhoun (The MIT Press, Cambridge, MA, 1992), pp. 109–42.

22. Keith Michael Baker, 'Defining the Public Sphere in Eighteenth-Century France: Variations on a Theme by Habermas', in *Habermas and the Public Sphere*, ed. Calhoun, pp. 181–211.

23. Kathryn Dodd, 'Cultural Politics and Women's Historical Writing: The Case of Ray Strachey's *The Cause*', *Women's Studies International Forum*, 13 (1990) pp. 127–37.

24. One local study has indicated the growth of women's private enterprise and employment, linked to expanding publication: Susan Skedd, 'Women Teachers and the Expansion of Girls' Schooling in England, c. 1760–1820', in Hannah Barker and Elaine Chalus (eds), *Gender in Eighteenth-Century England: Roles, Representations and Responsibilities* (Longman, London and New York, 1997), pp. 101–25.

25. Stephen Howard, '"A Bright Pattern to All Her Sex": Representations of Women in Periodical and Newspaper Biography', in Barker and Chalus, *Gender in Eighteenth-Century England*, pp. 230–49.

26. Hannah Barker, 'Women, Work and the Industrial Revolution: Female Involvement in the English Printing Trades, c. 1700–1840', in Barker and Chalus, *Gender in Eighteenth-Century England*, pp. 81–100.

27. Nancy Armstrong, *Desire and Domestic Fiction: A Political History of the Novel* (Oxford University Press, New York, 1987).

28. Donna Landry, *The Muses of Resistance: Laboring-Class Women's Poetry in Britain, 1739–1796* (Cambridge University Press, Cambridge, 1990); Roger Lonsdale (ed.) *Eighteenth-century Women Poets: An Oxford Anthology* (Oxford University Press, Oxford and New York, 1989).

29. Anne I. Robertson, *Myself and My Relatives: A Story of Home Life* (Sampson Low, Son & Co, London, 1863); *The Story of Nelly Dillon*, 2 vols (T. Cautley Newby, London, 1866).

30. Geoff Eley, 'Nations, Publics, and Political Cultures: Placing Habermas in the Nineteenth Century', in *Habermas and the Public Sphere*, ed. Calhoun, pp. 289–339.

31. Anna Clark, *The Struggle for the Breeches: Gender and the Making of the British Working Class* (Rivers Oram Press, London, 1995).

32. Kathryn Gleadle, *The Early Feminists: Radical Unitarians and the Emergence of the Women's Rights Movement, 1831–51* (Macmillan, Basingstoke, 1995); Jane Rendall, 'The Citizenship of Women and the Reform Act of 1867', in Hall, McClelland and Rendall, *Defining the Victorian Nation*.

33. Josephine Butler, *Our Christianity Tested by the Irish Question* (London, 1887?), p. 8.

34. Leonore Davidoff, 'Regarding Some "Old Husbands Tales"', p. 258.

35. Linda Kerber, 'Separate Spheres, Female Worlds, Woman's Place: The Rhetoric of Women's History', *Journal of American History*, 75 (1988), pp. 9–39; Nancy Hewitt, *Women's Activism and Social Change. Rochester, New York 1822–1872* (Cornell University Press, Ithaca and London, 1984), and 'Beyond the Search for Sisterhood: American Women's History in the 1980s', *Social History*, 10 (1985), pp. 299–321.

36. Jane Rendall, *The Origins of Modern Feminism: Women in Britain, France and the United States, 1780–1860* (Macmillan, London, 1985).

37. Jose Harris, *Private Lives, Public Spirit: Britain 1870–1914* (Oxford University Press, Oxford, 1994) p. 95.

38. These papers were given at the Warwick conference 'The Power of the Petticoat: Women in British Politics, 1780–1860', 27 May 1998, University of Warwick.

39. Catherine S. Williams, 'The Public Law and Women's Rights: The Nineteenth-century Experience', *Cambrian Law Review*, 23 (1992), pp. 80–103; Brian Keith-Lucas, *The English Local Government Franchise* (Basil Blackwell, Oxford, 1952), pp. 164–5.

40. *Second Annual Report of the Manchester National Society for Women's Suffrage* (Manchester, 1869); *Newcastle Chronicle*, 20 May 1869; *Bury Times*, 26 June 1869.

41. *Hansard*, New Series vol. 1, Old Series vol. 196, Appendix, cols 1973–6, 7 June 1869.

42. Anna Clark, 'Gender, Class, and the Nation: Franchise Reform in England, 1832–1928', in *Re-reading the Constitution: New Narratives in the Political History of England's Long Nineteenth Century*, ed. James Vernon (Cambridge University Press, Cambridge, 1996), pp. 239–53.

43. K. T. Hoppen, 'The Franchise and Electoral Politics in England and Ireland, 1832–1885', *History*, 70 (1985), pp. 202–17.

44. Catherine Hall, 'The Nation Within and Without', in Hall, McClelland and Rendall, *Defining the Victorian Nation*.

6

The Difficulties of Gender in France: Reflections on a Concept

Michèle Riot-Sarcey, translated by *Emily Salines*

Much, if not everything, has been said on the conflictual relations of historical analysis based on gender and the writing of social, political or economic history. In all countries, women historians more than anyone else complain about the very low level of women's integration in History in the global sense of the word. However, the French approach to history is rather specific, as the tensions between French historians on the question of gender suggest.

Let me try to clarify a situation which, all things considered, remains rather confused. Semantic differences, linked to questions of grammar, and often brought forward in order to explain the lack of use of the word 'genre' (gender) in France, are only convenient pretexts used to avoid exploring the reasons for an entirely different rejection – this one not so easily admitted. The identification of one method with another blurs things even further. Debate is then avoided and the core of the problem remains; indeed, many French historians confuse uncritically women's history and gender history. For example 'Women's History or Gender Studies' implies that the history of a social category can replace the history of hierarchies.[1] In addition, the optimistic views of a few women historians further contribute to avoiding the question of methodological differences: 'without using easily the term (gender) or the "isms" and "post" prefixes, [women's history] has widely taken on the directions opened by *gender*, including its complex theories of gendered analysis of practices and the deconstruction of discourse'.[2] Such an observation is however not easily verified in the research published to date. The most common attitude is to adopt a distant look at a North American practice. 'Thus were proposed a historical category – *gender* – and a method of discourse analysis – deconstruction – which could only seduce minds in love with novelty.'[3]

To an even greater extent, Mona Ozouf's book has seduced minds which were more ready to reject 'imported concepts' than to engage with the aporias of national history. It is preferable to search for a specificity of French history, which is proud of its 'moderate feminism' which 'does not have the ambition to reinterpret universal history in the light of women's history', but instead tries to discover 'the ever so revealing presence of the feminine' in the heroines of the past.[4]

Thus I believe that in France, history, and, more specifically, women's history, has not really assimilated the openings offered by the problematics of the construction of differences, nor the logical consequences of the use of gender. Cultural differences are partly responsible for this, and the polysemy of the word *genre* may possibly add to the confusion: in French '*genre* refers to grammatical gender, but also literary genre, and there is also the use of genre as a philosophical notion and as a classifying category in natural history'.[5] In theory, the fundamental questions are raised by historians such as Michelle Perrot who, referring to the innovative ideas of critical sociologists, states without hesitation: 'we are many women – and men – who think that gender, as a category of thought and culture, comes before sex and modulates it'.[6] In practice, however, and apart from a few exceptions, women's history in France is reluctant to engage in a historical analysis which would take into account the founding role of hierarchy, which is central to gender. (Eleni Varikas was the exception to the rule of silence in this domain. Her pioneering work remained for long an outsider's study. Having created the concept of gender consciousness, she is now used in France as an almost unique reference.)

The question of the use or non-use of the word is less important than the theoretical implications of the way in which one thinks history.

As Françoise Thébaud stresses in her book, one can undoubtedly say that 'the prestige of history as a discipline, linked to the affirmation of the Nation and the Republic, plays an important role in education and culture and claims to be an objective and universal discourse'.[7]

Once such pregnant presuppositions are established, it is all the more difficult to give visibility to female individuals and groups made to remain unthinkable by the concept of universality. Hailed as the prerogative of a founding history of modernity, rooted in 'the people's spirit' by two centuries of exemplary education – exported to new democracies – national history cannot absorb a gendered view of the rules of its systems without risking the destabilisation of a past which remains the guarantee of democracy precisely when its very representation is in crisis.

Now, this prestige is much damaged today. As a consequence, it provides the occasion for a critical reassessment of French history, and more particularly French political history. The writing of history, reluctant as it is to question ideas taken for granted, has played a large role in the creation of a harmonious picture of the relationship between men and women. Thus the concept of the complementarity of roles has made it possible to hide the social construction of identities and groups, avoiding therefore a wider reflection on relations of domination.

Michel Foucault's statement is still valid today: 'The history of power struggles, and therefore of the real conditions for exercising and keeping power, is almost entirely invisible, untouched by knowledge'.[8]

This view was indeed outlined by the female authors of an important article, published in 1986 in *Annales*: 'The subtle structure of powers and counter-powers which forms the hidden pattern in the social fabric is what should be analysed following an approach (much inspired by Foucault) which would introduce into it the element of the relation between the sexes'.[9] Even though, the analysis of the relation between the sexes is not equivalent to a reflection on gender 'in the singular' which 'helps to move the focus, the divided parts, towards the principle of partition itself' and in which 'hierarchy is a constitutive aspect'.[10] Gender implies, as we know, that the social and political structure is looked at in its historicity.[11]

Moreover many women historians are currently stressing the limits of this analytical method, after having engaged in its tumultuous practice. To understand this rejection, we must make a historiographical detour in order to try and decode the unthinkable of a historical approach closely linked to the political present.

In France, the weight of positivism is well known and is still weighing on the methods currently in use. Voices are regularly raised to attack young researchers attracted by the study of 'representations' in preference to 'practices', which are a modern version of 'facts', dear to positivism.

Auguste Comte himself waged a war against 'metaphysical' history. Keeping to *facts* was for long an unquestioned rule, which is always being actualised. René Rémond, for that matter, pays tribute to his positivist pre-cursors, who paid attention to 'the politics which order themselves around and structure themselves according to the State'.[12] This is why the question of universal suffrage in its singular applications is not relevant. Universality is in itself a conquest of the country of human rights. 'Our country having been the first great European country to adopt universal suffrage, which it gradually extended to most of election processes, and having practised it ever since with no other interruption than those imposed by the two world wars, the historians of political life have at their disposal a continuous series of consultations which includes all the types of political elections, as well as social or professional elections.'[13]

Who votes does not matter much since using the word universality guarantees it. The truth established by the utterance does not in any way imply the questioning of the masculine dimension referred to by the word. It is not necessary to explain it since the vast majority of contemporaries use the phrase. The strength of the *doxa* is enough to tell the truth. Uni-versality, specifically male, has become commonplace after the objections of the feminists, who did not give the same meaning to words, were brushed aside. So the acceptance of these objections, generally made ridiculous, has become impossible.

The point of view of some has become an accepted fact, a useful invariant in the founding base of the idea of the complementarity of the sexes. French historians have indeed preferred talking about the loving, rather than conflictual relations (seen as 'against nature') between men and women. Here too Auguste Comte's views have been the strongest. In 1848, he stated that 'the proletariat and women are without doubt the auxiliaries of the new general doctrine [i.e. positivism]', and went on to say that 'for this reason in all human societies, public life belongs to men and women's existence is essentially domestic'.[14] This perception of men's world has become a 'social fact' which male and female historians have tried to study, throughout the history of the family, birth, death, the body and private life.

More than any other country, France has been keen to restore facts to the visibility of their coming into being. From this point of view, the 'feminine' *fact*, the *fact* of women, has remained marginal to the movement of history, since for the most part it is inscribed in '*la longue durée*'.

The discursive construction of *fact*, what is at stake in the interpretations of events, the importance of the historicity of words and concepts, their instrumentalisation, have long remained marginal to historians' questions. In other words, everything which is at play in the meaning of words, discourses and the founding values of a nation, its institutions and its rules, is removed from the historical narrative, because it is inaccessible to an intelligibility of fact, being hidden in the shadow of the appearances of a sense of history. I believe that this is why the 'linguistic turn', as we like to call it this side of the Atlantic, is so badly understood or traditionally transformed in France, where it is only referred to in relation to the excesses of postmodernism, which history rejects entirely. Seen as belonging to the realm of philosophers and discourse, as separate from reality, practice and actions, the reflection on the construction of reality through discourse could be looked at theoretically without being the object of a specifically historical study. I do not wish to enter in the dispute between the unconditional believers in method and the enemies of the language *fact* in the name of the social *fact*,[15] but I believe that the debate hides an incapacity to think the conflictual relations of the construction of a reality through discourse, the resistance it creates and the identities it constructs.

Thinking gender implies not limiting oneself to the effects of reality. Nicole Loraux, whose specialism is Greek history, does not use gender as an analytical tool but instead looks at history through the separate parts of society hidden by political discourse. It can be argued that Nicole Loraux's problematic is similar to that introduced by gender study: 'Because "the mask of ideology" is made up of its silences, rather than of what it says, one must accordingly look at the absent words in civic discourse, for instance at *krátos*, a word which tends to be hidden, absent from oratory flights which prefer the word *arke*, the name of institutional power, which is shared and always renewed in the uninterrupted succession of magistrates in the centre of the city.'[16]

Clearly, such a method makes it necessary to leave the beaten track of the *facts*, which have become the only proof of reality, because they are retained and classified by contemporaries as part of a process to establish their representativeness.

The history of the division of roles and of the construction of differences cannot do without the analysis of semantic fields, and this well beyond the argument introduced by the all too famous linguistic turn. Because 'semantics necessarily refer to the referents as a whole',[17] it forces us to reach the signified by highlighting the instrumentalisation of universal principles such as, for example, liberty and equality. As we know, these principles have served all regimes in discourse, but have essentially remained the privilege of a layer of society largely identifiable by the interests it defends in practice. This is why the choice of discursive utterances reveals what is at stake in meaning, which is often what is at stake in power, since 'language functions as a machine to produce meaning'.[18] The analysis of these phrases helps to explain the creation of hierarchies about which the signifier says nothing, a point which hardly receives the interest of political historians. And women historians encounter some difficulties in going beyond the traditional paths of history in order to reach the invisibility of unequal divisions, which are however clearly noticed by ethnologists and anthropologists. Nicole-Claude Mathieu was a particularly interesting pioneer in the undressing of the apparent neutrality of language, 'one of the constitutive elements of social relations':

> Behind the lack of attention to women in the description of facts, behind their being made invisible as social actors, the lack of or poor integration of their physical or mental activities in the theoretical models of the functioning and structure of societies, behind their linguistic treatment as non-human animates or even inanimates, can be found a conceptualisation of the sexes which is inherited from naturalism, and more precisely an idea of the biological nature of women in its link to sociological matters.[19]

Particularly influenced by 'François Simiand's felicitous phrase' of a knowledge of history through the traces left by the past,[20] French historians have long been resistant to the historicity of words and concepts made prominent by Reinhart Koselleck. They have preferred the path of the logic of a historical reading, and, from the 1930s, mainly an economic logic. 'Positivism' having in appearance been swept aside by the historians who founded the *Annales*, the present of crises helping to understand the past, economic phenomena became considered as the crucial factors in the explanation of history. So, as the focus moved to the temporal rhythm of men, to the quantitative aspect of things, conflictual relations and more particularly domination relations became irrelevant. In this view of the past, from Lucien Febvre to F. Braudel, 'when a specific event is mentioned, it tends to be looked at only in its exemplariness; there is no place for the historical fact out of its representative nature [*représentativité*]'.[21] But what is *représentativité* if not a construction made up by successive strata of meanings which have formed the basis of values, norms of exchange means, contemporary opinions and identities, which may be discovered by historians through classifiable discourse evidence and practices?

The easiest route – explaining the past by economic factors – away from any reflection on the domination of the male gender, was chosen by the large majority of French historians. This made it possible for structuralism and Marxism to coexist happily, without the need to worry about the gendered presuppositions on which social rules were being built.

This was soon replaced by a history of *mentalités*, which is specific to French historiography. The void thus created enabled the renewal of political history, still attached to the description of visible manifestation in the public space, which is, as we know, inaccessible to women. According to its practitioners, '*mentalités* describe the generic specificity of a particular social group at a given time and in a given space'.[22] There the group is looked at in itself and there is no reason to reflect on its constitution as a social construct. Its existence is enough for the community to appear. This form of history has become more established through the international reputation of some of its historians. Women infiltrate it fully through the study of the family, maternity, ways of being and behaving in relation to 'femininity'. Present in the couple, they cannot have access to deviant *mentalités* as critical subjects, but through fiction or through force depending on the gender which constructs them as other. Michel Vovelle's study is exemplary in this respect: 'let us classify the dream of female emancipation within anticipations which are probably too strong to take part in this 10-year adventure. There is some naivety in some feminist authors' conclusion that the dream of fraternity is hypocritical because monopolised by men.'[23] Whenever gender is in question, history is avoided, and historians refer to psychology or have recourse to value judgements. Gender history really does not have a place in French history.

Just ten years ago, some historians were lamenting the slippages in the history of *mentalités*, which had 'become the refuge for historical objects which had been excluded by "normal history". Mentalities then turn into substances ... It must be noted that this drifting off towards substantialism contradicted the first distributive function of the history of *mentalités* and that the new objects found rightly their place in general or social history, or else structured themselves into micro-totalities which do not belong to *mentalités*: women's history (gender studies) has been defining itself for the last few years as an independent discipline (something like the history of the difference between men and women)'.[24]

At that time, a poorly identified object found little place in the various historiographical trends, but today it has come into its own under this single name. A recent issue of *Annales* (October–December 1998) devotes to it a full section, listing together works dealing with gender as well as women's history books.

Unquestionably, the success of *A History of Women*, edited by Michelle Perrot and Georges Duby,[25] as well as the substantial audience for the journal *Clio*, are undoubtedly clear indications of the importance of this history which has now outgrown its marginal stage. It has had to impose its presence by making women visible in the domains of a human community dominated by struggles of clans, orders and classes, victim of wars between nations, and subject to the contradictions of divergent economic and social interests, advancing at the pace of the evolution of exchanges and attempting to overcome the conflicts of representations. The traces of the past were thus rediscovered and recomposed following these main trends. They ensured in turn that historical explanations came first by becoming a law common to all historians. As a consequence, not following those paths was equivalent to not following the rules for reading, understanding and analysing the phenomena of the past. French history has chosen to present itself as the inheritor of the pioneers of human rights and tried to exert its influence across frontiers, sure of its achievements. The institutionalisation of the professional community of historians has granted some the power to lay down the historical law under pretexts of 'scientificity' and 'objectivity'.[26] The confusion between knowledge, methods, subjective approaches and normative models for historiographical construction has not been very helpful in the integration of different problematics which fell outside the branded paths maintained by the institutions. Hence it was particularly difficult to make acceptable a shift in the historical gaze which is entirely foreign to recognised subjects and academic fields: the feminist shift, which is the only one able to subvert the categories of thought. Looking at past societies according to their initial hierarchical system, searching the category of woman to uncover the construction of a subordinated group rather than one which was complementary, meant going beyond the beaten track of French history. French history saw itself as justified by its ancient universal conquests. It could not accept their instrumentalisation. In no way could the dominant figure be embodied by man since in France more than elsewhere the citizen represented the individual devoid of his own interests.

This is why it was first necessary to bring to the surface women's *traces,* which were buried under the rubble of the revolutionary spirit and the remains of class struggles. As Michelle Perrot wrote in 1987:

> At first, women's history was that of their oppression. Battered, betrayed, humiliated, raped, underpaid, abandoned for mad and imprisoned women ... An inventory of feminine sufferings was made, sometimes without a questioning of the mechanisms of domination, focusing on effects. This history is necessary, but it is also depressing.[27]

It became more than necessary to make visible ordinary women. Then came the study of feminine sociabilities, their places, their practices; then there was an attempt to understand women's activities. Their roles, their professions, their functions, their places soon found a niche in history journals.[28] Always running in parallel to the real history, but with a slight shift from the dominant explanatory models, in France, as in many other countries, women's history has not been allowed to develop within the main directions chosen by historians, be it at the EHESS (École des Hautes Études en Sciences Économiques et Sociales) or within the framework of the various history journals, from *Annales* to *Mouvement social*. They are more and more present, without changing however the dominant categories of thought. Political history, whether conceptual or institutional, remains particularly unconcerned by the lack of symmetry between the roles and status of men and women.

Logically speaking, the departure from women's history as a category cannot be achieved outside history since it is history which has created it.[29] Consequently, it seems impossible to consider the object 'women' without tackling the question of the political rules at the source of which the category was created. This was my objective, begun in *La Démocratie à l'épreuve des femmes*, and pursued in *Le Réel de l'utopie* in which I widened up the field of research to include utopians, most of whom have remained nameless individuals taken out of history.[30]

Globally, in France, the analysis of the practices of allocation of social roles as the basis of social hierarchy still needs to be tackled. Women's history has not overcome the obstacle of the critique of the political. The method matters more than the use of the word 'gender' as an analytical tool.

The history of *representations*, which has taken the place of *mentalités* over the last twenty years, has played an important role in uncovering the discourse constructions applied to women. Writers, advertisers, politicians have all taken their turn in order to say what women should be. In one of her articles, Michelle Perrot picks up François Guizot's views on women's frivolity. 'The great man', who is the ideal, 'the creator of modern politics', distances himself very strongly from the woman, who cannot be great, and at worst is the 'little woman' of Paris. Of course, such discourse is revealing and adds to the multiplicity of normative texts in this domain. It is perfectly representative of the views of nineteenth-century men, and it also plays an important role in parallel to the formation of the rules of representative government. Now this liberal system bases social hierarchy on the privilege of the male head of household's reason ('*la raison du père de famille*'):

> No matter how simple society is, it has other business than just the family, business which demands abilities which neither women nor minors possess. No matter whether deliberations occur in a savage tribe or in an already enlightened city, no matter whether their subject is a war-like expedition or the adoption of a civil law, there is no doubt that naturally and generally neither women, nor minors, are able to rule on, reason, such interests.[31]

The 'naturalisation' of women served as a basis for the hierarchic system of representative democracy whose rules were accepted by all political parties.

As a consequence, and well beyond the representations of identity and culture, the construction of differences has influenced all political practices: from the *Code civil* to the creation of the citizen, via school curricula.

Although it has been possible to achieve the exclusion of women from the city in silence, this exclusion becomes visible in the symbolic domination of which the traces are gradually erased as it becomes integrated socially. It belongs to the 'unthought' of politics the 'suppressed' of conflicts.[32] It structures the whole of a democratic system, but does not belong specifically to it.

This is exactly why it is important not to be satisfied with the readable traces of the past which foreground most often agreement, belonging, even collective resistance, within a group of rules of which the presuppositions remain in the shadow of utterances. What is at stake in power where women are particularly concerned, is rarely explicit, underlying the play of relations between equals. This is Nicole Loraux's conclusion: 'But the historian of Greece must know that to give a meaning to the word "city", he must carry on unearthing from the *pólis* the founding omission of what its unity implies, which might temporarily be division.'[33]

However, today in France, 'faced with the backward surge of the great explanatory models',[34] the conditions which make it possible to question contemporary presuppositions, to analyse the process of subjection, to bring to light the differential hierarchy of the sexes, are all met. 'Historians have understood that the very categories they were working with had a history, and that social history was necessarily the history of the reasons and the uses of these categories.'[35]

The concept of gender will probably not be used more widely than in the past. It will be all the less used as confusion often rules in other countries where, like sex, and by assimilation to it, gender tends to be in turn essentialised, a fact which does not help at all in the study of the formation of hierarchies through the division of roles and of the sexes. But the method can still be used. 'If we reorientate our gaze towards unrepresented groups and individuals, which are rarely considered as subjects of their own history, but instead are always objects of representation, I think that we can understand, through the study of the conflictual relations, the process of formation of the political system', which precedes the construction of norms and social values which govern gender hierarchy.[36]

Notes

1. Alain Bourreau, 'Propositions pour une histoire restreinte des mentalités', *Annales ESC*, 1989, p. 1493

2. Françoise Thébaud, *Ecrire l'histoire des femmes* (ENS Editions, Fontenay-Saint-Cloud, 1998), p. 166.

3. Anne Marie Sohn, *La France démocratique: mélanges offerts à Maurice Agulhon* (Publications de la Sorbonne, Paris, 1998), p. 47.

4. Mona Ozouf, *Les mots des femmes* (Paris, Fayard, 1995), p. 12.

5. Christine Planté, 'La confusion des genres', in *Sexe et genre: de la hierarchie entre les sexes* (Seuil, Paris, 1991), p. 51.

6. Michelle Perrot, *Les femmes ou les silences de l'histoire* (Flammarion, Paris, 1998), p. 393.

7. See Thébaud, *Ecrire l'histoire des femmes*, p. 88.

8. Michel Foucault, *Dits et Ecrits* (Gallimard, Paris, 1994), vol. II, p. 224–5.

9. Colectif, 'Culture et pouvoir des femmes: essai d'historiographie', *Annales ESC*, 2 (mars–avril 1986) p. 286.

10. Christine Delphy, 'Penser le genre: quels problèmes?', in *Sexe et Genre*, p. 92.

11. See Joan Scott, *Only Paradoxes to Offer: French Feminists and the Rights of Man* (Harvard University Press, Cambridge, MA, 1996).

12. René Rémond, *Pour une histoire politique* (Seuil, Paris, 1988), p. 17.

13. Rémond, *Pour une histoire politique*, p. 28.

14. Auguste Comte, *Discours sur l'ensemble du positivisme, ou exposition sommaire de la doctrine philosophique et sociale propre à la grande république occidentale* (1848), pp. 3 and 205.

15. See on this Gérard Noiriel, *La Crise de l'histoire* (Belin, Paris, 1996).

16. Nicole Loraux, *La Cité divisée* (Payot, Paris, 1997), p. 53.

17. Emile Benveniste, *Cours de linguistique générale* (Gallimard, Paris, 1974), vol. 2, p. 64.

18. Benveniste, *Cours*, p. 97.

19. Nicole Claude Mathieu, *L'Anatomie politique* (Côte-femmes, Paris, 1991), p. 107.

20. Marc Bloch, *Apologie pour l'histoire ou métier d'historien* (1941; Cahiers des Annales, 3, Armand Colin, Paris, 1964), p. 21.

21. Alain Corbin, *Au Berceau des Annales* (Presses de l'institut d'études politiques de Toulouse, 1983), p. 132.

22. Robert Muchembled, 'Mentalités, cultures, sociétés: jalons pour un débat', in *Mentalités: histoires des cultures et des sociétés* (Imago, Paris, 1988), p. 9.

23. Michel Vovelle, *La mentalité révolutionnaire* (Editions sociales, Paris, 1985), p. 215.

24. Allain Bourreau, 'Propositions pour une histoire restreinte des mentalités', p. 1493.

25. Michelle Perrot and Georges Duby (eds), *Histoire des femmes*, 5 vols (Plon, Paris, 1991–2).

26. Noiriel, *La Crise de l'histoire*.

27. Michelle Perrot, 'Quinze ans d'histoire des femmes', *Sources, Travaux Historiques, Femmes: universalité et exclusion, Revue de l'association Histoire au présent*, 12 (1987).

28. Thébaud, *Ecrire l'histoire des femmes*, pp. 79, 81.

29. See Michèle Riot-Sarcey, 'Women's History in France', *Gender & History*, 9 (1997), pp. 15–35.

30. Albin Michel, Paris, 1994 and 1998.

31. François Guizot, 'Du droit de suffrage dans les petites sociétés' (1837), cited in *Histoire de la civilisation en Europe* (Hachette, Pluriel, Paris, 1985), p. 383.

32. Nicole Loraux, *La Cité divisée* (Payot, Paris, 1998), pp. 81–2.

33. Loraux, *La Cité divisée*, pp. 38–9.

34. Roger Chartier, *Au bord de la falaise* (Albin Michel, Paris, 1998), p. 10.

35. Chartier, *Au bord de la falaise*, p. 12.

36. M. Riot-Sarcey, *Le Réel de l'utopie*, pp. 33–4.

7

The Body as Method? Reflections on the Place of the Body in Gender History

Kathleen Canning

In the course of the past decade we have been faced with a veritable flood of books, articles, dissertation proposals and conference panels on various aspects of body history, or bodies in history. Many, even most of these studies merely invoke the body or allow 'body' to serve as a more fashionable surrogate for sexuality, reproduction, or gender without referring to anything specifically identifiable as body, bodily or embodied. In contrast to other keywords in the history of women and gender, such as 'patriarchy', 'class', or 'gender', which have been the subject of intense debate among feminists and across disciplines, 'body' remains a largely unexplicated and under-theorised *historical* concept. Interestingly, the debates surrounding Judith Butler's notable *Bodies That Matter*, for example, have not resounded widely among historians of women, gender or bodies.[1] Despite the deep involvement of many feminists in interdisciplinary arenas of Women's Studies, it is still more common to seek methodological clarity in the pages of another historical study than in a philosophical text like Butler's.[2] So historians grappling with methodological issues raised by 'the body' might be more inclined to turn to more specific case studies of body histories, such as Barbara Duden's imaginative *Woman Beneath the Skin: A Doctor's Patients in 18th Century Germany*, which explores how women 'of a vanished world' perceived and experienced their bodies, to the path-breaking special issue of *Representations*, edited by Catherine Gallagher and Thomas Laqueur, *The Making of the Modern Body*, or to the field-defining volumes *Fragments for a History of the Human Body*.[3]

The first part of this essay explores the current fascination with body histories and ponders the simultaneously unspecific and yet seductive invocation of the body in many recent histories. I contemplate the reasons the body has remained an elusive presence in most of our fields of national or chronological specialisation until recently and reflect on the potentialities and limitations of the concept of the body, on the methodological implications of placing bodies at the heart of historical investigation. The second part briefly explores the conceptual and methodological implications of recuperating and incorporating the body into my own project on citizenship and the crisis of nation in Germany after the First World War.

Analysis of the body has offered important new insights into the histories of the Enlightenment and the French Revolution, the history of welfare states and social policy, and more recently of imperialism, the First World War, and the rise of fascism. In some historical studies, bodies, as signifiers, metaphors or allegorical emblems, promise new understandings of nation or social formation. In others the body – as a site of intervention or inscriptive surface – specifies and expands our grasp of the processes of social discipline or the reach of the interventionist welfare state, of medicalisation, professionalisation, rationalisation of production and reproduction. The body histories that have left a historiographical mark (in the sense of convincing readers that bodies are significant objects of historical investigation) have sought most frequently to analyse the body as a signifier – of nation or state power, of social formations or dissolutions, of moral or hygienic visions and dangers, as a site of intervention or inscriptive surface 'on which laws, morality, values, power, are inscribed'.[4] From Carole Pateman's incisive delineation of the distinct political meanings of male and female bodies in French Enlightenment thought, to Lynn Hunt's 'family romance' of the French Revolution and her analysis of the many bodies of Marie-Antoinette, to Dorinda Outram's reading of the 'changes in the public presentation and public significance of the bodies of individuals', the history of the body in the Enlightenment and the French Revolution has helped elucidate the transformation of public space, the role of culture in the revolution, and the banishment of women (on the basis of their embodiment, argues Pateman) from the emergent public sphere.[5] Casting a somewhat different light on the relevance of the body to the formation of civil society in Germany, Isabel Hull's recent book *Sexuality, State and Civil Society in Germany, 1700–1815*, regards male rather than female embodiment as a crucial aspect of emergent civil society and of definitions of citizenship in eighteenth-century Germany. 'Whereas collective estate, or *Stand*, had once organized society', she argues, 'the individual citizen now founded civil society. Stripped of social status and regional inflection, the citizen had to be based on universal principles adhering to the only distinguishing feature he had left: his body'.[6]

The study of bodies, particularly symbolic bodies, during the periods of the Enlightenment and the French Revolution, has probably yielded the most sophisticated results thus far in a field we can only vaguely call 'body history'. In many other areas of gender history – sexuality, reproduction, labour, and welfare state, four crucial areas of inquiry, as reflected in the pages of this journal during its first decade – bodies have figured more often implicitly than explicitly. In studies of beauty, prostitution, witchcraft, or female circumcision, for example, the body is so obviously present that it often seems unnecessary to comment upon or theorise its presence.

Attempting to trace the place of the body in the gradual shift from women's history to gender history brings us headlong into a confrontation with the complex sex/gender distinction, which has significant implications for a conceptual-methodological reflection on bodies in history. As Donna Haraway argued some years ago, 'the political and epistemological effort to remove women from the category of nature and to place them in culture as constructed and self-constructing social subjects in history' caused the concept of gender 'to be quarantined from the infections of biological sex'.[7] In a similar vein, Moira Gatens contends that the perceived 'dangers of biological reductionism' propelled the embrace of gender and the repudiation of sex in feminist analytical vocabulary. In her essay 'A Critique of the Sex/Gender Distinction', Gatens seeks to retain a theory of sexual difference while firmly rejecting the notion that all such theories are plagued by essentialism or biologism. In place of a view of the body as a passive mediator of social inscriptions, which accompanied the sharp demarcation of gender and sex, Gatens asserts that 'the body can and does intervene to confirm or deny various social significances'.[8] Seeking to define femininity and masculinity in relation to female and male bodies, Gatens makes clear why this relationship is anything but arbitrary: 'there must be a qualitative difference', she claims, between the kind of femininity 'lived' by women and that 'lived' by men.[9] Thus the repudiation of sex in favour of gender left sex inextricably linked to body, and body stigmatised with biologism and essentialism. This explains in part the apprehension many feminist historians have shown towards a more explicit theoretical or methodological engagement with the body as a historical concept.

As one outcome of the displacement of sex by gender, the discursive body has figured more prominently in the last decade of gender history than Barbara Duden's 'body as experience'. Yet it is difficult to overlook the fact that the emphasis on the body's symbolic dimensions has also remained superficial in many instances: the symbolic body remains immaterial/dematerialised, as it grows increasingly difficult to conceive of social relations in terms of associations between bodies as specific loci of experience or identity formation. While the embrace of the discursive body might be traced back to the extraordinary influence of Michel Foucault on the study of both bodies and gender, in the field of history there is also a more practical explanation for its prevalence. Sources that chart the discursive construction of male and female bodies at the levels of state, church, social reform, science, medicine, or law are, namely, much more readily accessible than those that might offer insights into the body as a site of experience, memory, or subjectivity.

Another legacy of Foucault is the 'social body', which emerged according to the anthropologist David Horn at the boundary between the economic and the political, the public and the private, the natural and the discursive, in the course of the nineteenth century and was defined in 'that modern domain of knowledge and intervention carved out by statistics, sociology, social hygiene and social work'.[10] Examinations of 'social bodies' therefore often leave obscure the differences between the social bodies of men, women and children, the distinct experiences of those who inhabited the 'moral' social spaces and those who inhabited the crowded terrain of 'embodied "others" ... the sick, the criminal, the mad, the unemployed, the infertile'.[11]

If discursive and social bodies have frequently figured as abstractions, studies of individual or collective 'material' or bodily experiences often have the reverse problem: they are often overly concrete, undertheorised or cast too simply in terms of resistance/subjection.[12] Joanna Bourke's *Dismembering the Male: Men's Bodies, Britain and the Great War*, which pursued the relatively new topic of male corporeality in war, unfortunately remains limited within an excessive concreteness, by which 'male corporeality' is defined in the most empirical sense of the 722,000 corpses of British soldiers. Also notable is her disavowal of the symbolics of bodily dismemberment and mass death. With respect to those men maimed or disfigured by the war, Bourke argues that, despite the 'shocking suddenness of wartime disfigurement', a few years after the war had ended, the scars and deformities no longer held a unique significance in British society; rather, 'they joined a wider population of disabled men, women and children'.[13]

The search for the 'material' body reflects, in part at least, an unease with the prevalence of the discursive or Foucauldian body. This unease has led some scholars to pose extraordinarily fruitful questions, for example, regarding the effacement of the specificities of the 'bodies of the disciplined' whose corporealities are ultimately subsumed into 'a universalized body worked upon in a uniform way by surveillance techniques and practices'.[14] N. Katherine Hayles asks, for example, 'how actual bodies, in their cultural and physical specificities, impose, incorporate and resist incorporation of the material practices he [Foucault] describes'. Hayles points out that the Foucauldian body marks the 'absorption of embodiment into discourse' while the hallmark and still influential study by Elaine Scarry, *The Body in Pain*, emphasises 'that bodily practices have a physical reality which can never be fully assimilated into discourse'.[15] Yet Scarry's main pursuit is the intricate relationship between bodily pain and language or, more specifically, the political consequences of pain's resistance to 'objectification in language'.[16] While Bourke's study of dismembered male bodies sheds light on what Scarry terms 'the most radically embodying event in which human beings ever collectively participate', Bourke's attention to the material body is far less subtle than Scarry's. For Scarry probes how the deep alterations of the bodies of massive numbers of participants 'are carried forward into peace', how 'the record of war survives in the bodies, both alive and buried'. She asks how the soldier's 'unmaking' or deconstruction of himself, his consent 'to empty himself of civil content "for his country"', reverberates in the rebuilding of the nation. Ultimately the body's pain and its silencing through the realm of politics has profound meanings far beyond the individual or collective (material) injured body, namely for 'immaterial culture', for 'national consciousness, political beliefs, and self-definition'.[17] Judith Butler's *Bodies That Matter* has persuasively assailed the tendency of feminists to read the body's 'materiality' as that which is irreducible, that which 'cannot be a construction' and offered in its place a highly suggestive examination of the genealogy of materiality by which matter is understood 'not as site or surface, but as a *process of material-ization that stabilizes over time to produce the effect of boundary, fixity, and surface we call matter'*.[18]

A final complexity, if one attempts to define a field of 'body history', is that slippage commonly occurs between individual bodies as sites of experience/agency/resistance and social bodies, formed discursively, or between bodies as sites of inscription/intervention and notions of nation, class or race as 'reified bodies'. It is then often difficult to discern how these divergent bodies are contingent and constitutive of one another. Summarising some of these more problematic aspects of body histories in an article provoca-tively entitled 'Why all the Fuss about the Body?', the historian Carolyn Walker Bynum argues that the current preoccupation with the body oper-ates on the basis of 'totally diverse assumptions' and definitions of the body within and across different fields. In Bynum's view the absence of 'a clear set of structures, behaviors, events, objects, experiences, words, and moments to which *body* currently refers' has rendered current discussions of the body within and across disciplines incommensurate and often mutually incomprehensible.[19]

The work of conceptualising the body is further encumbered not only by the wholly diverse understandings of the body, even among scholars in the same field, but also by the particular valence of the body in popular culture, which infiltrates into our academic discussions and renders the task of defining a conceptual frame or methodology an even more confusing enterprise. Bryan Turner, author of a number of works on the 'sociology of the body', explains the current fascination of social scientists with the body in terms of the shifts in economic and social developments, towards an emphasis on 'pleasure, desire, difference and playfulness which are features of contemporary consumerism' and he also points to the influence of the women's movement and the transformation of the role of women in the public sphere. Others point to the conversion of the 'project of the self, as the principal legacy of individualism, into the project of the body'.[20] The October 1997 issue of *Lingua Franca* carried a short piece, 'Pieces of You', that seemed to confirm these views, declaring 1997 the 'year of the Body Part', referring not only to Paula Jones's legal deposition describing President Clinton's genitals, but also to the publication in the July *New York Times* of an illustrated article entitled, 'The Whole Body Catalogue: Artifi-cial Parts to Mix and Match', which included a shopping list of 'available body parts'.[21] Similarly the January 1997 issue of the intriguing bi-lingual English–Russian magazine *Colors: A Magazine about the Rest of the World* was entitled 'Shopping for the Body' and included similar rubrics on 'extensions' (prostheses), 'maintenance' (cosmetic surgery), 'transformation' (electric shock, seaweed packs, working out), 'purification', 'recreation, 'personal hygiene', and 'protection'.[22] Scholarship, the *Lingua Franca* article claims, has been similarly 'driven by a culture fixed on the fragment', by a characteristically postmodern 'rejection of all forms of totality, including the corporeal'.[23]

The incommensurability of representations of the body across the lines of popular culture and academe, across and within the individual disciplines, might appear to reinforce this rejection of totality or to encourage a frivolous embrace of the body (or body parts) as mere adornments in our scholarly projects. Indeed, the recognition that the body is, as Bryan Turner describes it, 'at once the most solid, the most elusive, illusory, concrete, metaphysical, ever present and ever distant thing – a site, an instrument, an environment, a singularity and a multiplicity' makes the question of 'body as method' a particularly daunting one.[24]

Further dilemmas that cannot be resolved within the bounds of this essay include the location of bodies in time and space. Certainly implicit in this discussion thus far has been a presumed but unexplicated 'modern' body, one that requires historicisation and demarcation from medieval or early modern bodies. Barbara Duden has suggested that 'a violent process began in the seventeenth century' by which 'the body as the embodiment of localized social vitality was symbolically broken', for example through witch trials. In the course of the eighteenth century the body as 'the vague corporeality of popular culture' became offensive and in the last third of the century 'the study and cultivation of the body politic' became a matter of state policy. As states, medical professionals, and social reformers began to wield new knowledges of health and hygiene, 'the new body assumed a central place in the self-image of the bourgeoisie'.[25] This is undoubtedly what Isabel Hull means when she suggests that 'a modern person's sense of self ... must always have a strong bodily anchor to it', that the imbrication of body and self has a particular salience in the phase of history known as 'modernity'.[26] Locating bodies spatially, nationally, and as inscribed by ethnicity and race, is obviously another critical methodological task. So it may be useful to interrogate the notion or presumption of a nationally bounded body, especially in the wake of a rich and wide-ranging historiography on gender and colonialism/imperialism which, even if not attentive to imagined or lived bodies as framing concepts, has uncovered the body projects of empire and traced the links between domesticity in the metropoles and the conquest of 'the sexual and labor power of colonized women'.[27]

While this brief discussion has highlighted several dilemmas in the theory and practice of body history – bodies that are singularly discursive or abstract, bodies that are excessively material and undertheorised, bodies that are not made visible at all – feminist scholarship in the disciplines of literary studies and philosophy has effectively critiqued the gender/sex distinction, boldly sought to dissolve the divide between discourse and materiality with respect to bodies, and sought to redefine the key words agency, subjectivity, and positionality in terms of the body. While on the one hand resisting the allure of biological essentialism, feminist philosopher Elisabeth Grosz for example also refuses the 'process of sanitization, of neutralization, of decorporealization of the concept "body"' that accompanied 'the discursivation of bodies'.[28] The literary scholar Leslie Adelson introduces her *Making Bodies, Making History* with the contention that 'there is an assuredly multifaceted reality of human bodies that does not exist outside discourse and is yet not by any means subsumed by it'.[29] Acknowledging the powerful influence of Michel Foucault on our understandings of how 'power is inscribed on and by bodies through modes of social supervision and discipline as well as self-regulation' and of how bodies are 'moulded by a great many distinct regimes', Elisabeth Grosz nonetheless emphasises that all of those processes that mark the body through specific rituals and practices – punishment, torture, medicalised observations, sexuality and pleasure – denote bodies that represent 'an uncontrollable, unpredictable threat to a regular, systematic mode of social organisation'. Positing a place for agency in the discursively constituted subject, Grosz contends that the body is not only marked by coercive forces, but is 'internally lived, experienced and acted upon by the subject and the social collectivity'.[30] Moira Gatens's notion of the imaginary body also creatively bridges the purported gulf between discursive and material bodies: always socially and historically specific, imaginary bodies are constructed by 'a shared language; the shared psychical significance and privileging of various zones of the body; and common institutional practices and discourses which act on and through the body'. Imaginary bodies, she contends, provide 'the key or the code to the decipherment of the social and personal significance of male and female biologies as lived in culture, that is, masculinity and femininity'.[31]

Indeed, the notion of *embodiment* may be the most promising outcome of these fruitful debates and interventions. Embodiment, which Adelson terms 'crucial to any feminist enterprise', denotes a process 'of making and doing the work of bodies – of becoming a body in social space'.[32] So embodied practices are always contextual, inflected with class, ethnic, racial, gender and generational locations, with 'place, time, physiology and culture'.[33] A far less fixed and idealised concept than body, embodiment encompasses moments of encounter and interpretation, agency and resistance. So, as N. Katherine Hayles has argued, 'during any given period, experiences of embodiment are in continual interaction with constructions of the body'. Embodied practices, she argues, engender 'heterogenous spaces even when the discursive formations describing those practices seem uniformly dispersed throughout the society'.[34] Elisabeth Grosz's notion of 'counterstrategic reinscription' offers a perhaps parallel notion. In her view, the body 'as well as being the site of knowledge-power ... is thus also a site of resistance, for it exerts a recalcitrance, and always entails the possibility of a counterstrategic reinscription, for it is capable of being self-marked, self-represented in alternative ways'. The body's recalcitrance, it seems, might be seen as an example of one kind of 'embodied practice' imagined by Hayles. Subjects thus produced are not simply the imposed results of alien, coercive forces; the body is internally lived, experienced and acted upon by the subject and the social collectivity.[35]

Memory represents perhaps another kind of embodied practice, one that is particularly intriguing in that embodied memories are most likely to be both materialised and mediated discursively. Scarry points to Bourdieu's study of 'hidden pedagogies', such as 'cultural manners', passed from one generation to the next, and his contention that 'the principles embodied in this way are placed beyond the grasp of consciousness, and hence cannot be touched by voluntary, deliberate transformation, cannot even be made explicit'. Scarry's own study points to the embodiment of 'political identity', which 'is usually learned unconsciously, effortlessly, and very early, and expressed in gestures, habits, postures and demeanors, which are nearly impossible to unlearn'.[36] The concepts of embodiment, bodily reinscription and bodily memory may help to make more specific the fluid and porous concept of body and to chart historical change in and through bodies which the presumed fixity of 'body' seems to defy. Mapping a conceptual space in which bodies encounter, incorporate, intervene and resist dominant discourses through the notions of embodiment and reinscription should perhaps be accompanied by a rethinking of the term discourse as well. Judith Butler's apt comments on feminist unease with the notion of 'construction' and her suggestion to rethink the prevalent understanding of discourse as that which is always 'artificial and dispensable' should help to elucidate the material outcomes of discursive inscriptions, the ways in which they are materialised and embodied.[37]

In modern German history the body has figured most significantly in the study of the Weimar and Nazi periods, encompassing the highly charged discourses and practices of interwar natalism and sexual reform, the campaigns for birth control and abortion rights, as well as the emergence of the 'new woman', the single 'women of the metropolis' whose bodies became markers for all that the First World War had transformed in the relations between the sexes.[38] The body is an even more explicit presence in recent studies of the Nazi 'racial state', figuring as a signifier of both racial purity (the 'Aryan' body) and racial pollution (the Jewish body, the deformed, handicapped or ageing body) in the Nazis' 'barbarous utopia', as an object not merely of intervention, but of mutilation and annihilation.[39] As Leslie Adelson notes, reference to the six million Jews the Nazis murdered 'signifies in no uncertain terms the ineluctable embodiment of history' (a point that is underscored by the enormous popularity of Daniel Goldhagen's best-selling and intensely graphic account of the 'face-to-face' extermination of Jews by 'ordinary Germans', in which the bodies of both victims and killers are explicitly present).[40] Klaus Theweleit's influential two-volume study of 1978, *Male Fantasies*, offers an intriguing examination of the meanings of female bodies for male fascist subjectivities, suggesting that the violent destruction of bodies and disordering of gender during the First World War is crucial to understanding the exterminationist drive of the Nazi state. While Theweleit's text left little dispute about the salience of bodies to fascist fantasies and practices, it left unexplicated the precise links between male fears of engulfment after World War I and the perpetration of Nazi violence and, ultimately, genocide a quarter century later.[41]

Attention to the body as method of reading key moments in the transformations of the war and postwar period uncovers a crisis that went far deeper than the disintegration of political regimes, which implicated the female body in the crises of nation, citizenship, and class that followed the collapse of the Kaiser's rule. In my current project, *Embodying Citizenship: Gender and the Crisis of Nation in Weimar Germany*, I probe the relevance of the body to the ruptures of nation, state, and political culture which occurred at the end of the First World War. Certainly, the body is of particular consequence at this juncture in German, indeed modern European, history. As Eve Rosenhaft has suggested, through the collective experience of mobilisation, unique to this 'total war', the limits of bodily endurance, and the integrity of the material body itself, were tested, stretched, and massively exceeded, both in the trenches and on the home front.[42] The shock of the war's violence towards both national and individual bodies, juxtaposed with the embodied sufferings of those who remained at the home front – hunger, cold, illness, anxiety, and grief – render this historical moment one in which both bodily inscription – by states and armies – and the reinscriptive, embodying responses of citizens and soldiers – through revolution, political violence and social protest – were particularly acute. Indeed, this embodied and violent moment of rupture, spanning the years 1917–24, was seared into the consciousness and history of the twentieth century by the violence it spawned in the late 1920s and early 1930s. The larger goal of this book project is to explore how the ideologies and practices of gender were ruptured, violently, even traumatically, and inscribed in the political culture of the Weimar Republic. Theweleit's unconventional masterpiece of the late 1970s, which suggested that the disordering of gender during the war and the fantasies of 'women, floods, bodies', of rape, murder and dismemberment it produced in male Freikorps activists, remains highly suggestive in this regard.[43] The recent work of Maria Tatar and Beth Irwin Lewis on the 'Lustmord' series of left male artists, such as Otto Dix and George Grosz, suggests that the 'five years of unchained atavistic impulses', described by medical doctor and sex reformer Magnus Hirschfeld, the brutalisation of sex behind the lines (in enemy brothels, for example), and the 'pathological and perverse forms of sex', which Hirschfeld claimed took place in the trenches, spurred fantasies of lustful murder and mutilation even among progressive, not only among pre-fascist, men.[44]

These are among the most dramatic examples of the experiential chasm that probably existed between the war front and home front. In an evocative essay, 'Militarization and Reproduction in World War I Germany', Elisabeth Domansky points to the everyday gulf between men, who were to protect the nation against the external enemy, and women, whose task was to protect the 'national body' from internal enemies, that is, disease, physical weakness and immorality.[45] Domansky suggests that the distinct bodily experiences of trenches and home front – dismemberment and death of men at the front; hunger, overwork, illness and immiserisation of women on the home front – created both important commonalities and disparities in male and female subjectivities after the war, from their shared desires to reclaim traditional roles in the family to the ways they positioned themselves in the new arenas of labour and sexual politics during Weimar.[46]

The first part of my book examines the significance of embodiment for the experiences and social identities of citizenship as articulated during a prolonged moment of politicisation – 1918–24 – which drew unprecedented numbers of women into the realm of formal and informal politics. Specifically, I examine ways in which embodied deprivations of the home front fostered protest which ultimately articulated working women's desire for citizenship in the broadest participatory sense. The concept of citizenship provides an interpretative grid for my investigation of the prolonged period of crisis that begins with the strikes, food riots, and political protests on the home front in 1917–18; it spans the collapse of the war effort, the November Revolution and the inception of Weimar as a 'non-nation'; it encompasses the process of casting and enacting women's citizenship in the People's Revolutionary Council and the Weimar National Assembly. Here I focus on the particular salience of male and female embodiment to the visions of citizenship that took shape during the highly contested process of drafting the Weimar constitution. How was female embodiment – motherhood, marital status, wartime service – cast in the debates about female suffrage? In what sense was the new constitution envisioned as a site of resolution and reconciliation of the stark divisions of wartime? How far did the constitution reach in attempting to mend the (embodied) ruptures of both war and revolution?

In the second part of the book I explore the symbolism of the wounded body, not mainly through an examination of the (embodied) cult of the 'fallen soldiers'[47] but in terms of a body that figured conspicuously in the November Revolution of 1918 and that came to signify a traumatic rupture in the founding of Weimar democracy – the body of Rosa Luxemburg. Luxemburg, the 'brilliant and fiery leader' of the prewar Socialist left and founder of the German Communist Party, became the quintessential 'red rifle woman' of Theweleit's *Male Fantasies* when she led the Spartacist Revolt in Berlin in January 1919.[48] Her brutal murder, along with that of her comrade Karl Liebknecht, lived on not only as the ultimate symbol of the indelible division of Socialists and Communists that fractured Weimar democracy, but was also enshrined in the culture of the Communist Left, which commemorated their leaders' deaths each January with 'sacred public rituals that consecrated the militant activism ... of the party's founding leaders and succeeding generations'.[49] Although Luxemburg herself disavowed nearly all particularities of women's politics (or bodies), her mutilated corpse, found six months after her murder at the bottom of the Landwehr canal in Berlin, left an explicitly gendered legacy for the political culture of the labour movement during the Weimar Republic. Her body, unlike Liebknecht's, was manifestly female (a Jewish body as well), one whose symbolics attested to the violent anti-Semitism, anti-Communism and hatred of women that was woven together in the ideology of the Freikorps.[50] It will undoubtedly be very difficult to link the symbolism of Rosa Luxemburg's body to the nearly invisible gender politics of the November Revolution, but I approach both as shaped by the violent polarisations of wartime, between people and state, class and nation, trenches and home front, women and men.

In the book's third section I investigate the campaign for expanded maternity protection during the mid 1920s in the context of the discourses of sexual reform, natalism and eugenics that criss-crossed with those of the expanded Weimar welfare state. Launched by the German Textile Workers' Union, which represented over 300,000 women workers during the mid 1920s, the campaign began as an inquiry into the effects of factory work on the pregnant woman's body. Its startling revelation of the high rates of stillbirth, miscarriage and illness among female textile workers soon transformed the inquiry into a vigorous campaign at the level of national parliament for expansion of maternity protection. The photographic representations of the pregnant female body at work, compiled by the socialist physician Max Hirsch, their swollen abdomens pressed up against moving machinery in each photo, transformed what Thomas Laqueur calls 'the statistical body' into 'the lived (female pregnant) body' that now had a bearing on national social policy.[51] This campaign marked a shift in labour politics, at least those of this largely female union, towards the foregrounding of the body in its day-to-day political work, which was visible as well in the demonstrations and conferences female union activists organised in subsequent years on the issues of abortion, pregnancy, birth control and housework. Of particular relevance here is the genesis of this shift: how does this campaign relate to the other, middle-class, social democratic, and communist social movements that mobilised bodies around the issues of sexual reform, birth control, abortion rights during Weimar? To what extent were female union activists the impetus behind these campaigns, exerting pressure from below upon the male leadership, or was this shift instigated by the predominantly male leadership in order to pre-empt or thwart dissent or protest within the union or to incite a new battle against employers or the Christian unions?

This third area of inquiry opens the way to an exploration of the processes of embodiment and reinscription, of the significance of bodily memories of war, revolution and postwar political violence. Here I am returning to an endeavour I began in an article of 1994 that suggested that women workers' contradictory experiences of war, revolution, and demobilisation opened the way for the transformations of consciousness and subjectivity during the postwar period.[52] The war represented an indisputable turning point in the body's politicisation: the escalated policing by the pro-natalist military dictatorship of the spheres of work, consumption, and sexuality and women's acute sense that, in Domansky's terms, 'the front was everywhere', that the front was inscribed in their bodies, meant that women experienced their bodies as sites of intensified intervention and regulation (and perhaps also as political weapons) in the aftermath of war, revolution and demobilisation.[53] I hope to follow the traces of those transformed subjectivities into the explosive politics and culture of the early years of the Weimar Republic and to analyse how they were expressed in the numerous skirmishes between men and women in the realm of formal labour politics during the 1920s.

My call for historical specificity in analysing bodies, inscriptions, and embodiment may not instate the body as the stable concept Caroline Bynum desires, one grounded in 'a clear set of structures, behaviors, events, objects, experiences, words and moments', but I hope that it might help us contemplate the very different methods required for reading the body as symbol versus reading the processes of embodiment, inscription and reinscription.[54] I also hope that the body histories I have outlined, even if broken into fragmentary vignettes, make clear the merits of charting the connections and convergences of the material and the discursive that make bodies such difficult objects of historical analysis and such intriguing sites of memory, agency and subjectivity.

Notes

I would like to thank Leonore Davidoff, Eleni Varikas and Keith McClelland for their incisive comments on this essay, which helped me revise and expand its scope considerably. I would also like to thank Eve Rosenhaft, Antoinette Burton, Uta Poiger, Lynn Thomas, Helmut Puff and Hubert Rast for astute comments and criticisms of earlier drafts of this chapter.

1. Judith Butler, *Bodies that Matter: On the Discursive Limits of 'Sex'* (Routledge, London and New York, 1993).

2. The same can be said of other provocative feminist texts on female bodies, including the work of Australian feminists Moira Gatens and Elisabeth Grosz. See, for example: Moira Gatens, *Imaginary Bodies: Ethics, Power and Corporeality* (Routledge, London and New York, 1996); and Elisabeth Grosz, 'Bodies and Knowledges: Feminism and the Crisis of Reason', in *Space, Time, and Perversion*, ed. Elisabeth Grosz (Routledge, London and New York, 1995), pp. 25–43. Also see Grosz's *Volatile Bodies: Toward a Corporeal Feminism* (Indiana University Press, Bloomington, 1994).

3. Barbara Duden, *Woman Beneath the Skin: A Doctor's Patients in 18th Century Germany*, trans. Thomas Dunlap (Harvard University Press, Cambridge, MA, 1991).

Although Duden's study relies upon the 8-volume study on the 'diseases of women', compiled by the physician Johann Storch of Halle during the period 1721–40, she makes a compelling case that the bodily experiences of Storch's 1,650 female patients were not 'medically determined', rendering Storch a witness to 'an orally transmitted popular concept of the body'. See pp. 23, 36–7, 66. See also: Thomas Laqueur and Catherine Gallagher (eds), *The Making of the Modern Body: Sexuality and Society in the 19th Century*, special issue of *Representations* (Spring 1986); Michael Feher with Ramona Nadoff and Nadia Tazi, *Fragments for a History of the Human Body*, 3 parts (Zone Books, New York, 1989–91).

4. Elisabeth Grosz, 'Bodies and Knowledges: Feminism and the Crisis of Reason', in *Space, Time, and Perversion*, ed. Grosz, (Routledge, New York, 1995), p. 33.

5. Carole Pateman, *The Sexual Contract* (Stanford University Press, Stanford, 1988), and Carole Pateman, 'The Fraternal Social Contract', in *Civil Society and the State*, ed. John Keane (Verso, London, 1988), pp. 101–28; Lynn Hunt, *The Family Romance of the French Revolution* (University of California Press, Berkeley, 1992); and Dorinda Outram, *The Body and the French Revolution: Sex, Class and Political Culture* (Yale University Press, New Haven, 1989). See also the recently translated book by Antoine de Baecque, *The Body Politic: Corporeal Metaphor in Revolutionary France 1770–1800* (published in France in 1993; Stanford University Press, Stanford, 1997).

6. Isabel Hull, *Sexuality, State and Civil Society in Germany 1700–1815* (Cornell University Press, Ithaca, 1995), p. 5.

7. Donna Haraway, *Simians, Cyborgs, and Women: the Reinvention of Nature* (Routledge, New York and London, 1991), p. 134.

8. Gatens, *Imaginary Bodies*, pp. 3–4, 10.

9. Gatens, *Imaginary Bodies*, pp. 4, 9.

10. David G. Horn, *Social Bodies: Science, Reproduction, and Italian Modernity* (Princeton University Press, Princeton, 1994), pp. 3–4, 10. See also Martin Hewitt, 'Bio-politics and Social Policy: Foucault's Account of Welfare', *Theory, Culture, and Society*, 2 (1983), pp. 67–84.

11. Here I am both citing and entering into dialogue with Horn, *Social Bodies*, pp. 3, 12. Mary Poovey's brilliant study *Making a Social Body* (University of Chicago Press, Chicago, 1995) suggests that 'social body' is perhaps best understood as an abstraction.

12. These arguments can be traced back to a conversation with Atina Grossmann in a panel discussion, 'Reading the Body in the History of the Weimar Republic', at the German Studies Association's Twenty-first Annual Conference, September 1997.

13. Joanna Bourke, *Dismembering the Male: Men's Bodies, Britain and the Great War* (University of Chicago Press, Chicago, 1996), pp. 27, 35, 251.

14. N. Katherine Hayles, 'The Materiality of Informatics', unpublished paper, p. 9. Prof. Hayles shared this paper with me when we were both fellows at the Stanford University Humanities Center (1992).

15. Hayles, 'The Materiality of Informatics', p. 10; Elaine Scarry, *The Body in Pain: The Making and Unmaking of the World* (Oxford University Press, New York, 1985).

16. Scarry, *The Body in Pain*, ch. 1.

17. Scarry, *The Body in Pain*, pp. 71, 112–14, 122.

18. Butler, *Bodies that Matter*, p. 9 (emphasis in the original).

19. Caroline Bynum, 'Why all the Fuss about the Body? A Medievalist's Perspective', *Critical Inquiry*, 22 (Autumn 1995), p. 5.

20. Bryan S. Turner, *The Body and Society*, 2nd edn (Sage, London, 1996), pp. 2–4, 20–21. Here Turner refers to Chris Shilling's *The Body and Social Theory* (Sage, London, 1993).

21. Emily Eakin, 'Pieces of You', *Lingua Franca* (October 1997), pp. 21–2.

22. The editorial offices of *Colors* are located in Paris and its editorial staff appears to be strewn across the world, lending it a global character. The editorial introduction reads: 'The body. Everybody's got one. But when it comes to having sex, cleaning ears, working out or taking a pee, people treat their bodies differently – and with lots of different products. What can you learn about a culture from all these items? To find out, *Colors* went shopping. We browsed beauty salons in Tokyo, street markets in Bogota, and a bionics laboratory in Edinburgh to discover what people buy for their bodies and why. We hope you find something in your size.' The cover photo is of a 'pubic wig', a 'fluffy clump of recycled human hair', known as a 'night flower' in Japan and worn on the vagina. Cost: $270. *Colors*, 18 (December 1996—January 1997).

23. Eakin, 'Pieces of You', p. 21. Eakin points to the recently published studies *Venus Envy: A History of Cosmetic Surgery* (Johns Hopkins University Press, Baltimore, 1997) and David Hilman and Carla Mazzio's *The Body in Parts: Fantasies of Corporeality in Early Modern Europe* (Routledge, London and New York, 1997).

24. Turner, *Body and Society*, p. 43.

25. Duden, *Woman Beneath the Skin*, pp. 10–11, 13–15.

26. Isabel Hull, 'The Body as Historical Experience: Review of Recent Works by Barbara Duden', *Central European History*, 28 (1995), p. 74.

27. Anne McClintock, *Imperial Leather: Race, Gender and Sexuality in the Colonial Contest* (Routledge, New York and London, 1995), p. 3. See here in particular McClintock's ch. 1, 'The Lay of the Land: Genealogies of Imperialism', and ch. 2, '"Massa and Maids": Power and Desire in the Imperial Metropolis', pp. 21–131, and Anne Stoler, 'Making Empire Respectable: The Politics of Race and Sexual Morality in 20th-Century Colonial Cultures', *American Ethnologist*, 16 (1989), pp. 634–60.

28. Elisabeth Grosz, 'Bodies and Knowledges: Feminism and the Crisis of Reason', in Grosz, *Space, Time and Perversion*, p. 31.

29. Leslie Adelson, *Making Bodies, Making History: Feminism and German Identity* (University of Nebraska Press, Lincoln, 1993), p. 2.

30. Grosz, 'Inscriptions and Body-Maps: Representations and the Corporeal', in *Feminine, Masculine and Representation*, ed. Terry Threadgold and Anne Cranny Francis (Allen & Unwin, Boston/Sydney, 1990), pp. 65, 71–2. See also Grosz, *Volatile Bodies*.

31. Gatens, *Imaginary Bodies*, p. 12.

32. Adelson, *Making Bodies*, p. xiii; Turner, *The Body and Society*, p. xiii.

33. Hayles, 'The Materiality of Informatics', pp. 10–12.

34. Hayles, 'The Materiality of Informatics', pp. 11–12.

35. Grosz, 'Inscriptions and Body-Maps', pp. 64–5.

36. Scarry, *The Body in Pain*, p. 110. Here Scarry cites Pierre Bourdieu, *Outline of a Theory of Practice*, trans. Richard Nice (Cambridge University Press, Cambridge, 1977), pp. 94–5.

37. Butler, *Bodies That Matter*, pp. xi, 4–5.

38. On the history of body and gender during the Weimar Republic, see: Renate Bridenthal, Atina Grossmann, Marion Kaplan (eds), *When Biology Became Destiny: Women in Weimar and Nazi Germany* (Monthly Review Press, New York, 1984). See also Cornelie Usborne, *The Politics of the Body in Weimar Germany: Reproductive Rights*

and Duties (University of Michigan Press, Ann Arbor, 1992); Atina Grossmann, *Reforming Sex: The German Movement for Birth Control and Abortion Reform 1920–1950* (Oxford University Press, Oxford and New York, 1995); Maria Tatar, *Lustmord: Sexual Murder in Weimar Germany* (Princeton University Press, Princeton, 1995); Katharina von Ankum (ed.), *Women in the Metropolis: Gender and Modernity in Weimar Culture* (University of California Press, Berkeley, 1997).

39. See Michael Burleigh and Wolfgang Wippermann, *The Racial State: Germany 1933–1945* (Cambridge University Press, Cambridge, 1991).

40. Adelson, *Making Bodies*, p. 23; Daniel Jonah Goldhagen, *Hitler's Willing Executioners: Ordinary Germans and the Holocaust* (Knopf, New York, 1996). Also see Raul Hilberg's poignant analysis of the popularity of Goldhagen's book, 'The Goldhagen Phenomenon', *Critical Inquiry*, 23 (Summer 1997), pp. 721–8.

41. Klaus Theweleit, *Male Fantasies*, vol. I, *Women, Floods, Bodies, History* (first published in 1977 in Germany; University of Minnesota, Minneapolis, 1987). Vol. 2 is entitled *Männerkörper: Zur Psychoanalyse des Weissen Terrors*.

42. Here I am paraphrasing Eve Rosenhaft's comments on an earlier draft of this paper, delivered to the European Social Science History Conference, Amsterdam, April 1998.

43. Theweleit, *Male Fantasies*, vol. I.

44. Tatar, *Lustmord*, and Beth Irwin Lewis, 'Inside the Windows of the Metropolis', in *Women in the Metropolis*, ed. von Ankum. Hirschfeld is quoted by Lewis, p. 219.

45. Elisabeth Domansky, 'Militarization and Reproduction in World War I Germany', in *Society, Culture, and the State in Germany 1870–1930*, ed. Geoff Eley (University of Michigan Press, Ann Arbor, 1997), p. 455.

46. Domansky, 'Militarization and Reproduction'.

47. George Mosse, *Fallen Soldiers: Reshaping the Memory of the World Wars* (Oxford University Press, New York, 1990).

48. Theweleit, *Male Fantasies*. For a new interpretation of Rosa Luxemburg's role in German communism, see Eric Weitz, *Creating German Communism 1890–1990* (Princeton University Press, Princeton, 1997).

49. Weitz, *Creating German Communism*, pp. 179–80.

50. Weitz, *Creating German Communism*, pp. 179–80. Weitz does not explore the different ways in which Luxemburg's and Liebknecht's murders were symbolised or commemorated but his discussion of the commemorations led me to reflect on this.

51. Thomas Laqueur, 'Bodies, Details, and the Humanitarian Narrative', in *The New Cultural History*, ed. Lynn Hunt (University of California Press, Berkeley, 1989), pp. 194–5.

52. Kathleen Canning, 'Feminist History After the "Linguistic Turn": Historicizing Discourse and Experience', *Signs*, 19 (1994), pp. 368–404.

53. Domansky, 'Militarization and Reproduction'. This citation is from an earlier version of the essay which was presented to the conference on the Kaiserreich, held at the University of Pennsylvania in February 1990, p. 9.

54. Bynum, 'Why all the Fuss about the Body?', p. 5.

8

Gender and Science

Ilana Löwy

The heading 'gender and science' covers several distinct issues. One is the question of the consequences of the new focus on 'gender' for our understanding of the history of science and medicine. A second is the study of the effects of feminism, or more broadly, of changes in women's status brought about by the women's movement, on science and technology. A third is the investigation of the role of gendered assumptions in the construction of scientific knowledge. The fourth focuses on the effects of the exclusion of women from the scientific enterprise as regards the universality and objectivity of science. While these issues may seem distinct – the first interrogates history, the second concrete practices of present-day scientists, and the third and fourth the production and validation of scientific know-ledge – they are often lumped together and are occasionally confused.[1]

The more narrowly defined subject of the effects of introducing the variable 'gender' into the history of science, medicine and technology also has several distinct aspects.[2] Numerous researchers, especially those in-spired by the feminist movement, have taken to the task of 'uncovering' the hidden women in the sciences: the 'anonymous helpers', the 'devoted wives', and above all the women who have made direct contributions to science and whose names have been obliterated and erased in numerous ways. An akin, but not identical topic is the study of the institutionalisation of science, and the ways this, which entailed the exclusion of all the prac-tices excluded from 'official' science, transformed the knowledge held by women either into an inferior category of practical skills (as opposed to the scientific enterprise) or as 'superstition' and 'folk knowledge'.[3] Other studies have followed the influence of masculine values on the development of science.[4] An additional area of interest is the history of the constitution of the image of 'woman' as antithetical to that of the 'scientist', and of the ways the education of women barred their access to the sciences. This chapter focuses, however, on a different problem: the consequences of the introduction of the concept of gender on studies of scientific and medical practices. It will be limited, in the main, to historical studies of twentieth-century biomedicine, and will be focused on the way science deals with the differences between the sexes.[5]

Once historians of science were interested mainly in the deeds of 'great men of science'. In the last thirty years they have also become increasingly interested in the multiple ways science operates on a micro- and macro-level. They study laboratories and instruments, patterns of communication among scientists, organisational and administrative practices, or the role of norms and standards in the diffusion of scientific knowledge and practices. The interest in gender neatly fits this new perception of science. It calls attention to the fact that scientists operate within the framework of a society divided according to gender lines, that their minds are located in sexed/gendered bodies (until recently, nearly exclusively male ones), and that this fact may, and often does, affect the knowledge they produce. On the other hand, one may argue that the scientists of the past (white, upper-class males) who produced knowledge grounded in the self-evident 'natural' hierarchy between the sexes and between human races, were led astray by their preju-dices. The addition of the gender dimension to studies of 'outdated' science may help us to understand better the interactions between science and society in the past, but need not affect our perception of present-day science (progressive, bias-free, and produced by men and women belonging to numerous national and ethnic groups) as a reliable source of knowledge about the natural world. A focus on twentieth-century biomedicine may allow us, by contrast, to examine the validity of scientific assumptions which under-lie our understanding of the natural world, the genesis and the present status of scientific definitions of masculinity and femininity, and the ideological basis of science-based technological interventions in the domain of sexuality and reproduction. The latter can be seen as opening new opportunities, but also as creating new dilemmas, and their ambivalent, and occasionally controversial status is reflected in historical studies which investigate their origins and development.

The development of the concept of gender (to describe either the social expressions of masculinity and femininity, or, for feminists, the systems of signs and symbols which denote relations of power and hierarchy between the sexes) led, in the 1970s, to a distinction between gender (presumably social and constructed) and sex (presumably biological and given at birth). However, in the 1980s, partly under the influence of social studies of science, investigators became interested in the social and cultural construction of bio-logical sex. While the majority of human beings are non-problematically classified as 'males' or 'females' on the basis of their anatomy and their physiology, a certain number of individuals do not fit the 'natural' criteria of either category. In the nineteenth and early twentieth century, scientists adhered to the non-complicated assumption that sex is determined by the presence of sexual glands (ovaries or testes) and by substances secreted by these glands. Individuals with ambivalent external genitalia were automatically classified as belonging to the sex of their sexual glands (gonads), independently of their experience and self-perception (the only exceptions were the rare cases of true hermaphroditism, that is, the simultaneous presence of male and female sexual glands in the same individual).[6]

The discovery of the 'sexual chromosomes' (XX for women, XY for men) complicated this picture. Scientists observed numerous variants of the usual chromosomal formula (the absence of one or both of the sexual chromosomes, the duplication or triplication of a chromosome) and in some cases had difficulty defining precisely what the 'chromosomal sex' of a given individual was. Moreover, they also noted that the different levels of sex determination – anatomical, glandular, hormonal and chromosomal – are not necessarily concordant (an anatomical female might be a chromosomal male, and vice versa; some individuals who saw themselves as 'normal' men or women were found to be 'chromosomal freaks'), making the definition of the 'true' biological sex of a given individual problematic. In 1980, scientists hoped that the new techniques of molecular biology would lead to the identification of the genetic (and thus, presumably, the most fundamental) level of sex determination. Their starting point was the assumption that woman is a 'sex by default'. The basic structure of a human embryo, they proposed, is female, but half of the embryos are later transformed into males by a masculinity-determining gene, while those which fail to receive the 'added value' of masculinity, remain females. The search for the putative masculinity-defining gene, however, led to a further complexification of the determination of biological sex. The genetic determination of sex was found to be submitted to several levels of positive and negative regulation, and to be only partly convergent with anatomical, hormonal and chromosomal data.[7]

The search for the 'master gene' or 'master molecule' which defines sex is mainly of interest to scientists (although the definition of woman as a 'sex by default' is not). By contrast, the practical problems of definition of biological sex are illustrated by experts' attitudes to management of intersexed infants (children born with intermediary sexual characteristics, because of either anatomical, hormonal or chromosomal abnormality). Feminist researchers have recently become interested in this topic, seen as a privileged locus of observation of relationships between sex and gender, and between the biological and the social definition of masculinity and femininity. They have pointed to the importance of doctors' presuppositions of what the essence of 'femininity' or 'masculinity' is in the process of definition of the social sex of an intersexed infant. In addition, these children are a direct (if extreme) illustration of the thesis that gender determines sex.[8] The decision to assign a given gender to an intersexed child has been (until recently at least) almost automatically followed by a surgical and hormonal treatment, the goal of which is to harmonise the child's biological sex with their attributed gender. Thus boys born with a small penis (a congenital anatomical malformation) but who otherwise have normal male characteristics (the presence of testes, of male hormones, chromosomal formula 46, XY) were often surgically and hormonally transformed into girls, because their inability to penetrate a woman was seen as an absolute obstacle to the acquisition of male gender identity.[9]

The conviction that the appropriate education, as a girl, of an infant born as a biologically normal although anatomically imperfect boy, grew out of studies made by John Money and Anke Erhardt. Money and Erhardt's well-known book *Man & Woman, Boy & Girl* (1972) is often presented as one of the first investigations which postulated, to echo Simone de Beauvoir, that one is not born but rather made a woman (or a man). On the other hand, the same book has also been attacked for its stereotypical representation of putative male or female traits, supposedly fixed by hormonal influence before birth. The book, in fact, represents both points of view. Its understanding of the biological determination of sex is grounded in the 'organisational theory' (elaborated in the 1950s), which postulated that the effect of sexual hormones on the brain structure during embryonic development accounts for the sexual orientation of individuals, their overall behaviour and their innate capacities.[10] Money and Erhardt's descriptions of girls who were 'masculinised' in utero by exposure to high doses of male hormones, follow the postulates of the 'organisational theory' and at the same time conform to the most stereotypical and (today largely outmoded) representations of gendered behaviour. According to Money and Erhardt, 'normal' girls play with dolls, are interested in nice clothes, and strongly prefer motherhood over professional work. The abnormality of the hormonally 'masculinised' girls was revealed by the fact that they were not attracted by dolls, liked simple, functional clothes, and declared that they wished to combine motherhood and career. On the other hand Money and Erhardt claim, following, in particular, their observation of the case of a 'biologically normal' boy educated as a girl after an accidental loss of penis in infancy, that the biological make-up of an individual can be successfully modified through an appropriate education.[11]

In 1972, Money and Erhardt presented an optimistic story, and suggested that the negative effect of ambivalent biological sex might be corrected through socialisation into a well-defined gender role. Later, researchers found that many among the intersexed children raised in their 'attributed sex' had important physical and mental problems when reaching adolescence and early adulthood. The surgically crafted sexual organs were seldom fully functional, while the best efforts of their educators did not prevent frequent problems of sexual identity. Some of the opponents of the concept of social shaping of sexual identities proposed that these difficulties (especially in Money and Erhardt's exemplary case of a 'biological boy' turned into a 'social girl') attested to the strength of the unavoidable 'call of nature'.[12] An alternative explanation would be that intersexed children raised by parents conscious of their 'abnormality', submitted from their early childhood to heavy medical treatments, often suffering from sexual problems and living in a society which does not easily tolerate sexual ambivalence, can hardly be expected to escape personality problems.[13]

Feminist scholars have carefully displayed the difficulties created in the past by arbitrary attribution of gender/sex identity to intersexed children. It is more difficult to provide concrete solutions for the parents of such children. Scholars, but also intersexed individuals themselves, seem to agree that the previous practice of irreversible surgical and hormonal treatment of intersexed children at birth often did more harm than good. As grown-ups, intersexed individuals can either accept the ambivalence of their sexual organs and, if applicable, of their sexual drive (the greater tolerance of homosexuality and of bisexuality may facilitate such accommodation), or, alternatively, opt for a surgical and hormonal solution which will help them become as close as possible to 'normal' men or women.[14] This proposal, however, leaves open the central question of the conditions which may allow new-born intersexed children to grow up without excessive psychological harm. It is not impossible for an adult to find a social 'niche' which tolerates atypical sex/gender identity, but there are no similar, sheltered 'niches' for small children. Parents and doctors, a surgery textbook explains, want a rapid solution to the problem of the sexual ambivalence of a child: 'after a baby is delivered, the first question asked by the parents is typically "Is it a boy or a girl?" Furthermore, the social pressures placed on the parents when the sex of the new-born is indeterminate compels the medical and surgical team caring for the baby into a rapid diagnostic paradigm for gender assignment, in response to this *social emergency*.'[15] The concrete dilemmas of intersexed infants, born into a world in which there is no room for individuals who do not conform to the male/female dichotomy, elude easy answers.

The introduction of gender into studies of recent biology has questioned the – supposedly scientific and objective – descriptions of the physiology of women's bodies. The anthropologist Emily Martin has shown that the usual descriptions of menstruation in medical books and in popular science books are invariably in terms of waste and loss. The shedding of uterine endometrium is connected with the absence of pregnancy, and is formulated in purely negative terms. Educated women (unlike working-class ones) adopt as a rule the 'scientific' explanation of menstruation as the secretion of 'unnecessary' tissue and blood. This explanation is not, however, Martin argues, the only one compatible with the observed phenomenon of shedding of the uterine lining and regrowth of a new tissue. Other biological phenomena in which a tissue is shedded and then replaced by another, for example the permanent replacement of the stomach lining, are described in terms of renewal and growth. The difference is especially striking when one contrasts the scientific descriptions of menstruation – a monthly waste – with those of the production of sperm – an amazingly efficient production. The observation that only a few (at best) of the millions of spermatozoids produced in a male's lifetime will serve to produce offspring is not translated into the terms of a wasteful biological mechanism. Similarly, menopause is invariably described as a diminishment of a woman's biological potential, not as a positive change and a redirection of the body's biological resources towards different tasks.[16]

The introduction of the concept of gender into the history of endocrinology (especially in the studies of Diana Long-Hall, Nelly Oudshoorn and Adele Clarke) has similarly displayed the gendered assumptions underlying investigations of male and female hormones.[17] The concept that specific molecules have 'sexed' identities originated in the convergence of two distinct lines of investigation: the study of human reproduction and the investigation of mechanisms which maintain the stable internal environment of the body (homeostasis). The encounter of the two led to the concept of the role of substances secreted by the sexual glands in the determination of secondary sexual characteristics. The argument that reproductive organs, or their secretions, affect numerous vital functions, was propagated through the widely publicised experiments of the French physiologist Charles Eduard Brown-Sequard, who in the late nineteenth century promoted the rejuvenating effects of testicular transplants and extracts, and was consolidated through the development (in 1905) of the concept of 'internal secretions' (later renamed 'hormones') by the British researcher Ernest Starling.[18]

In the early twentieth century scientists assumed that substances secreted by testes have a 'masculinising' effect, and those secreted by ovaries a 'feminising' one. The perfection of methods of purification and testing of hormones later led, historians of endocrinology have shown, to the blurring of the very idea of the existence of 'male' and 'female' hormones. Molecules, it so happens, resist sexualisation. Scientists found that both ovarian and testicular extract could introduce the growth of uterus in castrated female rabbits (a standard test for 'feminising' substances) or the growth of accessory glands in castrated male rats (a standard test for 'masculinising' ones). They concluded that ovaries and testes secrete both 'masculinising' and 'feminising' substances, and that the appropriate level of analysis is not the organ, but the chemical substances it secretes. Further studies revealed, however, that purified sexual hormones had various physiological effects, some of which were not connected with sexual functions. Worse, identical molecules could, under different circumstances, induce 'masculinising' or 'feminising' effects. At first these contradictory effects were attributed to the impurity of the hormonal preparations, but highly purified hormone preparations and synthetic hormones behaved in the same way.

The accumulation of often contradictory observations about hormones secreted by the sexual glands, and observation of the close structural resemblance between the 'male' and 'female' hormones, led in the 1930s to the proposal to change the name of these substances and abolish the reference to their putative male or female nature. This proposal was rejected, and future development strengthened, in the main, the sexualisation of these molecules.[19] Their names reinforced sexualised stereotypes. The 'male' hormones were renamed 'androgens' ('male-making'), a very general term, while the female hormones were called 'oestrogens', that is, substances which induce the cyclical changes related to oestrus, the period of female fertility. The new name firmly linked female (but not male) hormones with reproduction and cyclicity. The link was not merely rhetorical. Female, but not male hormones, rapidly achieved the status of therapies for 'female disorders'. The fundamental assumption that women's health (and more broadly, women's identity) is dependent on the functioning of their sexual organs, coupled with the existence of a medical sub-speciality – gynae-cology – focused on women's reproductive health (and the absence of such a speciality addressed to men), led to the rapid diffusion of treatments based on female hormones.[20] The efficacy of the early therapeutic uses of organ extracts and of hormone preparations remains questionable, but their popularity in the 1920s and 1930s consolidated the relations between women, hormones and biomedical research. The possibilities of commer-cialisation of female hormones stimulated further fundamental investigations into the effects of hormones on the female body, and these investigations led, in turn, to development of new uses for female hormones, the most spectacular of which was the development of the contraceptive pill in the 1950s.[21] In the absence of a parallel practical stimulus to investigate hor-mones in men, studies which could potentially have traced in detail the effects of changes in hormone levels in the blood on men's behaviour, moods, or professional performances, never took place. Women, but not men, became increasingly identified with their 'hormonal bodies'.[22]

Two debates focused attention on the problematic aspect of interpreting female bodies in hormonal terms: the one on premenstrual syndrome (PMS) and the one on hormone replacement therapy for menopause (HRT). Debates on PMS focused on the reality of this phenomenon, asking whether it is a 'true' organic pathological disorder, a psychosomatic affection, or an invention of women-hating doctors and a profit-seeking drug industry. PMS – a mid-cycle personality change in women, leading to depression, irritability, anger flashes and in some cases physical symptoms as well – was first described in the early 1930s but became widely known mainly thanks to the studies of the English endocrinologist Katherine Dalton. Dalton, who opened the first PMS treatment clinics, and became an advocate of the treatment of this condition (and later testified in trials in which the defence argued for diminished clinical responsibility in women who committed crimes when supposedly suffering from 'pre-menstrual tension'), explained later that her involvement with this topic stemmed from observation of the suffering of women with marked PMS symptoms.[23] Feminist writers pointed to the consequences of attributing the manifestation of feminine anger to hormonal causes, and to the fact that there were no studies focused on the potential positive effects of the feminine hormonal cycle (and no inves-tigations whatsoever about the possible influence of hormones on male behaviour).[24] On the other hand, women who claimed that they were suffer-ing from PMS symptoms were pleased to receive recognition and attention, and were often satisfied with the results of therapies they received (hormonal treatments, tranquillisers, and psychotherapy were all reported to be efficient as PMS treatments).[25]

While the very existence of PMS was questioned by feminists, the debates on menopause (defined as the cessation of menses in women, usually around the age of fifty) did not focus on the (uncontested) existence of the phenomenon but on the frequency and severity of physical symptoms which accompany the cessation of menstruation, and on the desirability of medical treatment of menopause, especially through prolonged administration of female hormones. Menopausal symptoms, anthropologists have argued, are not a universal biological phenomenon. Margaret Lock, who studied menopause in Japan, found that Japanese women rarely suffer from 'hot flashes', the most frequently mentioned symptom of menopause in the West. They also tend to attribute their health problems to ageing, rather than to menopause.[26] On the other hand, Western cultures have, from the early nineteenth century on, perceived menopause as a dangerous period in women's lives. The perception of the nature and extent of the danger, and the recommendations about how to deal with it, have however varied greatly in different historical periods, as Joy Barbe has shown, and have been closely related to perceptions of the 'right' societal role for woman. In the nineteenth century, menopause was seen as a dangerous period for a woman, which, however, if safely overcome could lead to a renewal of health and vitality. The tendency to treat menopausal women with glandular extracts was developed in the interwar era and was enthusiastically adopted by many women (including some of the prominent advocates of women's rights). Its immediate popularity may be explained by the fact that preparations aiming at preserving a woman's vitality were in agreement with the ideal of women of the 1920s and 1930s: youthful, energetic and thin. After World War Two, the image of the ideal woman shifted to that of spouse and mother, and later grandmother. At the same time, doctors became less enthusiastic about hormonal therapies and argued that a 'well adjusted' woman, happy in her feminine role, should not suffer from menopausal troubles.[27]

The return of the 'youthful ideal' in the 1960s, coupled with the steady increase in the number of women in the workforce, led to a regaining of the popularity of hormonal therapy for menopause, advocated again mainly as a way for women to preserve their femininity and vitality. In the 1980s the arguments in favour of HRT shifted from the preservation of female attractiveness to that of the preservation of health. HRT, experts argued, protects ageing women from osteoporosis and heart disease.[28] The latter claims remained controversial, however, and the adversaries of this therapy pointed to increased risks of cancer for women on HRT. The medicalisation of menopause was strongly criticised by feminists (especially in the US), who denounced the manipulation of women by doctors and the pharmaceutical industry, and proposed an alternative 'feminist' model of menopause based on its perception as a natural phenomenon and as an opportunity for growth and change.[29] This model, the anthropologist Patricia Kaufert explains, was nevertheless influenced by the medical view of menopause, and it shares some of the basic assumptions of the medical view, above all the perception of menopause as an important event in a woman's life. Feminists, it is true, present menopause as a positive event. On the other hand, however, their tendency to glorify the reproductive functions of the female body makes positive valorisation of menopause difficult. In addition, while the medicalisation of menopause presents women as 'deficient' but does not blame them for this deficiency, a view which presents menopause as a 'natural event' tends to implicitly blame women who do not develop the 'right' attitude and a healthy lifestyle, and therefore 'fail' to have an eventless menopause (a view which, paradoxically, recalls the opinion, popular in the 1950s, that women who are well adapted to their feminine role are protected from the negative effects of menopause).[30]

To sum up, the increased use of female hormones as drugs can be seen as a mixed blessing. It has allowed the development of efficient contraception, and the treatment of numerous hormone-related disorders. It has also linked female bodies with hormones, with cyclical function, and with the perception of the ageing female (but not male) body as essentially flawed, providing a new, scientific context for the traditional perception of women as 'closer to nature'. Paradoxically, this naturalisation (or rather re-naturalisation) of women's bodies was effected in the main through a large-scale diffusion of substances produced by the pharmaceutical industry (one may note that the main male hormone, testosterone, has an important symbolic role but is much less often used as a drug than the female hormones). One should add, however, that the massive use of hormones by women was not the result of a plot organised by paternalist doctors and greedy industrialists. Besides their enthusiastic endorsement of the contraceptive pill, women also actively participated in the medicalisation of menstruation, of pregnancy and childbirth, and of menopause, and frequently the rapid diffusion of new therapies was at least as much the result of their pull as of the industrialists' push. Women's support for hormonal therapies can be related to the role of these therapies in alleviating physical discomfort, but also to indirect benefits from the reclassification of complaints once labelled 'psychosomatic' (read, imaginary or hysterical) as respectable hormonal disorders, and from the fact that the legitimating of their 'female complaints' allowed them to obtain attention, sympathy and care.[31]

Historians interested in gender have pointed to the partly contingent and partly cultural reasons which led to the redefinition of women's (but not men's) bodies as ruled by sexual hormones, and to the societal consequences of this imbalance.[32] Their studies remind us that it could have been otherwise. We could have had cyclical, 'hormonal men', or alternatively a natural world without specific 'sexual hormones'. In such a world, molecules would have escaped sexualisation/gendering, secretions of endocrine glands could have been classified according to, for example, structural criteria, and the substances today labelled 'sexual hormones' could have been included in a much larger family of 'growth and differentiation agents'. On the other hand, a 'historical fiction' is exactly that – a fiction. During the twentieth century, sexual hormones have become integrated into the world view of individuals living in industrialised countries. The majority of feminist historians, anthropologists, sociologists, and health activists share, like nearly all educated women, a biomedical framework of understanding of their bodily experiences. They interpret, filter, eliminate and amplify their physical sensations through a grid which incorporates a hormonal perception of the female body. This perception shapes the ways women conceptualise their similarities and their differences with men, and affects their efforts to fight against the transformation of these differences into means of discrimination.

Researchers interested in relationships between gender and science have questioned in a radical way the notions of universality, rationality and objectivity in the sciences. Feminist researchers have teamed with those interested in social and cultural studies of the sciences, and with students of non-Western scientific practices, in order to question the ways science has been used as a tool for reinforcing the hegemony of the Western world, and to question the perception of science as a 'view from nowhere' and as a 'culture outside culture'. Sandra Harding proposes developing a 'standpoint epistemology', Wendy Faulkener and Elisabeth Kerr advocate the multiplication of vantage points on science (including a multiplicity of feminist points of view), while Donna Haraway calls for a science which incorporates passion, critical point of view, solidarity and responsibility.[33] Standpoints, it is assumed, will integrate the points of view of individuals excluded up to now from the edifice of science, and this will make science more, not less objective. Enlargement of the basis of elaboration of scientific knowledge in order to include the point of view of social groups previously excluded from such elaboration may, and often does, improve the quality of this knowledge. This is not, however, an unproblematic issue. Londa Schiebinger has noted that military researchers have a strong and well-defined standpoint but this fact does not, by itself, justify the inclusion of their point of view in the elaboration of new knowledge.[34] One may argue that Schiebinger's argument is purely rhetorical: military research always has, and continues to have, an important influence on the development of the sciences. However, the inclusion of groups genuinely excluded under more traditional arrangements from the domain of the construction of new scientific knowledge may also present problematic aspects.

The inclusion of AIDS patients in decisions concerning clinical investigation of therapies against this pathology is frequently given as an example of positive effects of taking local knowledge into account when applying science.[35] The participation of AIDS patients in the elaboration of clinical trials of new therapies has led to modifications in the organisation of these trials and to a partial redefinition of the norms of 'good clinical research'. On the other hand, the patients' influence was at its apex in a period during which there was no efficient treatment for AIDS, and doctors and researchers grappled in the dark. The development of more efficient therapies for this pathology led to the reinforcement of the role of big pharmaceutical companies which produce anti-HIV drugs. The patients' organisations which were active in an earlier stage in shaping the form and content of clinical trials and promoting a parallel expertise, have reverted in the main to the important but less innovative role of consumers' associations. They fight for high-quality medical services, for enlarged access to new drugs, for greater governmental subsidising of anti-AIDS therapies, and are occasionally 'enrolled' by pharmaceutical firms to campaign for a given product.[36]

The story of AIDS activism illustrates the difficulty of separating the lofty goal of enlarging the basis of scientific knowledge through cooperation, contradiction and debate between the beholders of different points of view, and the much more pedestrian problems of choices imposed by late twentieth-century technoscience, which inseparably mixes cognitive, social, political and economic interests. The argument that science is rarely a 'pure' activity, isolated from the rest of society, can be used in two ways. It may sustain the argument that an 'impure' activity which, far from being grounded in a single and non-controversial 'scientific method', depends on multiple variables (cognitive, technical, institutional, social, cultural, economic, political) and on numerous contingent and non-predictable elements, may benefit greatly from inclusion of the experience of groups previously excluded from the edifice of science. It may at the same time indicate some problematic aspects of the 'opening' of scientific and technological debate in a fundamentally unequal and unjust society in which a 'strong objectivity' may drift towards the 'objectivity of the strong', and may transform the ideal of a fully democratic technoscience into the reality of a lobby-driven one.

The persistence of gendered inequalities in our society has led to a parallel persistence of ambivalence in the consequences of attention to gendered issues in the sciences. Emily Martin's 'romance of the egg and the sperm' shows that the shift from one set of metaphors (the 'traditional' representation of a passive egg penetrated by an active spermatozoid) to another (the 'progressive' representation of a cooperation of the egg and the sperm in the fertilisation process) may at the same time open the way to the use of this new perception to mobilise a new range of metaphors, some of which are hostile to women. The positive effect of this shift – the abandonment of the stereotype of the inert, inactive egg which is 'transported' or 'drifts' into the fallopian tube until it is 'assaulted' and 'penetrated' by the agile sperm cell, and its replacement by images in which both the egg and the sperm are active partners in fertilisation – has led in parallel to the revival of images in which the huge egg draws, attracts and engulfs a small, defenceless spermatozoid. In these new images the egg, likened to a spider waiting in her web, becomes a female aggressor who 'captures and tethers' the sperm with her sticky zona. The old images, which referred to the classic stereotype of passive females and aggressive males, are replaced by equally classic stereotypes of devouring mothers and 'femmes fatales'.[37] Similarly, the examples discussed in this chapter – the shaping of hormonal bodies and the treatment of sexually ambivalent individuals – show how the introduction of the concept of gender into science has opened new opportunities for women and for 'atypical men', while at the same time it has closed other avenues and made some choices (including the choice not to use a new technology) difficult.[38]

The main issue here is therefore the impossibility of treating the issue of gender and science as a separate topic, isolated from all the other implications of gender *and* of science. Scientific ideas and practices do not exist in the void. If we accept the basic tenet of the investigators who have studied the relationships between gender and science, namely that science is a sociocultural activity inseparable from the time and place of its pro-duction, it is reasonable to assume that this activity will mirror present-time ambiguities of women's status. The same principle may apply to historical investigations too. Divergent evaluations of the past and present con-sequences of scientific developments, such as hormonal contraception, treat-ment of pseudo-hermaphroditism, surgery for sex-change, in vitro fertilisation, or hormonal therapy of PMS and menopause, reflect the simultaneous ex-istence of multiple definitions of masculinity and femininity, of numerous trends of feminism, and above all the fact that we live in a society in which the concrete advances of women cannot mask the fact that they continue to be discriminated against in old and in new ways (and through numerous combinations of both), and that the main locus of this discrimination continues to be their sexed bodies.

Notes

1. Some of the papers given at the conference 'Science , Medicine and Technology in the 20th century: What Difference Has Feminism Made' (Princeton University, 2–3 October 1998) discussed historiographic issues, others debated the role of feminists in changing scientific practices, and still others were interested in the ways the new visibility of women has modified the way scientists look at natural phenomena. A recent book by Londa Schiebinger, *Has Feminism Changed Science?* (Harvard University Press, Cambridge, MA, 1999), traces the contribution of women to the development of scientific disciplines, the role of women as consumers of science and technol-ogy, and the changes interest in gender has brought to the content of scientific investigations.

2. For a review of these directions, see Ludmilla Jordanova, 'Gender and the His-toriography of Science', *British Journal of the History of Science*, 26 (1993), pp. 469–83.

3. Londa Schiebinger, *The Mind Has No Sex: Women in the Origins of Modern Science* (Harvard University Press, Cambridge, MA, 1989); Michèle Le Dœuff, *Le Sexe du savoir* (Aubier, Paris, 1998).

4. Evelyn Fox Keller, *Secrets of Life, Secrets of Death: Essays on Gender, Language and Science* (Routledge, London, 1992).

5. For more general surveys on gender and science, see for example Elisabeth A. Kerr and Wendy Faulkner, 'On Seeing Broken Spectres: Sex and Gender in Twentieth-Century Science', in *Science in the Twentieth Century*, ed. John Krige and Dominique Pestre (Harwood Academic Publishers, London, 1997), pp. 43–60; Jordanova , 'Gender and the Historiography of Science'; Evelyn Fox Keller and Helen Longino (eds), *Feminism and Science* (Oxford University Press, Oxford, 1996).

6. Alice Domurat Dreger, 'Hermaphrodites in Love: The Truth of Gonads', in *Science and Homosexualities*, ed. Vernon A. Rosario (Routledge, London, 1997), pp. 46–66.

7. Cynthia Kraus, 'La Bicategorization par sexe: problèmes et enjeux des recherches en biologie sur la détermination du sexe chez les humains', in *L'Invention du naturel: les sciences et la fabrication du féminin et du masculin*, ed. Delphine Gardey and Ilana Löwy (Editions des Archives Contemporaines, Paris), in press.

8. Ruth Hubbard, 'Gender and Genitals: Constructs of Sex and Gender', in *Science Wars*, ed. Andrew Ross (Duke University Press, Durham, 1996), pp. 168–79; Susanne J. Kessel, 'The Medical Construction of Sex: The Management of Intersexed Infants', *Signs: Journal of Women, Culture and Society*, 16 (1990), pp. 3–26. For the history of medical treatment of hermaphrodites, see Alice Domurat Dreger, *Hermaphrodites and the Medical Invention of Sex* (Harvard University Press, Cambridge, MA, 1998).

9. Anne Fausto-Sterling, 'How to Build a Man', in *Science and Homosexualities*, ed. Rosario, pp. 219–25.

10. Marianne van den Wijngaard, *Reinventing the Sexes: The Biomedical Construction of Femininity and Masculinity* (Indiana University Press, Bloomington, 1997). 'Organizational theory' was recently mobilised to support the claim of differences in brain stucture between 'straight' and homosexual men. Simon Le Vay, *Queer Science: The Use and Abuse of Research Into Homosexuality* (The MIT Press, Cambridge, MA, 1996).

11. John Money and Anke A. Erhardt, *Man & Woman, Boy & Girl: The Differentiation and Dimorphism of Gender Identity from Conception to Maturity* (Johns Hopkins University Press, Baltimore, 1972), pp. 118–25.

12. Bill and Anne Moir, *Why Men Don't Iron: The Real Science of Gender Studies* (HarperCollins, London, 1998), p. 103.

13. Fausto-Sterling, 'How to Build a Man'.

14. Domurat Dreger, *Hermaphrodites and the Medical Invention of Sex*, pp. 197–9.

15. Patricia K. Donahoe, David M. Powell and Mary M. Lee, 'Clinical Management of Intersex Abnormalities', in *Current Problems in Surgery, 1991* (Mosby-Year Book Inc., Littleton, MA, 1991), pp. 515–79, at p. 519. My italics.

16. Emily Martin, *The Woman in the Body: A Cultural Analysis of Reproduction* (Beacon Press, Boston, 1987).

17. Diana Long-Hall, 'Biology, Sex-Hormones and Sexism in the 1920s', in *Women and Philosophy*, ed. Max Wartofsky and Carol Gould (Putnam, New York, 1975), pp. 81–95; Nelly Oudshoorn, *Beyond the Natural Body, Archeology of Sex Hormones* (Routledge, London, 1994); Adele Clarke, *Disciplining Reproduction: Modernity, American Life Sciences and the Problem of Sex* (University of California Press, Berkeley, 1998).

18. Merriley Borrel, 'Organotherapy and the Emergence of Reproductive Endocrinology', *Journal of the History of Biology*, 18 (1985), pp. 1–30. Chandak Segoopta, 'Glandular Politics: Experimental Biology, Clinical Medicine and Homosexual Emancipation in Fin de Siècle Central Europe', *Isis*, 89 (1998), pp. 445–73.

19. Nelly Oudshoorn, 'Endocrinologists and the Conceptualization of Sex, 1920–1940', *Journal of the History of Biology*, 23 (1990), pp. 163–86.

20. Ornella Moscucci, *The Science of Women: Gynecology and Gender in England, 1800–1929* (Cambridge University Press, Cambridge, 1990).

21. On the history of the contraceptive pill, see Lara Marks, *Sexual Chemistry: An International History of the Pill* (Yale University Press, New Haven, forthcoming).

22. Oudshoorn, *Beyond the Natural Body*.

23. Katherine Dalton, *The Premenstrual Syndrome and Progesterone* (Heineman, London, 1977).

24. Gail Vines, *Raging Hormones: Do They Rule Our Lives* (Virago, London, 1993); Emily Martin, 'Premenstrual Syndrome, Work Discipline and Anger', in *The Politics of Women's Bodies: Sexuality, Appearance and Behavior*, ed. Rose Weitz (Oxford University Press, Oxford, 1998), pp. 221–41.

25. Richard C. Friedman (ed.), *Behavior and the Menstrual Cycle* (Marcel Dekker, New York and Basel, 1982).

26. Margaret Lock, *Encounters With Aging* (California University Press, Berkeley, 1992).

27. Joy Webster Barbe, *From 'Goodwives' to 'Menoboomers': Reinventing Menopause in American History* (unpublished PhD thesis, University of Minnesota, 1994).

28. Bettine Leysen, 'Medicalization of Menopause: From "Feminine Forever" to "Healthy Forever"', in *Between Monsters, Godesses and Cyborgs: Feminist Confrontations with Science, Medicine and Cyberspace*, ed. Nina Lykke and Rosi Braidotti (Zed Books, New York, 1996), pp. 173–92.

29. Anne Fausto-Sterling, *Myths of Gender: Biological Theories about Women and Men* (Basic Books, New York, 1985), pp. 90–122.

30. Patricia A. Kaufert, 'Myth and Menopause', *Sociology of Health and Illness*, 4 (1982), 141–66.

31. Catherine Kohler Riessman, 'Women and Medicalization: A New Perspective', in *The Politics of Women's Bodies*, pp. 46–63.

32. On the reasons for the absence of efficient male contraception, see Nelly Oudshoorn, 'Shifting Boundaries between Industry and Science: The Role of WHO in Contraceptive R&D', in *The Invisible Industrialist: Manufacturers and the Production of Scientific Knowledge*, ed. Jean-Paul Gaudillière and Ilana Löwy (Macmillan, London, 1998), pp. 345–68.

33. Sandra Harding, 'Rethinking Standpoint Epistemology: What Is "Strong Objectivity"', in *Feminist Epistemologies*, ed. L. Alcoff and E. Potter (Routledge, New York and London, 1993); Donna Haraway, 'Situated Knowledges: The Science Question in Feminism and the Privilege of Partial Perspective', *Feminist Studies*, 14 (1988), pp. 575–99; Kerr and Faulkner, 'On Seeing Broken Spectres'.

34. Schiebinger, *Has Feminism Changed Science?*, p. 184.

35. For example, Harry Collins, 'The Science Police', *Social Studies of Science*, 29 (1999), pp. 287–94.

36. Steven Epstein, *Impure Science: AIDS, Activism and the Politics of Knowledge* (University of California Press, Berkeley, 1996).

37. Emily Martin, 'The Egg and the Sperm: How Science Has Constructed a Romance Based on Stereotyped Male–Female Roles', *Signs: Journal of Women, Culture and Society*, 16 (1991), pp. 485–501.

38. Marylin Strathern, *Reproducing the Future* (Manchester University Press, Manchester, 1992).

9

Work, *Gender & History* in the 1990s and Beyond

Efi Avdela

Work has been at the centre of feminist historical research in many countries since the 1970s. Influenced and challenged by the development of social history and the Marxist paradigm prevailing in the field, feminist historians in Britain, France, the USA, Germany, and in other countries, set out to document the historical patterns of the sexual division of labour in industrial societies; women's constantly subordinated position in the labour market; the connections between their paid and unpaid work; and their experiences of and responses to exploitation. Debates about the relations between women and the labour movement, between feminism and socialism or between patriarchy and capitalism radicalised this enterprise according to the different historical traditions and political circumstances prevailing in each country.[1]

As studies proliferated in the 1980s, it became clear that the issue of women's work in industrial societies took to task the established wisdom in the history of work in a variety of ways: by documenting women's presence in workplaces, unions, and protests, feminist historians integrated women into labour history and called into question the public/private divide; by highlighting the inability of the analytical categories of traditional labour and working-class history, such as class consciousness, skill, or wage, to incorporate the experience of women workers, they criticised its implicit masculinist assumptions; and by investigating the varying contents and meanings of femininity and masculinity at play in labour relations, they stressed the importance of gender in processes of class formation. Soon after the 'new' labour history turned from the study of working-class institutions to the study of class formation through social and cultural transformations, feminist historians turned from women to the conceptualisation of gender as an analytical category of historical analysis, a shift closely related to the growing interest in questions of identities and the increasing awareness of the significance of cultural factors in the gendering of work and class identities.[2] This process was not linear and presented significant variations depending on the national traditions of both labour history and women's history scholarship.

By the end of the 1980s, having amply demonstrated that the study of class could no longer be separated from the study of gender, feminist historians were advocating a new gendered history of work. American historian Ava Baron addressed the issue at the beginning of the 1990s and identified four problems that women's labour history had yet left unresolved, setting out the agenda for future research: take women's labour history out of its ghetto; explain the mechanisms of sexual difference in labour relations; theorise women's and men's 'consent' to oppression; and understand differences among women. According to Ava Baron, the quest for a gendered labour history required new conceptual tools and new theoretical approaches: connecting discursive constructions and experiences, historicising gendered subjectivities, linking agency and language, theorising the interrelation of gender, class and race, and producing historically and culturally specific, partial explanations.[3]

In this chapter I will seek to examine to what extent the above agenda has been met by research on work and gender during the last decade, taking as an example the ten volumes of *Gender & History* (1989–98). Explicitly dedicated since its first issue in 1989 to the study of gender in history, yet not specialised on the topic of work, the journal is a privileged witness to a double set of developments: on the one hand, methods and concepts applied to the study of work and gender, and on the other hand, the significance of this topic in gender history at large. The journal has been scanned for articles, but also reviews and review essays dealing with work understood in a broad sense: men and women workers, industrial and agricultural labour, employment and crafts, the workplace, labour unions, labour movement, strikes, work identities, class formation, working-class culture, working-class families and working-class life. The sample on which this overview will be based comprises more than fifty contributions unevenly dispersed throughout the ten years, presenting a net concentration in volumes 1, 5 and 9, and a notable decline toward the end of the decade.

Breaks in the isolation and segregation of women's labour history, the first problem identified by Ava Baron, can be detected in the journal in two respects: on the one hand, in the engagement with central questions of the history of work reformulated through the perspective of gender; and on the other hand, in the increasing participation of male historians of work. Indeed, the 1990s are more generally marked by the growing acknowledgement by male historians of the contribution of gender history to labour history. As Jürgen Kocka, one of the most prominent representatives of established European social history, has recently recognised, gender history poses 'the most momentous' challenge to traditional working-class and labour history, especially in respect of the social and cultural dimensions that link the 'public' domain of paid work to the 'private' domain of family, kinship and community.[4] Other historians have also acknowledged that feminist historiography has transformed the conceptualisation of class formation in working-class history, demonstrating its gendered character.[5] Yet this acknowledgement is far from being universal and there are more than a few examples of labour historians who continue to ignore women as well as gender in their studies.

Gisela Bock and Judith Bennet, in their seminal articles in the first volume of the journal, have demonstrated, albeit from different perspectives, how findings in research on work and gender have transformed our understanding of the past by undermining naturalist explanations of women's subordination in as well as out of the labour market.[6] Indeed, one of the early criticisms addressed by feminist historians to established working-class history has been that the historical construction of its central analytical categories, and especially its focus on materialist explanations, was based on the acceptance of seemingly 'natural' dualisms that in fact constituted hierarchical relations and had gendered meaning: work/family, public/private, politics/society.[7] Feminist labour historians have questioned these dualisms and have persistently 'pushed' the 'boundaries' of the field, insisting on the permeability and interrelation of the public and private spheres. More particularly, they have demonstrated the centrality of family life to working-class communities, its relevance to trade union activism, as well as the interconnection of the sexual division of labour in the family and in labour relations.[8]

The rejection of the public/private dichotomy is taken up in the journal from its outset, with several authors stressing the interdependence of the two spheres.[9] For example, in pleading for the necessity to go beyond this dichotomy and place gender 'in the wider world', Alice Kessler-Harris has suggested the study of subjectivity as a means to consider gender as one of the many parameters of identity of working women and men.[10] Yet, this explicit rejection of the public/private dichotomy is not evoked by most of the other authors, who seem to take it for granted.[11] The interrelations between work and family in the social construction of gender and in the shaping of masculinities and femininities has been more openly raised in reviews and review essays published in the journal.[12] However, although the blurring of boundaries between paid work and domesticity, workplace and family is repeatedly evoked in the papers under consideration, work is still implicitly equated with the public realm, be it the workplace, working-class life, working-class protest or the role of the state in moulding gendered versions of working-class identity. Family is very seldom the focus of analysis of the workplace and work identities. At any rate, it does not seem that the suggestion, recently and, I believe, fruitfully formulated by Alice Kessler-Harris, to study the workplace and gendered identities at work from the perspective of the family has yet been adequately put into practice by historians.[13] Furthermore, most of the time work and class mean industrial work and the working class. Few of the articles study domestic or agricultural work, services or clerical work, or even middle-class professions, and research on work in periods prior to the nineteenth century is barely represented.[14] It would seem that the innovative research of the 1980s on the role of gender in middle-class formation has not found its sequence in the journal.[15]

Of particular interest in this respect are the articles that link women's paid work to a wider conception of class formation, dealing with the relation of class and gender beyond the workplace. The questions asked extend the relevance of gender to the history of work: when studying the auxiliaries created by American skilled workers' wives in the 1920s, for example, Susan Levine argues for an understanding of working-class culture that includes concerns of consumption and the standard of living formulated outside the workplace and trade unions.[16] Workers' strategies of resistance to dominant conceptions of family and decency are analysed by Lynn Adams for nineteenth-century Germany, and Barbara Littlewood and Linda Mahood for Victorian Scotland.[17] In a similar vein, Donna J. Guy highlights how public health policies in Argentina at the turn of the century which prescribed the ideal gender and class behaviours of the 'masses' affected the structuring of the public sphere, the body politic and the nation.[18] The last two studies also underline the representation of sexuality in public discourses on women's work. Other contributions explore the relation between women's work, the welfare state and citizenship, while a special issue is dedicated to the protection of maternity, a topic that has been at the centre of important recent research.[19] These and other studies disclose the role of the state in negotiating, structuring and fixing the public/private dichotomy and gender identities through state policy: in a study on factory legislation in mid nineteenth-century England, Robert Gray documents the gendered character of protection and the effect of industrial reform in the crystallisation of gender segregation of jobs, a thesis long argued by feminist historians.[20] These studies broaden our conception of who belongs to the working class and emphasise women's agency in resisting, negotiating and adapting conditions prescribed for them by others. Yet, if class and gender are considered to be relational, it should be noted that their association with race, or ethnicity, is rarely examined.[21]

The increasing number of male historians of work publishing in the journal is the second sign of the growing integration of gender and labour history. Focusing mainly on the study of masculinity, these authors use the perspective of gender to revisit some of the main themes of labour history, and at times of their own research, as in the case of Keith McClelland and Robert Gray.[22] However, they are not alone in this endeavour. In fact, historicising masculinity in the formation of gender identities at work constitutes the journal's main contribution and corresponds to the second of the problems identified by Ava Baron.[23] The need to historicise masculinity and its historical construction along with that of femininity, and to study male institutions, are guidelines for research already advocated in the Editorial of the first issue.[24] The focus of many of the relevant articles on the construction of masculinity in the workplace and in unions reveals the existence of multiple, changing and often conflicting versions of male identity, thus undermining the traditional universal category of the 'worker' in labour history and documenting the culturally bounded formation of

gender and class identities. It is worth noting, however, that for many contributors masculinity seems to be better captured in action, such as strikes,
or in conflicts generated in the workplace and in unions.[25] Men at home
or the relation of men to domesticity are seldom at the centre of analysis.[26]
At the same time, though, masculinity is always defined as relational: male
identity appears to be shaped in relation to women,[27] other men,[28] children,[29] or all of the above,[30] but also to change through time and in action.[31]
On the other hand, the study of all-male institutions remains rather under-
developed. Yet the few cases included in the sample show the importance
of male bonding, for instance in German guilds or in South African gold
mines, in reproducing the dominant working-class male ideal.[32] Some articles
also underline the role of the state in the process of fixing masculine
working-class identities through policies of protection at work and social
welfare.[33]

The historical exploration of masculinity in the journal summons some
of the most inventive methodological approaches. Several authors pay particular attention to the cultural representations of male power through idioms
of honour,[34] heroism, manliness, combativity and justice,[35] or through
the model of respectability and autonomy,[36] highlighting the importance of
language in the formation of subjectivity. Some of the most insightful
studies depart from crisis situations, such as strikes, in order to analyse how
conflicting discursive practices inform action and constitute shifting identities
in a complex configuration of power relations: the analysis of the Lancashire
Weavers' strike of 1878, the New England textile workers' revolts of the
1870s, the Great Sea strike of 1890 in Australia and New Zealand, done by
Sonya Rose, Mary Blewett and Bruce Scates respectively, combine the
study of language, in the sense of the struggle over the meaning of working-
class gendered identities, with detailed record of action, thus bounding
agency in a specific historical context.[37]

Skill, one of the classical topics of labour history which has been at the
forefront of feminist criticism since the 1970s, is investigated by several
studies from the point of view of its cultural and social construction and its
relevance in the formation of gendered identities at work. The essays stress
the process of deskilling and its divergent gendered meaning, as in the case
of the American printing industry,[38] the different content and meaning of
skill for men and women workers, the relation of skill to the wage, the
sexual division of labour, or the status of a particular job.[39] In other words,
they address the question 'how and why sexual difference becomes
culturally and politically significant for the gendering of work'.[40]

The focus on male identities, however, does not always find its equivalent in the consideration of female identities. The problem is not of the
journal only. As several reviewers remark, much of the literature on work
and gender does not participate in discussions about the fluidity of the
categories of gender and femininity. As a result, different 'femininities', that
is the distinct gendered subjectivities of women and their consequences for

feminist theory and the theory of gender – the fourth problem in Ava Baron's list – would appear to need further investigation.[41] In the journal, the significance of work in the formation of female subjectivity as well as differences among women are examined in several articles: for example, Aarwen Mohoon and Miriam Glucksmann study different versions of subjectivity and identity. The former has examined the case of women working in the steam laundry industry in the beginning of the century in America, while the latter has compared women working in weaving or in informal paid jobs.[42] Those studies that pay particular attention to the unstable meanings of gender identities, such as those cited above or the one by Ava Baron on the changing definitions of sexual difference among American printers, document conflicting versions of both masculinity and femininity, highlighting their relational construction.[43] However, it seems that generally speaking the new sophisticated analysis concerning the fluidity of gender identities in labour and working-class history has not yet been adequately applied to femininities. As a result, feminine identity is sometimes treated in a more one-dimensional way, somehow undermining the relational character of gender.[44]

Historicising femininity along with masculinity in the study of the construction of gender identity and its significance in shaping workers' lives can provide insights to the third conceptual problem listed above, i.e. women's and men's 'consent' to oppression. According to Ava Baron, 'To understand men's or women's role in reproducing hierarchies of class and gender we must understand men's and women's efforts to construct and to defend a collective gender identity'.[45] In challenging one of the central theses of British working-class historiography on the Victorian decline of working-class radicalism and the compromise between capital and class, for example, Sonya Rose applies gender analysis to draw attention to practices that produce not only institutionalised 'consent' but also 'non-institutionalised forms of resistance'.[46] The fragility of 'consent' was in its turn the product of the homogenising discourse of trade union leaders that denied differences among workers. In another case, Mary H. Blewett emphasises the struggle over the multiple and unstable meanings of working-class subjectivity at play both between workers and employers and among workers themselves, which is also a struggle over the meaning of practices construed as being 'deferential' or 'defiant'.[47] Finally, for Margaret Hobbs the only way to understand instances of women's collusion with men in campaigns against some categories of women, as in the case of the Depression, is to consider them as cases of struggle over the preservation of particular definitions of gender identity.[48] Theorising subjectivity and the way subjects are constituted through discursive practices embedded in power relations upon which they act meaningfully, is the research strategy proposed by these and other scholars.

However, not all authors in our sample share the same theoretical and methodological options. The variety of approaches is more apparent in definitions of gender in relation to work. In the Editorial of the first issue gender was defined as both lived relations and a symbolic system referring to and sustaining power relations, a process operating at all levels, and the agenda was set for the investigation of historical changes in definitions of gender and for the questioning of the dominant binary oppositions.[49] Yet, in practice gender is seldom explicitly defined. In one of the rare debates published in the journal on the usefulness of a 'gender-neutral understanding of work', historians Alice Kessler-Harris and Margaret Hobbs both defend a relational and historically specific conception of gender, yet each one perceives this differently. For Hobbs, gender informs all aspects of life and its relational character can be better understood in the 'shifting nature of gender boundaries'.[50] Kessler-Harris, on the other hand, argues for an understanding of gender as a metaphor, for the need to 'comprehend the relationship of gender to the range of meaning systems that shape the lives of men and women'.[51] And in her own study published in the journal, Ava Baron perceives gender as a dynamic social process constituting power relations.[52]

Most of the contributors, however, do not define gender, or work for that matter. Focusing mainly on the study of working or working-class women, a number of authors employ the notions of experience, consciousness and reality in order to promote women's agency, and analyse the interrelation of work and family in the historical construction of gender identities. Inscribed in the line of empirical social history informed by decades of feminist criticism, they insist on the importance of material circumstances and social relations, even when they take language and meaning into consideration. In this they share the options explicitly defended by most of the reviewers in our sample. In as much as reviews and review essays can be considered to be more representative of the journal's methodological preferences, it is worth noting that they regularly express an open scepticism toward the usefulness of the 'linguistic turn' in historical research on gender and work.[53] In my view, these are indications that the journal is closer to the British tradition of feminist historical scholarship that is said to be consciously attempting to relativise the poststructural contention about the discursive construction of gender and class, as exemplified in the work of Joan Scott, by promoting empirical research on the relation between these categories and their contested and changing meanings.[54] Moreover, no examples of clear-cut postmodernist approaches are to be found in the journal. Those studies that analyse language in the construction of gender and class identities rather opt for what is known as the 'middle ground',[55] combining the quest for meaning with the agency of historical subjects. In that sense they apply the corrective that 'discourses may constitute individuals, but it is individuals trying to remake their world that constitute the stuff of history'.[56]

As is to be expected from an English language journal, the majority of essays under consideration refer to England and the USA, with individual papers on Germany, France, Argentina, Scotland, Sweden, Norway, South

Africa, the Soviet Union, Canada, and Greece. This is not a small scope of countries and conforms to the explicit commitment expressed in the Editorial of the first issue, to promote contributions that cut across place.[57] However, the cases correspond, to varying extents, to what is known as the 'industrialised world', testifying that research on work has not yet been developed in respect to other parts of the world, as has been recently done for other topics.[58] Furthermore, no attempts at comparisons across countries are to be found in the sample. As a result, research on work and gender, as portrayed in the journal, does not seem to participate in the move to go beyond the idea of 'exceptionalism' in labour history, and widen the dominant paradigms by extending research to a larger range of cases as well as by promoting comparative approaches.[59]

In this chapter I have tried to trace the main trends in historical scholarship on work and gender as depicted in the ten volumes of *Gender & History.* In spite of the partial character of the sample, this inquiry has indicated some of the directions that research on this topic is taking and will have to pursue in the 2000s in order to fully integrate gender in the study of work and class. Part of a larger movement toward reformulating labour and working-class history's questions, paradigms and narratives, these directions contribute to further 'pushing the boundaries' of the field. They constitute a response to the 'crisis' of labour history and point toward an integrated history of work in the broadest sense possible.[60] First there is a need for more theoretically informed research that would employ combined methodologies. Redefining work as well as gender will contribute to fully surmounting the public/private dichotomy and will further integrate work, family and community in our research. Historicising femininities along with masculinities, both in the public and the private realm, seems to be the next task that research on work and gender is facing. Finally, a gendered history of work would have to go beyond peculiarities and exceptionalisms, toward systematic comparison and the widening of the dominant paradigm.

However, the move toward the interrelation of public and private, work and family, as well as toward the construction of identities, their fluidity, multiplicity and transformation, calls into question to what extent work can continue to constitute a distinctive area of historical investigation. It seems to me that 'work' is no longer a field of research; it is rather a point of entry for studying people in the past, one of many others. By incorporating public and private, structure and agency, experience and language, reality and representation, gender and class and race, this gendered history of work should at the same time accept its partiality. And as feminist history and theory have already claimed, partiality is not a weakness but an option. In this respect, specific, contextualised, particular research on work and gender contributes to the feminist assertion that the study of history can only disclose 'partial truths'.[61]

Notes

1. For accounts on the relation between women's history and labour history, see for Britain: Catherine Hall, 'Feminism and Feminist History', in her *White, Male and Middle Class: Explorations in Feminism and History* (Polity Press, Cambridge, 1992), pp. 1–40; and Jane Rendall, '"Uneven Developments": Women's History, Feminist History, and Gender History in Great Britain', in *Writing Women's History: International Perspectives*, ed. Karen Offen, Ruth Roach Pierson and Jane Rendall (Macmillan, London, 1991), pp. 45–57; for France: Françoise Thébaut, *Écrire l'histoire des femmes* (ENS Editions, Fontenay/Saint-Cloud, 1998), pp. 48–50; for the USA: Ava Baron, 'Gender and Labor History: Learning from the Past, Looking to the Future', in *Work Engendered: Toward a New History of American Labor*, ed. Ava Baron (Cornell University Press, Ithaca and London, 1991), pp. 1–46; for Germany: Ute Frevert, Heide Wunder, Christina Vanja, 'Historical Research on Women in the Federal Republic of Germany', in *Writing Women's History*, ed. Offen, Pierson and Rendall, pp. 291–331; more generally: Gisela Bock, 'Women's History and Gender History: Aspects of an International Debate', *Gender & History* (hereafter *G&H*), 1 (1989), pp. 7–30.

2. See, among others, Joan Wallach Scott, *Gender and the Politics of History* (Columbia University Press, New York, 1988); Sonya O. Rose, *Limited Livelihoods. Gender and Class in Nineteenth Century England* (Routledge, London, 1992); Leonore Davidoff and Catherine Hall, *Family Fortunes: Men and Women of the English Middle Class, 1780–1850* (Routledge, London, 1987).

3. Baron, 'Gender and Labor History', pp. 1–46, esp. pp. 16–35.

4. Jürgen Kocka, 'New Trends in Labour Movement Historiography: A German Perspective', *International Review of Social History*, 42 (1997), pp. 67–78, esp. pp. 71–2. For the influence of the public/private dichotomy on the construction of labour history's categories of analysis, see Sonya O. Rose, 'Gender and Labor History: The Nineteenth-Century Legacy', *International Review of Social History*, 38 (1993), pp. 145–62, the very reference in J. Kocka's article.

5. See Keith McClelland, 'Introduction', in *E. P. Thompson: Critical Perspectives*, ed. H. J. Kaye and K. McClelland (Polity Press, Cambridge, 1990), p. 4; Geoff Eley, 'Is All the World a Text? From Social History to the History of Society Two Decades Later', in *The Historic Turn in the Human Sciences*, ed. Terrence J. McDonald (The University of Michigan Press, Ann Arbor, 1996), pp. 193–243; and Geoff Eley, 'Playing it Safe. Or: How is Social History Represented? The New *Cambridge Social History of Britain*', *History Workshop Journal*, 35 (1993), pp. 206–20; also most of the contributors in Lenard R. Berlanstein (ed.), *Rethinking Labor History: Essays on Discourse and Class Analysis* (University of Illinois Press, Urbana and Chicago, 1993).

6. Bock, 'Women's History and Gender History'; Judith Bennett, 'Feminism and History', *G&H*, 1 (1989), pp. 251–72.

7. Baron, 'Gender and Labor History'; Rose, 'Gender and Labor History: The Nineteenth-Century Legacy'; Leonore Davidoff, 'Regarding Some "Old Husbands" Tales: Public and Private in Feminist History', in her *Worlds Between: Historical Perspectives on Gender and Class* (Polity Press, Cambridge, 1995), pp. 227–76.

8. Laura L. Frader and Sonya O. Rose, 'Introduction: Gender and the Reconstruction of European Working-Class History', in *Gender and Class in Modern Europe*, ed. Laura L. Frader and Sonya O. Rose (Cornell University Press, Ithaca and London, 1996), pp. 1–33, esp. pp. 13–19. See also Gay L. Gullickson, 'Commentary: New Labor History from the Perspective of a Women's Historian', in *Rethinking Labor History*, ed.

Berlanstein, pp. 200–213; and Ruth Milkman, 'New Research In Women's Labor History', *Signs,* 18 (1993), pp. 376–88.

9. See in *G&H*: Alice Kessler-Harris, 'Gender Ideology in Historical Reconstruction: A Case Study from the 1930s', 1 (1989), pp. 31–49; also Wendy Goldman, 'A "Non-Antagonistic" Contradiction? The Waged and Unwaged Labor of Soviet Women', 3 (1991), pp. 337–44; and the following review essays: Bonnie Smith, 'Havens No More? Discourses of Domesticity', 2 (1990), pp. 98–102; Carol Elizabeth Adams, 'White-Blouse and White-Collar: Work, Culture and Gender', 2 (1990), pp. 343–8; Nancy Grey Osterud, 'Gender and Industrialization', 3 (1991), 97–103; Louise Tilly, 'Women and Work, plus Gender', 4 (1992), pp. 90–95; Lena Sommestad, 'Rethinking Gender and Work: Rural Women in the Western World', 7 (1995), pp. 100–105.

10. Kessler-Harris, 'Gender Ideology in Historical Reconstruction'.

11. See Miriam Glucksmann, review of Alice Kessler-Harris, *A Woman's Wage: Historical Meanings and Social Consequences* (The University Press of Kentucky, Lexington, 1990), *G&H*, 3 (1991), p. 369, and her remark that the public/private dichotomy is not so relevant for British and European women's history, while in the context of American women's history it is related to the debate around the concept of 'female sphere' and its inadequacy for understanding working-class women's lives. For the American debate see references in Susan M. Reverby and Dorothy O. Helly, 'Converging on History', in *Gendered Domains: Rethinking Public and Private in Women's History,* ed. Dorothy O. Helly and Susan M. Reverby (Cornell University Press, Ithaca and London, 1992), pp. 1–24.

12. See *G&H* review essays in note 9 and Rosemary Pringle, 'Rethinking Gender and Work', 5 (1993), pp. 295–301.

13. Alice Kessler-Harris, 'Treating the Male as "Other": Redefining the Parameters of Labor History', *Labor History,* 34 (1993), pp. 190–204.

14. See in *G&H*: for agricultural work: Sommestad, 'Rethinking Gender and Work', and Lena Sommestad, 'Able Dairymaids and Proficient Dairymen: Education and De-Feminization in the Swedish Dairy Industry', 4 (1992), pp. 34–48; service work is dealt with mainly in reviews: Carol Elizabeth Adams, 'White-Blouse and White-Collar'; Margaret Hedstrom, 4 (1992), pp. 426–9; and Ellen Jordan, 9 (1997), pp. 156–9; as well as in: Ellen Jordan, 'The Lady Clerks at the Prudential: The Beginning of Vertical Segregation by Sex in Clerical Work in Nineteenth-Century Britain', 8 (1996), pp. 65–81; for middle-class professions: Carol Dyhouse, 'Women Students and the London Medical Schools, 1914–39: The Anatomy of a Masculine Culture', 10 (1998), pp. 110–32; Ida Blom, 'Changing Gender identities in an Industrializing Society: The Case of Norway c. 1870–1914', 2 (1990), pp. 131–47; and Joyce S. Pedersen, 10 (1998), pp. 333–4 (review); for historical periods preceding the nineteenth century: Merry E. Wiesner, 'Guilds, Male Bonding and Women's Work in Early Modern Germany', 1 (1989), pp. 125–37; Tilly, 'Women and Work, plus Gender'.

15. See, among others, Davidoff and Hall, *Family Fortunes*; Catherine Hall, *White, Male and Middle-class: Explorations in Feminism and History* (Polity Press, Cambridge, 1992); Ute Frevert (ed.), *Bürgerinnen und Bürger: Geschlechterverhältnisse im 19. Jahrhundert* (Vandenhoeck und Ruprecht, Göttingen, 1988); Ute Frevert, 'Classe et genre dans la bourgeoisie allemande du XIXe s.', *Genèses,* 9 (1991), pp. 5–28; Mary Ryan, *Cradle of the Middle Class: The Family in Oneida County, New York, 1790–1865* (Cambridge University Press, Cambridge, 1981).

16. Susan Levine, 'Workers' Wives: Gender, Class and Consumerism in the 1920s United States', *G&H*, 3 (1991), pp. 45–64.

17. In *G&H*: Lynn Abrams, 'Concubinage, Cohabitation and the Law: Class and Gender Relations in Nineteenth-Century Germany', 5 (1993), pp. 81–100; Barbara Littlewood and Linda Mahood, 'Prostitutes, Magdalenes and Wayward Girls: Dangerous Sexualities of Working Class Women in Victorian Scotland', 3 (1991), pp. 160–75; see also Ginger S. Frost, '"I Shall Not Sit Down and Crie": Women, Class and Breach of Promise of Marriage Plaintiffs in England, 1850–1900', 6 (1994), pp. 224–45.

18. Donna J. Guy, 'Public Health, Gender, and Private Morality: Paid Labor and the Formation of the Body Politic in Buenos Aires', *G&H*, 2 (1990), pp. 297–317.

19. See in *G&H*: Hilary Land, Introduction to special issue on 'Motherhood, Race and the State in the Twentieth Century', 4 (1992), pp. 283–92; Jane Lewis, 'Women's Agency, Maternalism and Welfare', 6 (1994), pp. 117–23 (review essay); Renate Howe, 'Gender and the Welfare State: Comparative Perspectives', 8 (1996), pp. 138–42 (review essay). See also Linda Gordon (ed.), *Women, the State, and Welfare* (The University of Wisconsin Press, Madison, 1990); Seth Koven and Sonya Michel (eds), *Mothers of a New World: Maternalist Politics and the Origins of Welfare States* (Routledge, New York and London, 1993); Jane Lewis (ed.), *Women and Social Policies in Europe: Work, Family and the State* (Edward Elgar, Aldershot, 1993); Gisela Bock and Pat Thane (eds), *Maternity and Gender Policies: Women and the Rise of the European Welfare States 1880s–1950s* (Routledge, New York and London, 1991); Susan Pedersen, *Family, Dependence, and the Origins of the Welfare State: Britain and France 1914–1945* (Cambridge University Press, Cambridge, 1993); Leora Auslander and Michelle Zancarini-Fournel (eds), *Différence des sexes et protection sociale (XIXe–XXe siècles)* (Presses Universitaires de Vincennes, Paris, 1995); Alisa Del Re, *Les femmes et l'Etat-providence: Les politiques sociales en France dans les années trente* (L'Harmattan, Paris, 1994); and Anne Cova, *Maternité et droits des femmes en France (XIXe–XXe siècles)* (Anthropos, Paris, 1997).

20. In *G&H*: Robert Gray, 'Factory Legislation and the Gendering of Jobs in the North of England, 1830–1860', 5 (1993), pp. 56–80; see also note 19, and for the case of Greece, Efi Avdela, 'Contested Meanings: Protection and Resistance in Labor Inspectors' Reports in Twentieth Century Greece', 9 (1997), pp. 310–32. Also Ulla Wikander, Alice Kessler-Harris and Jane Lewis (eds), *Protecting Women: Labor Legislation in Europe, the United States, and Australia, 1890–1920* (University of Illinois Press, Urbana, 1995); Mary Lynn Stewart, *Women, Work and the French State: Labour Protection and Social Patriarchy, 1879–1919* (McGill-Queen's University Press, Kingston, Montreal and London, 1989); and Joan Scott, 'La travailleuse', in *Le XIXe siècle*, ed. Geneviève Fraisse and Michelle Perrot, volume 4 of Georges Duby and Michelle Perrot (eds), *Histoire des femmes en Occident* (Plon, Paris, 1991), pp. 419–44.

21. The attention given to race or ethnicity in historical scholarship on gender and class is less developed in Britain than in America. See Hall, *White, Male, and Middle Class*.

22. In *G&H*: Keith McClelland, 'Some Thoughts on Masculinity and the "Representative Artisan" in Britain, 1850–1880', 1 (1989), pp. 164–77; Gray, 'Factory Legislation and the Gendering of Jobs'; see also Bruce Scates, 'Mobilizing Manhood: Gender and the Great Strike in Australia and Aotearoa/New Zealand', 9 (1997), pp. 285–309; Theodore Koditschek, 'The Gendering of the British Working Class', 9 (1997), pp. 333–63.

23. See in *G&H*: Wiesner, 'Guilds, Male Bonding and Women's Work in Early Modern Germany'; Elizabeth Faue, '"The Dynamo of Change": Gender and Solidarity in the American Labour Movement of the 1930s', 1 (1989), pp. 138–58; Cynthia Cockburn, Introduction to 'Forum: Formations of Masculinity', 1 (1989), pp. 159–63; McClelland, 'Some Thoughts'; Ava Baron, 'Questions of Gender: Deskilling and Demasculinization

in the U.S. Printing Industry, 1830–1915', 1 (1989), pp. 178–99; Ella Johansson, 'Beautiful Men, Fine Women and Good Work People: Gender and Skill in Northern Sweden, 1850–1950', 1 (1989), pp. 200–212; Sonya O. Rose, 'Respectable Men, Disorderly Others: The Language of Gender and the Lancashire Weavers' Strike of 1878 in Britain', 5 (1993), pp. 382–97; Mary H. Blewett, 'Deference and Defiance: Labor Politics and the Meanings of Masculinity in the Mid-Nineteenth-Century New England Textile Industry', 5 (1993), pp. 398–415; Scates, 'Mobilizing Manhood'; John Tosh, 3 (1991), pp. 220–22 (review); more generally on the issue: Bock, 'Women's History and Gender History'; David Morgan, 2 (1990), pp. 34–9 (review) and Frank Mort, 'Crisis Points: Masculinities in History and Social Theory', 6, pp. 124–30 (review essay). See also Ava Baron, 'On Looking at Men: Masculinity and the Making of a Gendered Working-Class History', in *Feminists Revision History*, ed. Ann-Louise Shapiro (Rutgers University Press, New Brunswick, New Jersey, 1994), pp. 146–71.

24. 'Why Gender and History?', *G&H*, 1 (1989), pp. 1–6.

25. See in *G&H*: for antagonisms in the workplace and workers' protest: Baron, 'Questions of Gender'; Rose, 'Respectable Men, Disorderly Others'; Blewett, 'Deference and Defiance'; Scates, 'Mobilizing Manhood'; for men in unions and parties: Faue, '"The Dynamo of Change"'; Karen Hagemann, 'Men's Demonstrations and Women's Protest: Gender in Collective Action in the Urban Working-Class Milieu during the Weimar Republic', 5 (1993), pp. 101–19; Robert Stuart, 'Gendered Labour in the Ideological Discourse of French Marxism: The Parti Ouvrier Français, 1882–1905', 9 (1997), pp. 107–29.

26. See A. James Hammerton, 'The Targets of "Rough Music": Respectability and Domestic Violence in Victorian England', *G&H*, 3 (1991), pp. 23–44; also McClelland, 'Some Thoughts'.

27. Wiesner, 'Guilds, Male Bonding and Women's Work'; Scates, 'Mobilizing Manhood'.

28. Faue, '"The Dynamo of Change"'; Scates, 'Mobilizing Manhood'; Blewett, 'Deference and Defiance'.

29. Baron, 'Questions of Gender'; Johansson, 'Beautiful Men, Fine Women and Good Work People'.

30. Rose, 'Respectable Men, Disorderly Others'.

31. Baron, 'Questions of Gender'; Blewett, 'Deference and Defiance'; Rose, 'Respectable Men, Disorderly Others'; Scates, 'Mobilizing Manhood'; Eleanor Gordon, *G&H*, 5 (1993), pp. 442–4 (review); Ellen Ross, *G&H*, 6 (1994), pp. 297–8 (review); Hammerton, 'The Targets of "Rough Music"'.

32. Wiesner, 'Guilds, Male Bonding and Women's Work'; Patrick Harris, 'Symbols and Sexuality: Culture and Identity on the Early Witwatersrand Gold Mines', *G&H*, 2 (1990), pp. 318–36; also Tosh, *G&H*, 3 (review).

33. Avdela, 'Contested Meanings'; Gray, 'Factory Legislation'.

34. Wiesner, 'Guilds, Male Bonding and Women's Work'.

35. Faue, '"The Dynamo of Change"'.

36. McClelland, 'Some Thoughts'; Rose, 'Respectable Men, Disorderly Others'; Blewett, 'Deference and Defiance'.

37. Rose, 'Respectable Men, Disorderly Others'; Blewett, 'Deference and Defiance'; Scates, 'Mobilizing Manhood'.

38. Baron, 'Questions of Gender'.

39. In *G&H*: Cockburn, Introduction; McClelland, 'Some Thoughts'; Johansson, 'Beautiful Men, Fine Women'; Arwen Mohun, 'Why Mrs Harrison Never Learned to

Iron: Gender, Skill and Mechanization in the American Steam Laundry Industry', 8 (1996), pp. 231–51; Harriet Bradley, 4 (1992), pp. 413–15 (review); Rosalind McClean, 6 (1994), pp. 144–5 (review).

40. Baron, 'Gender and Labor History', p. 21. For early feminist critics on the notion of skill in working-class history, see Barbara Taylor and Anne Phillips, 'Sex and Skill: Notes Toward a Feminist Economics', *Feminist Review*, 9 (1980), pp. 1–15; Mary Freifeld, 'Technological Change and the "Self-Acting" Mule: A Study of Skill and the Sexual Division of Labour', *Social History*, 11 (1986), pp. 319–43. See also Gullickson, 'Commentary'.

41. See in *G&H* remarks by Jutta Schwarzkopf, 7 (1995), pp. 130–32 (review); and Miriam A. Glucksmann, 'Some Do, Some Don't (But in Fact They All Do Really); Some Will, Some Won't; Some Have, Some Haven't: Women, Men, Work, and Washing Machines in Inter-War Britain', 7 (1995), p. 292 n. 9; also Bradley, 4 (review); and Ida Blom, 'Changing Gender Identities in an Industrializing Society'.

42. For contributions that examine the issues of the differences among women and of the fluidity of gender, see Pringle, 'Rethinking Gender and Work'; Mohun, 'Why Mrs Harrison Never Learned to Iron'; Glucksmann, 'Some Do, Some Don't'; Koditschek, 'The Gendering of the British Working Class'; Frost, '"I Shall Not Sit Down and Crie"'.

43. See note 37 and Baron, 'Questions of Gender'.

44. It would be interesting to relate this deficiency to the contention, recently put forward by a leading German historian, that the crystallisation of manliness has historically been more important than femininity in the construction of the norm on which the public and private dichotomy was based. See George L. Mosse, *L'Image de l'Homme: L'invention de la virilité moderne*, trans. Michèle Hechter (Abbeville, Paris, 1997).

45. Baron, 'Gender and Labor History', p. 30.

46. Rose, 'Respectable Men, Disorderly Others', p. 393.

47. Blewett, 'Deference and Defiance'.

48. Margaret Hobbs, 'Rethinking Antifeminism in the 1930s: Gender Crisis or Workplace Justice? A Response to Alice Kessler-Harris', *G&H*, 5 (1993), pp. 4–15.

49. 'Why Gender and History?', pp. 1–6.

50. Hobbs, 'Rethinking Antifeminism'; see also Cockburn, Introduction.

51. Alice Kessler-Harris, 'Reply to Hobbs', *G&H*, 5, pp. 16–19; for the notion of gender as metaphor, see also Guy, 'Public Health, Gender, and Private Morality'. See also Bock, 'Women's History and Gender History'.

52. Baron, 'Questions of Gender'.

53. See in *G&H*: Catherine Hall, 'Politics, Post-Structuralism and Feminist History', 3 (1991), pp. 204–10; Pringle, 'Rethinking Gender and Work'; Gordon, review of Baron (ed.), *Work Engendered*; and Schwarzkopf, review of Kathleen Canning, *Languages of Labor and Gender: Female Factory Work in Germany, 1850–1914* (Cornell University Press, Ithaca and London, 1996).

54. The remark is made by Koditschek, 'The Gendering'; also Alice Kessler-Harris, 9 (1997), pp. 160–64, review of the books by Sally Alexander, *Becoming A Woman And Other Essays In 19th And 20th Century Feminist History* (Virago Press, London, 1994), and Davidoff, *Worlds Between*; see Scott, *Gender and the Politics of History*. For historical differences and similarities between British and American historical scholarship on work and gender, see Judith L. Newton, Mary P. Ryan, Judith R. Walkowitz, Editors' Introduction, in *Sex and Class in Women's History*, ed. Newton, Ryan and Walkowitz, (Routledge & Kegan Paul, London, 1983), pp. 1–15; J. Rendall, '"Uneven Developments"', pp. 45–57; Baron, 'Gender and Labor History'; and Elisabeth Faue,

'Gender and the Reconstruction of Labor History: An Introduction', *Labor History*, 34 (1993), pp. 169–77.

55. See Eley, 'Is All the World a Text?'; Kathleen Canning, 'Feminist History after the Linguistic Turn: Historicizing Discourse and Experience', *Signs*, 19 (1994), pp. 368–404; Gullickson, 'Commentary'; Laura L. Frader, 'Dessent over Discourse: Labor History, Gender, and the Linguistic Turn', *History and Theory*, 34 (1995), pp. 213–30; Mary Poovey, 'Feminism and Deconstruction', *Feminist Studies*, 14 (1988), pp. 51–65; William H. Sewell, Jr., 'Review Essay: *Gender and the Politics of History*. By Joan Wallach Scott ...', *History and Theory*, 29 (1990), pp. 71–82; Mariana Valverde, 'As If Subjects Existed: Analysing Social Discourses', *Canadian Review of Sociology and Anthropology*, 28 (1991), pp. 173–87.

56. Baron, 'Gender and Labor History', p. 31. See also Rose, 'Respectable Men'; Avdela, 'Contested Meanings'; Scates, 'Mobilizing Manhood'; Frader and Rose, 'Introduction'.

57. 'Why Gender and History?', p. 4.

58. See for example the special issue on 'Feminisms and Internationalism', *G&H*, 10 (1998), ed. Mrinalini Sinha, Donna J. Guy and Angela Woollacott, as well as a number of papers scattered throughout the ten volumes.

59. See Frader and Rose, 'Introduction'; relevant remarks in Efi Avdela, 'Genere, famiglia e strategie del lavoro in Grecia', *Passato e Presente*, XV/41 (1997), p. 162; James E. Cronin, 'Neither Exceptional nor Peculiar: Towards the Comparative Study of Labor in Advanced Society', *International Review of Social History*, 38 (1993), pp. 59–75; and Jürgen Kocka, 'Comparative Historical Research: German Examples', *International Review of Social History*, 38 (1993), pp. 369–79.

60. Gullickson, 'Commentary'. For the debate around the 'crisis' of labour history, see among others Berlanstein (ed.), *Rethinking Labor History*; Eley, 'Is All the World a Text?'; and Patrick Joyce, 'Refabricating Labour History; or, From Labour History to the History of Labour', *Labour History Review*, 62 (1997), pp. 147–52.

61. See Jacquelyn Dowd Hall, 'Partial Truths', *Signs*, 14 (1989), pp. 902–11; and Gianna Pomata, 'History, Particular and Universal: On Reading Some Recent Women's History Textbooks', *Feminist Studies*, 19 (1993), pp. 7–50.

10

Close Relations? Bringing Together Gender and Family in English History

Megan Doolittle

One of the most corrosive assumptions of mainstream history is that it is only public events and lives which are important and meaningful. Neither gender nor family has a presence in this construction of what matters about the past, a vision which gender history has consistently sought to challenge, recognising that it has warped and silenced gendered relations of power and their historical specificities. Historians of the family have also sought to foreground the supposedly private realms of domestic life. Thus histories of gender and families have common starting points: the questioning of the historical enterprise as solely the province of public men invisibly supported by the familial and the female, and the revealing of ways that public events have been moulded by the social and personal relationships of gender and family.

'Legitimate' history has been shaped by a liberal conception of civil society and the state which saw the family as not only private, but a relic of the state of nature, remaining important only because families provided the springboard for freeing the male individual to become himself and to act in the public world. Back in the natural family, women, children, and other dependants were seen as living in an unchanging ahistorical world. Most histories of politics, the state, and even religion have focused on the struggles for institutional power, on national and imperial ebbs and flows, without considering how relationships of gender and family have permeated and shaped their developments. The low status of both gender and family history has reflected this construction: both are commonly trivialised, starved of research resources and lacking in academic clout.

Despite sharing this common starting point, there have been surprisingly few historical interpretations of English history which knit together both family and gender. Family history seems unable to respond to long-standing feminist critiques,[1] still dominated by empirical, local or comparative approaches, rooted in paradigms of modernisation. Gender history has moved in very different directions, deeply concerned with questioning history's grand narratives and methodological assumptions, but seemingly avoiding much exploration of family life, despite the family's profound importance in shaping gender relations and the key role gender plays in shaping families. It is this gulf, and the ways it is being bridged, which I wish to explore here, in the context of English historiography of the nineteenth and twentieth centuries, firstly by seeking explanations for each approach's seeming reluctance to engage with the other, and secondly by tracing their points of convergence and cross-fertilisation.

Why have these two fields with potentially so much in common shared so little? Louise Tilly wrote in 1987 that women's history made the early assumption that the family was the centre of women's oppression, and that the most urgent task was to uncover the stories of women who sought power *outside* the familial.

> 'Family', then, is not one of the categories in which history is conceptualised in the feminist journals. For most of their authors, family is contingent, relational to women as individuals, in politics, in work, in marriage, as spinsters, or within female networks, friendships or love affairs.[2]

Despite the critiques by black feminists of the view that families were necessarily oppressive,[3] and the many other developments in women's history since her analysis, the contingency of family remains an unfortunate legacy.

Five years later, Tessie Liu argued that historians of the family and of women had begun with many similar aims.[4] They had both been looking for 'true communities' in the past, for solidarities in the face of social change, but each strand necessarily undermined the other. While historians of the family looked for strategies employed by families to cope with industrialisation and to challenge the harsh relations of the market, historians of women sought out struggles for recognition and equality, often in the face of opposition both from women's actual families and from ideological constructions of their familial duties. The true community of family was thus disrupted by feminist claims that families were oppressive to women, and women's solidarity was undercut by women within families' apparent collaboration with their menfolk. Liu saw this is as an inevitable result of a shared search for an authentic self, originating with the yearnings of historians for the roots of true community, but in opposing contexts.

However, Liu pointed to developments in feminism and in history which she hoped would bring these conflicting projects closer together. She pointed to the processes by which the questioning of solidarity between women across class, race and other divides began to destabilise the category of 'woman' itself, a disruption which has developed into wide-ranging and fruitful debates.

However, families continue to remain sidelined in the rich and lively theoretical resources developed by gender historians which have emerged in the intervening years, and it is possible to put forward a number of possible explanations for this. Perhaps most understandably, the tendency of historians of women to take women out of their families, to explore their lives as individuals or as sisters (in a political sense), has acted as a corrective to our long absence in 'public' history. Thus histories of women's work and of women's political action have continued to occupy centre stage, tending to marginalise the importance of families.

In histories which are concerned with the shaping of social relations of gender, researchers have also avoided looking at families because of their connections with those aspects of life most closely connected with what is seen as the natural, the messy everyday business of life and death, the eating of meals and clearing up afterwards. Postmodern analyses of gender sometimes seem light years away from doing the laundry. In seeking to enhance the status of gender history, a turn towards abstract theory has served to put a safe distance between the historian and the trivial concerns of daily life, but at the expense of explorations of the familial.

Even work on the body which challenges all the boundaries of the natural and the social seems to slide away from physical experiences such as the pain of childbirth or the rumbling of hungry stomachs which mark the playing out of both gender and familial relations. An interesting example is the debate about sexual difference raised by Laqueur's argument for a paradigm shift in representations of gender, from an ancient model which saw male and female as two halves of a single sex, to a modern model of two complementary but distinct sexes.[5] He points to changing representations of sexual organs as an indication of this shift, but only in a context of sexual relationships. He does not go on to explore any links there may have been between sexuality and reproduction, links which are paradigmatically forged within a familial framework. Did the one sex model include a reciprocal notion of conception, pregnancy and giving birth, and did this change as medical discourses readjusted views of sexual difference?[6] Posing questions like this draws gender into the realms of the familial, widening and deepening the possibilities for analyses of sexuality and the body.

In histories of masculinity, men also seem to be studied outside their familial relationships, in terms of male identities associated with work, homosocial bonds, male sexuality, and the processes of acquiring masculinity in school and amongst peers. Constructions of masculinity are much less often explored in their domestic settings, in terms of family, kin or household relationships, despite the often observed reliance of men on having someone to 'do' for them, i.e. the services of their dependants.[7]

Thus historians interested in gender have developed interesting and fruitful theoretical tools and empirical research with which to question the categories and representations of gender but have tended not to turn these to the realm of the family. On the other hand, many historians of the family continue to unproblematically project their common-sense understandings of 'family' without questioning the categories of household, kinship and family, or other theoretical underpinnings, which gender (and other social historians) have sought to unpick and destabilise. This has allowed questions of gender to escape serious attention.

Many of the assumptions of family historians are rooted in their methods and sources. In Britain, the longstanding dominance of demographic studies has narrowed the questions which have been asked about families, particularly those which involve interpretations of meaning in familial relationships. Perhaps the most startling example has been the research into the fertility transition by demographers. As Alison MacKinnon pointed out, demographers have portrayed fertility as 'a characteristic of populations, rather than of persons',[8] depicting change as natural and universal in human societies. Deeper explanations for the fertility transition rarely go beyond a critique of the idea of a simple linear story of progress, to propose a more piecemeal and local series of changes.[9] However, some historians have suggested that gender relations might possibly be relevant to an issue involving the conception and birth of children, and that explanations which do not include both gender and familial relations can do little to explain such profound social processes.[10]

Demographic historians have relied on methodologies which are derived from quantitative and scientific models as a means of bolstering the status of the sub-discipline. They have also relied very heavily on particular kinds of records as primary sources, and this has often implied an uncritical acceptance of this data as objective evidence about families. Before the national census records, it is parish records of baptism, marriages and funerals which have been drawn upon, particularly in the technique of family reconstitution. Constructions of what counted as family were taken for granted, as historians in many parts of the world reassembled records of husbands, wives and children like complicated jigsaw puzzles.[11]

In investigating nineteenth-century families, census data has been used without examining the particular visions of household and family of those who designed it. These necessarily included specific gender and generational relations, mostly clearly seen in the mid nineteenth-century definitions of household as a group of dependants with a head who was typified as the husband and father. Gender relationships within households were thus assumed to fall into the dichotomous categories of independent male individual and dependent female or younger others, a model which was eventually to be labelled as the breadwinner and housewife roles. Inevitably, households were configured to fit this model in the processes of collection of census data. The best known example was the categorisation of all married women as 'unoccupied' from the 1881 census onwards, and the subsequent reclassification of married women in previous census statistics by Charles Booth and Alfred Marshall in the interests of constructing a consistent time series.[12] Thus attempts to use census material to establish family types and forms will inevitably be distorted by the vision of its original designers, as well as the assumptions of the historian.

Typologies of the family based on these records, which continue to fill the pages of family history journals, also mask the variety of family relationships which do not conform to boundaries of household. The early critiques by Harris and Chaytor of basing family history on household boundaries have yet to be fully integrated into the practices of family historians.[13] A recent micro-study by Di Cooper and Moira Donald of a nineteenth-century Exeter neighbourhood which supplemented census data with other local records, revealed not only that family connections reached beyond and between households, but also that within households, apparently unrelated members, particularly servants, were in fact closely tied to the 'family' through complex kinship, marriage and neighbourhood links.[14] Such research points to the inadequacies and assumptions which underpin studies which rely uncritically on the categorisation of demographic data. As more and more households are added to larger and larger samples, useful overviews of population patterns and local variations have emerged, but these can only provide a starting point or context for questions about what gendered family relationships were like and why they have changed over time.

The search for such interpretations by family historians who have begun from the individual voice, relying on personal sources such as diaries or prescriptive texts, has been criticised for its inbuilt bias towards the literate elite, in contrast to the cross-class evidence of demography.[15] But much of this work has also been dogged by a questionable set of assumptions about the relationship between families and modernisation: the view that the emergence of developed industrial society inevitably brings in its wake the modern nuclear family and the gender relations which seem natural to it. There is often an unacknowledged reliance on functionalist social theory which placed the modern family as an essential but separate adjunct to modern developed societies. Talcott Parsons's analysis of the modern nuclear family, wherein private affective relationships are contained and children are cared for, also includes a rigid gender divide between men and women's roles, which enables men to enter the public world of the market as part of a mobile labour force, free from constraints of extended kinship and yet supported both physically and emotionally.[16] This model of change from traditional to modern families has become part of the common sense of history, appearing in many guises including social policy debates (the decline of the extended family), models of economic development (the movement of production out of the household and into an impersonal market), and the popular pursuits of genealogists searching for their own traditional family to place on a family tree. Family historians have often absorbed this model without question, especially those working in the period of early industrialisation.

The findings of the Cambridge Group that the 'traditional' multi-generational household was not a common family experience in the early modern period in England might have thrown serious doubts about the supposed shift from traditional to modern families. But the picture painted by Laslett and others turned the paradigm on its head without questioning its assumptions, simply moving the emergence of the nuclear family further back in time, as a uniquely British prefiguring of modernisation.[17] Their methodology of family reconstitution dismissed household relationships of service, apprenticeship and visiting as irrelevant to family typologies. An early modern family without 'extra' relatives was thus classified as nuclear, whoever else may have shared the daily tasks and relationships within a household group, or whatever other familial connections were maintained between kin who were not co-resident. Thus, rather than challenging the modernisation paradigm, the backwards trajectory of the modern family has served to confirm its supposed strength and importance over long periods of social upheaval. The gender and generational relations which it presupposes are thus reinforced as having deep historical roots and continuities.

Modernisation theory has been shaken and stirred by wider historical debates about the nature and timing of industrialisation in the developed world, and in development studies where traditional/modern distinctions are increasingly challenged. The role of women in social and economic development and the varieties of ways that the familial engages with these processes in the contemporary world are now common concerns. But the issues raised by these challenges have yet to be widely explored, or even articulated, in the work of many family historians.

Perhaps even more important than the pervasiveness of modernisation models in family history, at least in terms of gender relations, is the widespread treatment of families/households as individual social actors. In much work based on household groups, there is a conflation of the various interests within households (or families), who are understood to develop and use strategies to survive and prosper. This approach has been the target of much feminist criticism, because it necessarily masks the internal differences of power and resulting struggles between members of households and families, reflected in and enforced through legal and cultural regulation, in which gender plays such an important part.[18]

Nowhere is this more problematic than in the distinctions of neo-classical economists between the public sphere of work and the market, and the private, domestic and affective relations of family and household. In neo-classical economic theory the family is viewed as a 'black box', within which market relations are supposed to be absent, and which therefore is not subject to economic analyses. This renders invisible a whole range of gendered exchanges of labour and money within households, classifying them as outside the economy. Family historians have by and large accepted this division between work and family, partly by claiming that there are few sources for 'private' exchanges within families but also by treating families and/or households as economic actors without questioning their internal dynamics.[19]

In sociological terms, tendencies to de-gender familial language have also been uncritically adopted in histories of the family. Thus mothers and fathers are described as parents, boys and girls as children, husbands and wives as spouses. Parenting, childhood and marriage are then discussed in ways which frustratingly underemphasise or conceal differences of power within these relationships.

In these ways, 'the family' has been understood as an object of research, a thing to be found, classified, and placed in wider processes of modernisation, rather than as networks of relationships, processes, rituals, practices, all of which not only include and reveal gender differences, but have also been fundamentally important in shaping gender relations. In the face of such critiques, family history has tended to retreat into microstudies of small communities at specific points in time, reluctant to generalise or to theorise any findings. In these studies, ironically, the voices of individuals are often silenced while local patterns and trends are extrapolated.

The meanings and dynamics of family relationships are also difficult to locate in that most individualised area of family history, genealogy. For those outside academic life, family history usually means the collecting of historical data about one's ancestors, most often in the form of filling in a family tree, a fixed model of kin relationships in a complex mixture of organic imagery of family trees and the dry detailing of names and dates. Genealogists are rarely explicit about what it is they seek, nor the assumptions about family they bring to their constructions of their roots.[20] The finding of individuals in the past who have some specific blood relationship to the searcher seems to encapsulate a whole range of ideas about what families consisted of in the past, and how people understood family relationships based on associations of kinship, lineage and tradition. Paradoxically, the genealogist traces the male bloodline to delineate what is more usually perceived as a private and feminised domain, an unacknowledged reflection of the dominance of inheritance of name and property in historical constructions of the family.

Thus the methodology of family-tree building is a gendered one, because it relies so heavily on names to make kinship links. Women's frequent lack of a life-long surname marks them as particularly elusive in the search for kin, but also signifies their lesser importance in the construction of family links downwards through generations, echoing their dependency on husband and father even in their capacities to be ancestors. Popular family history thus both downgrades those family stories which cannot be connected to the individual researcher by recognisable ties of blood, and reinforces preconceptions about gender and family.

The divisions between family and gender history are clearly deep and important ones and in some ways their differences have been exacerbated over the last ten years as each has tended to align itself with opposing theoretical and methodological strands. Each has in different ways led to many absences and silences in the histories of those familial relationships which are today seen as marginal such as kinship, siblings, domestic service, and institutional life. However, there is a growing body of work which begins to span both disciplines, seeking to move beyond each of their limitations.

In gender histories, the family has never been entirely absent, forming a significant focus in a wide range of research, including the work of Tilly and Liu themselves.[21] In the late 1980s, Leonore Davidoff and Catherine Hall's *Family Fortunes* brought to the foreground the far-reaching linkages between family relationships and the economic, political, and social shifts of an emerging industrial society, and thus the familial formed the core of Davidoff and Hall's exploration of gender relations in these processes. The debates which have subsequently arisen around the question as to whether the middle-class constructions of gender roles around the notion of separate spheres prefigured industrial growth or were part of the process of shaping a new industrial middle class, highlight the relevance of the connections between gender, family, class and industrialisation.[22] Anna Clark's work on the role of gender in the shaping of working-class political identities also integrates family with work and political action to show how questions of power between men and women were encountered and negotiated through familial relationships as much as the more 'public' arenas explored by previous social historians. These gendered and familial conflicts are shown as fundamental to the processes of class formation.[23]

Historians of women (and to a much lesser extent, those of men) have also moved towards approaches which focus on family relationships. For example, Ellen Ross's work on the London poor tells the stories of women as daughters, mothers, wives, neighbours, and welfare subjects. For these women, family has been shown as the warp and weft of their daily lives, as much more fundamental to their histories than public life or paid employment, although it is they, and not their families, which emerge as the historical subjects of Ross's work. Relationships between wives and husbands, between women and children, between women and their neighbours and local economies, and between women and public authorities are traced to reveal the workings of gender in these day-to-day interactions.[24] In writing on masculinity and families, John Tosh's work on the domestic worlds of middle-class men stands out as a fusion of individual stories and the wider social forces shaping manhood within families.[25]

Even though work which foregrounds both family and gender is still limited, the family hovers at the edges of a great deal of gender history. Networks of family and kin have underpinned the complex processes of negotiating gender for both men and women, and thus can rarely be completely absent. Even in the most political arenas of women's history, such as the suffrage movement, family connections continually leap out: the Pankhursts, the Potter sisters, the Garrett family are key social groupings based on familial connections, as relevant in shaping the movement as the individual women within them.

For historians of the family, the inclusion of gender issues has been rather more problematic. While many have acknowledged the inequalities between men and women, boys and girls which are played out within families and sought to include women as active subjects,[26] these efforts seem to have had a limited impact. One explanation for this is the apparent reluctance to question the historical subject itself: the family. The process of destabilising the category 'woman' and the parallel development of the idea of gender as a relationship has not been mirrored in a similar project of deconstructing 'family' and finding a language with which to analyse the diverse familial relationships which have been subsumed within it.

This contrasts sharply with developments in sociology and anthropology, where new conceptualisations of the family and kinship have become important areas for research and debate. David Morgan's definition of family in terms of practices, rather than social structure, is one fruitful avenue.[27] This approach can be seen in John Gillis's historical work on family rituals, an exploration of how families have shaped the meanings of time, space, relationships between generations, birth and death. In his broad sweep of family history in Western cultures, relationships of gender are central to familial meanings.[28]

A social constructionist approach to the family also points to the exploration of how families are defined and shaped by discourse, and the relationships of power which are enacted in these processes. Hugh Cunningham's investigation of the changing representations of poor children moved in this direction, showing how the story of the history of childhood was constructed as a national myth: 'it became part of the mental baggage of the British people, a romance in which both children and nation entered into hell, and were rescued to lead a new and better life'.[29] Other recent work on childhood by Anna Davin and Diana Gittins has moved towards a questioning of the standard boundaries of family, gender and generation. These very different understandings of childhood and the place of children in families challenge modernisation models which have portrayed the gradual liberation of children from parental and workplace exploitation by benevolent welfare and education systems.[30] Here the gendered webs of relationships between and among generations have begun to be explored.

The use of new sources and methodologies, especially oral history and autobiography, has also raised questions of meaning and interpretation in which both family and gender relations can rarely be ignored. Life stories and themed collections of oral interviews often focus on familial experiences, and questions of memory and constructions of the self which are raised in analyses of such evidence often include and link both their family and gender wellsprings.[31]

There are also longstanding topics and subjects for family historians which necessarily imply questions of gender. We have seen that in debates about population change, rooted most deeply in modernisation paradigms, uncertainties of family and gender have begun to be addressed. As Seccombe has pointed out it was through the unequal relations within and between families that fertility decisions were made.[32] Similarly, the continuing interest in marriage by family historians generates interesting work for which gender relations form a significant context.[33] In topics such as divorce, domestic violence, infanticide, and child abuse, gender and family are inextricably entwined with issues of power, and the implications of these conflicts in terms of gender can never be entirely absent.[34]

There is also an enormous popular interest in family history which goes beyond the naming of ancestors. Historical fiction has always found a central place for family drama as seen in the continuing popularity of the family saga, and many biographers have drawn heavily on the everyday, familial contexts of their subjects' lives. Both these strands have been taken up by feminist writers who have not hesitated to explore gender in the past within familial frameworks, from Toni Morrison to Margaret Atwood. Others, such as Margaret Forster, have drawn upon their own life stories to elaborate these themes.[35]

As the scramble continues for places at the local archive tables by those searching out scraps of information about 'their families', as family history societies flourish, and television teems with programmes which explore the family lives of older generations, it is perhaps a thankless task to begin undermining the foundations of this urge by questioning its central conceptual tools. But it is only by doing so that issues of gender can surface and demand attention. On the other hand, gender historians ignore the familial at their peril. As Hilde Nelson has pointed out:

> Feminists ... have had a great deal to say about any number of issues that would seem to cry out for at least ancillary treatment of families, yet by and large this treatment has been oddly absent – as if there were white spaces on the page just at the places where careful thinking about families is needed.[36]

If families occupy these uncomfortable blank spaces somewhere between the social and the natural, where gendered identities are shaped and played out at their closest to the processes of birth, death and physical survival as well as through the most elaborate social rituals and relationships, such territory is all the more rewarding for historians of gender.

Notes

I would like to thank Leonore Davidoff, Janet Fink, Katherine Holden and Keith McClelland for their helpful comments.

1. For example, Rayna Rapp, Ellen Ross and Renate Bridenthal, 'Examining Family History', which reported from a conference workshop of 1977, published in *Sex and Class in Women's History*, ed. Judith Newton, Mary Ryan and Judith Walkowitz (Routledge & Kegan Paul, London, 1983). For a recent critique, see L. Davidoff, M. Doolittle, J. Fink and K. Holden, *The Family Story: Blood, Contract and Intimacy 1830–1960* (Longman, London, 1999), ch. 2, 'The Family and the Historian'.

2. Louise A. Tilly, 'Women's History and Family History: Fruitful Collaboration or Missed Connection?', *Journal of Family History*, 12 (1987), p. 301.

3. Hazel V. Carby, 'White Women Listen! Black Feminism and the Boundaries of Sisterhood', in *Black British Feminism: A Reader*, ed. Heidi Safia Mirza (Routledge, London, 1997), p. 46.

4. Tessie Liu, 'The Politics of True Community in Social History: Assessing the Relationship Between Women's History and Family History', Conference Paper for *Family History and History of Gender*, University of Essex, 7 December 1991.

5. Thomas Laqueur, *Making Sex: Body and Gender from the Greeks to Freud* (Harvard University Press, Cambridge, MA, 1990).

6. On conception, the popular model until at least the late nineteenth century was of an active male principal and a passive female vessel. See Janet Blackman, 'Popular Theories of Generation: The Evolution of Aristotle's Works: The Study of an Anachronism'; in *Health Care and Popular Medicine in Nineteenth Century England*, ed. John Woodward and David Richards (Homes & Meier, New York, 1977). On pregnancy and childbirth, see John Gillis, *A World of Their Own Making: Myth, Ritual and the Quest for Family Values* (Basic Books, New York, 1996), pp. 159–65 and pp. 184–5, who argues that in early modern Europe, although women giving birth were ritually separated, the couvade, or sympathetic birth experiences of husbands, was common.

7. Michael Roper and John Tosh (eds), *Manful Assertions, Masculinities in Britain since 1800* (Routledge, London, 1991), includes two domestic pieces. Other masculinity literature often has very little.

8. Alison MacKinnon, 'Were Women Present at the Demographic Transition? Questions from a Feminist Historian to Historical Demographers', *Gender and History*, 7 (1995), p. 224.

9. Simon Szreter, *Gender, Class and Fertility* (Cambridge University Press, Cambridge, 1996).

10. For example, Wally Seccombe, *Weathering the Storm: Working-Class Families from the Industrial Revolution to the Fertility Decline* (Verso, London, 1993), ch. 5, 'Starting to Stop'.

11. E. A. Wrigley, *Population and History*, Weidenfeld and Nicolson, 1969, pp. 84–5. He shows the form used to record a reconstituted family, which only had spaces for husband, wife, their parents and their children, remarriage and marriage partners of children. Occupations for husband, husband's father and the wife's father were to be recorded. Because it was based on local records, family members who were born, married and buried elsewhere would go unrecorded.

12. Davidoff et al., *The Family Story*, p. 28.

13. Olivia Harris, 'Households and their Boundaries', *History Workshop*, 13 (1982), and Miranda Chaytor, 'Household and Kinship: Ryton in the Late Sixteenth and Early Seventeenth Centuries', *History Workshop*, 10 (1980).

14. Di Cooper and Moira Donald, 'Households and "Hidden" Kin in Early Nineteenth-Century England: Four Case Studies in Suburban Exeter, 1821–1861', *Continuity and Change*, 10 (1995).

15. For example, the seminal texts of Lawrence Stone and Philippe Aries were seen as generalising from the experiences of the wealthy classes. Philippe Aries, *Centuries of Childhood: A Social History of Family Life* (Jonathan Cape, New York, 1962, first published 1960); Lawrence Stone, *The Family, Sex and Marriage in England 1500–1800* (1977; repr. Penguin, Harmondsworth, 1979).

16. For a detailed analysis of Parson's ideas about the family, see David H. J. Morgan's, *Social Theory and the Family* (Routledge & Kegan Paul, London, 1975).

17. Seccombe, *Weathering the Storm*, pp. 57–9.

18. For the debates on using a family strategies approach, see Leslie Page Moch, et al., 'Family Strategy: A Dialogue', *Historical Methods*, 20 (1987).

19. Nancy: Folbre, 'Of Patriarchy Born: The Political Economy of Fertility Decisions', *Feminist Studies*, 9 (1983), p. 267.

20. See a tentative exploration of these issues in Michael Joyce, 'An Examination of Motivation for Research on Family History', and Trevor Hill, 'Genealogy – Kinship Studies or Family History?' *Genealogists Magazine*, 25 (1997).

21. Louise Tilly, *Politics and Class in Milan 1881–1901* (Oxford University Press, New York, 1992); Tessie Liu, *The Weaver's Knot: The Contradictions of Class Struggle and Family Solidarity in Western France 1750–1919* (Cornell University Press, Ithaca, 1994).

22. Robert Shoemaker, *Gender in English Society 1650–1850: The Emergence of Separate Spheres?* (Longman, London, 1998).

23. Anna Clark, *The Struggle for the Breeches: Gender and the Making of the British Working Class* (Rivers Oram Press, London, 1995).

24. Ellen Ross, *Love and Toil: Motherhood in Outcast London 1870–1918* (Oxford University Press, Oxford, 1993).

25. John Tosh, *A Man's Place: Masculinity and the Middle-class Home in Victorian England* (Yale University Press, London, 1999).

26. For example, Michael Anderson's work has consistently sought to push the possibilities of demographic analyses in these directions; see 'The Social Implications of Demographic Change', in *The Cambridge Social History of Britain 1750–1950*, vol. 2, *People and their Environment*, ed. F. M. L. Thompson (Cambridge University Press, Cambridge, 1990).

27. David H. J. Morgan, *Family Connections: An Introduction to Family Studies* (Polity Press, Cambridge, 1996), pp. 193–7.

28. John Gillis, *A World of Their Own Making.*

29. Hugh Cunningham, *The Children of the Poor: Representations of Childhood since the Seventeenth Century* (Basil Blackwell, Oxford, 1991), p. 17.

30. Anna Davin, *Growing Up Poor: School and Street in London 1870–1914* (Rivers Oram Press, London, 1995); Diana Gittins, *The Child in Question* (Macmillan, London, 1997).

31. For example, R. Samuel and P. Thompson (eds), *The Myths We Live By* (Routledge, London, 1990); Joanna Bourke, *Working Class Cultures in Britain 1890–1960*, (Routledge, London, 1994); D. Bertaux and P. Thompson, *Between Generations: Family Models, Myths and Memories* (Oxford University Press, Oxford, 1993).

32. Seccombe, *Weathering the Storm*, p. 157.

33. John Gillis, *For Better, For Worse: British Marriages, 1600 to the Present* (Oxford University Press, Oxford, 1985).

34. A. James Hammerton, *Cruelty and Companionship: Conflict in Nineteenth-Century Married Life* (Routledge, London, 1992); Shani d'Cruze, *Crimes of Outrage: Sex, Violence*

and Victorian Working Women (UCL Press, London, 1998); Margaret Arnot, 'Infant Death, Child Care and the State: The Baby Farming Scandal and the First Infant Life Protection Legislation of 1872', in *Continuity and Change*, 9 (1994); Louise Jackson, 'Child Sexual Abuse and the Law: London 1870–1914', unpublished PhD, 1997.

35. Margaret Forster, *Hidden Lives: A Family Memoir* (Penguin, Harmondsworth, 1996).

36. Hilde Lindemann Nelson (ed.), *Feminism and Families* (Routledge, London, 1997), p. 2.

11

Gendered Space: A New Look at Turkish Modernisation

Ferhunde Ozbay

Dominant theories of modernisation, both Marxist and non-Marxist, have paid little attention to gender subjectivities even though the concepts such as family, marriage, reproduction and childbearing have occupied an important place in these explanations.[1] The 'modern' family is usually defined as nuclear in form, isolated from work, and confined in a separate less secular world. However, such a uniform social entity has obviously been influenced and changed by social and economic forces and this abstract notion of family has rightly been seriously criticised by feminist social historians. It is a perspective that does not reflect the reality of various emerging forms of families, or of the gender and age inequalities within that unit, much less the active role of family members in shaping the processes of modernisation.[2]

These views of the family and its role in the development of modern, national societies have affected the way academic disciplines have been structured and the categories they use. For example, historical demography, which has dominated the study of changes in the birth rate and family size, operates with a set of particular notions about what should and what should not be studied and how it is to be done. According to Alison Mackinnon, in standard explanations of fertility decline the different and often contradictory voices of historical demographers and feminist historians can be heard. While the former focus is on the study of reproduction and regards women as one of a number of variables, the latter emphasises the meaning of love, sexuality and childbearing for both men and women.[3]

Nevertheless, the approach of historical demography, despite a somewhat mechanical explanation of social and cultural events, alerts social historians to the importance of social context. The concentration of historical demographers on issues around reproduction and mortality, issues which inevitably lead to considering gender relations in some form, has meant that mainstream historians could neglect, or even deny their historical relevance. For example, in his Inaugural Lecture as Regius Professor of Modern History in the University of Cambridge in 1984, G. R. Elton continued to maintain 'doubts about much of [that] work on children, women and marriage;

sometimes it does not seem overwhelmingly central to one's concerns ...
much social history has a charming quality of timelessness. The facts of birth,
copulation and death do not alter that much through the ages'.[4]

This splitting off of a crucial element in major historical change has had
political and social consequences for many non-Western societies, a way
of thinking which can be traced back to the way gender relations, particularly their power dimension, have been silenced within academic disciplines as well as the wider culture. However, in the last decade or so,
there have been new insights into issues around the modernisation of non-
Western societies which raise more general questions about how gender
has operated. Deniz Kandiyoti has made the point that, despite the omission
of the gender dimension of modernity within academic disciplines, sexuality,
family relations and gender identities were used in local discourses both as
products and signifiers of modernity and nationalism in Turkey.[5] Movements for women's emancipation which were often part of or at least linked
to both emerging nationalism and modernisation, had to work with whatever categories and understandings were available at the time. In particular
there was a certain predetermined view of the division of the public and
the private, and the place of the family within this was dominant.

The following empirical case of twentieth-century urban Turkey will try to
overcome some of the deficiencies resulting from such a narrow focus by
concentrating on changes in daily life throughout the period of modernisation. These changes incorporate the decisive decline in the number of
children born and raised by each woman as well as the move to a more
urban and industrial environment, both of which were entwined with a
cultural turning to a Western model.

In Turkey, the ongoing modernisation process had begun in the late
nineteenth century and spread throughout the country after World War II.
The dissolution of the Ottoman Empire and the establishment of a new
nation state in 1923, which marked the foundation of the Turkish Republic,
provided further ideological and legal bases for this process. Concern with
the family was a central theme of both Ottoman and Republican modernists,
although discourses on modernity among all persuasions tended to ignore
the importance of gender and class differences. A series of reforms adopted
among the urban middle classes were considered the most important
factors in the Turkish experience of modernisation. These reforms did include rights for women in terms of formal equality in education, work and
political participation with men. These rights have been the focus of gender
studies of modernity, which privilege the public domain. The more private
experiences around issues such as childbirth and family life have been
tucked under the rubric of medical history or, as we have seen above, been
left to the historical demographers.

Even within demographic studies of this period there are differing interpretations depending on the orientation of the commentators and the
methods they use, an often-unacknowledged difficulty, which has also

plagued attempts to introduce the gender dimension. For example, at the turn of the century Istanbul was a city of about one million inhabitants which, by the time of the first Republican census in 1927, had fallen to 691,000, of which 448,000 were Muslims.[6] The majority of non-Muslims were merchants, bankers or artisans, groups who had relatively more contact with European cultures and hence have been seen as pioneers of western-isation in Istanbul.[7] Considering only Muslim households, we would expect to see the most conservative elements in family life. Yet, contrary to expect-ations, the 1907 census of Istanbul's Muslim population shows a pattern of late marriage for both men and women, relatively low fertility and nuclear family households as prevalent. Only a negligible 2.2 per cent of house-holds were polygamous. Despite these census data, the image of Muslim Istanbul families in newspapers and journals of that time stressed 'orient-alist' features, complaining of early marriages, polygamy and high fertility and advocated late marriage and small numbers of children.[8] Deniz Kandiyoti interprets this contradiction as the desire of modernisers to distance them-selves from what was seen as traditional, to create a concept of the 'other'. 'They could formulate their vision of the modern family only with reference to an assumed prior state that was defective and in need of reform, regard-less of whether the patterns in question actually obtained in their society'.[9]

This puzzling contradiction also stems from approaches and sources used by both contemporary commentators and subsequent historians, especially the use of either quantitative or qualitative sources. In Turkish fiction as well as studies of Ottoman everyday life, large extended households living in *konaks* (mansions) were described as archetypal of Istanbul home life. Yet extended households such as these among the elite and middle class constituted less than one third of the total in the city.[10] The majority at this time were already living in nuclear family set-ups or in what were described as 'non-family' households (a telling choice of name in itself), the relatively large size of the latter being due to a high rate of widowhood. Thus the average household size in 1907 was 4.2 people and the total fertility rate 3.85 children.

It is true that in the first half of the twentieth century Istanbul, and perhaps a few other port cities such as Izmir, exhibited radically different social, cultural and demographic patterns from the hinterland. In 1940, for example, while the total fertility rate in Istanbul had declined to 2.4 children, it was around 7.0 children for the whole country.[11] The main shift in childbearing practice, which accompanied rapid urban development, rural transformation and industrialisation, took place only after 1950, and by the late 1990s the fertility rate for the whole of Turkey averages 2.6 chil-dren.[12] Although Istanbul's population has now reached nine million, the average household size in the city is about the same as at the turn of the century. Yet during this period, idealised home life has gradually been transformed from the *konak* (mansion) type of elite house to the white-collar, middle-class flat. Today throughout Turkey as well as in Istanbul only a modest proportion of multiple family households is found. These are no longer among wealthy, elite groups, but among lower-middle classes or the poor living in shantytowns.[13] But these, too, consider this as a temporary state, a household strategy made necessary by relative poverty.

Examining changes in the form and interior use of household space together with the interaction of an ideal and daily family life can illuminate the meaning of the family for individuals and its relation to the wider society and state, and avoid the limitations of a narrow focus on birth, marriage and death. Divisions between husbands and wives, children, 'blood' relations, servants and others who were included in definitions of family are understood in their literal places. Different disciplines have preferences about using the concepts of *family* and *household*. However, neither of these terms have clear definitions in terms of their boundaries. In this study these terms are used interchangeably and it is hoped that the spatial analysis which follows reduces the tension and confusion between the concepts. The form and internal use of household space may include both kin and non-kin members, yet at the same time such an analysis gives important clues about differentiation of members by blood or marriage relations, gender, age and class.

Throughout the nineteenth and early twentieth centuries, Ottoman urban houses had multi-functional rooms based on gender segregation. The living room where 'back-stage' living was carried out was called the *harem* and was also used for sleeping, eating and cooking. Female guests were entertained in these rooms, for the *harem* was a women's space and these quarters were closed to male guests. Men of the family could enter this room to rest, eat or be with their women in the family, but only when there were no other women present. Men's living space was the *selamlık*, a room where they ate their food apart from women and children and where they entertained male visitors. At night, the *selamlık* would also be used as a sleeping room. This room was better furnished than others in the house and was always kept in order. Women were not allowed in this room when the men were at home except to carry out domestic services. Boys up to age twelve lived together with women in the *harem* but then acquired rights to move into the *selamlık*, which became a sign of their manhood, while girls remained in the *harem*.[14] Note that circumcision ceremonies for the boys were organised around this age as a requirement of Islam and afterwards they could no longer go to the public baths with their mothers.[15] These spatial demarcations symbolise the way gender segregation was based on unequal rights, a clear material marker of men's dominant position.

However, it should be kept in mind that these were the households of the elite with hierarchies of status as well as gender and age. They were always staffed with a retinue of servants, paid and unpaid. No detailed statistics about the servants in Ottoman households exist although fiction writers and historians discussed their abundance. Ubucini claimed that there were one and a half million servants in the country in 1851.[16] According to him, in Istanbul alone there were 52,000 domestic slaves and the number of free servants was not less than 40,000; altogether they constituted about one third of the Muslim population living in the town. It was the privilege of Ottoman Muslim households to use both black and white slaves in domestic work, whereas non-Muslims could only use free servants. Successive attempts to ban the slave trade were effective in reducing the number of slaves by the end of the nineteenth century. Orphan and/or poor peasant girls who were taken into urban middle-class households in the name of 'protection' and 'goodwill' gradually replaced the former domestic slaves. The young women were called *evlatlıks*, which literally means 'adopted daughters'. During the years of successive wars and political turmoil (1911–22), many orphans were used as *evlatlıks*, and in later years this practice became institutionalised through the illegal purchase of peasant girls among middle-class households. This practice was banned, along with a general anti-slavery law, only in 1964. In fact, the use of residential servants began to fade away during these years as well. Living-in waged servants had higher status than *evlatlıks* since the former often had an urban background. European servants and, to some extent, native non-Muslims such as Greeks, Armenians and Jews as servants, were genuine status symbols in elite households. The combination of slaves, wage servants and *evlatlıks* would be found in these households, each having a different function, not only in terms of service but also as indicators of the household's social rank.

In such a situation, the mistress of the house did not actually participate in housework but was in charge of managing the establishment generally and directing the actual housework. Male servants acted as cooks, gardeners or coachmen. But those in charge of cleaning, washing and caring were women. The use of space in these houses was arranged to minimise contact between male servants and female members of the household. For example, male servants slept and took their free time in the basement or in a detached building in the garden. Food was delivered on 'dumb waiter' elevators or served only by women servants. But the servants themselves were divided by status levels. Experienced slaves were the most trusted and often had power over the other servants, that is young slaves, *evlatlıks* or waged servants. The spread of *evlatlık* practice among the middle-class households effected the decline of their status. After all, they were young peasant girls and either free or cheaper than any other type of servant labour.

Domestic work in this period, even within living memory, was hard, labour intensive and unrelenting. Technological developments in home appliances and housing were primitive in the early twentieth century. Running water and electricity were rare, central heating systems even more so. Under these circumstances, domestic help was vital in maintaining comfort as well as social standing.[17] Ideally the *harem*, or separate kitchen if there was one, would be large enough to let more than one woman work at the same time. In households where there were no domestic servants, female family members shared domestic responsibilities. Daughters were extensively involved in housework, while close or even distant female relatives either stayed with the family or regularly came to visit to help in domestic work and childcare.

Under these circumstances, a division of labour accompanied by status differentiation among the women in the household was inevitable. This was reflected in the spatial use of the house. There were set rules about who was allowed to do what and who was working, resting or sleeping where, who could go out, and who controlled supplies of food and cleaning materials, through devices such as keeping the keys to the cellar or store cupboards. The use of time also denoted status, for housework was an unending activity throughout the day, and time to spend outside the house was limited for both mistress and servants. Above all, women's place was seen as at the heart of the house. This meant that despite the dominant position of men, women's labour was both visible and important. Such unremitting bustle of housework indirectly limited the time adult men spent at home. Much of their daily lives was spent outside, at work, with friends in coffee-houses, or somewhere else, even after their formal work was over.

Gradually, the lifestyles associated with European cultures were welcomed by elite circles and among upper-middle-class, non-Muslim families, the first to make use of flats. During the Republican period in particular, officers and civil servants perceived the adoption of Western lifestyles as an indication of loyalty to the new political system.[18] However, Istanbul households took up the use of Western furnishings in a rather eclectic and piecemeal fashion.[19] Armchairs were the first to be adopted and were put, as might be expected, into the most public room, the masculine *selamlık*. Soon such features became widespread status symbols for upper-middle and middle-class households. However, the adoption of dining tables took longer, for the traditional order of the house did not change radically with just the adoption of armchairs in the *selamlık*. Household members did not have to sit in these armchairs, which were mainly used for guests, and it was difficult to shift dining habits, learned in childhood, which involved eating while sitting on the floor or off portable mats.

At first, too, bedsteads were put into the *selamlık* and were mainly for honorific purposes only. They were clearly meant to make public a certain status. For example, Duman mentions that he and his brother used the iron bedstead in their *selamlık* during their circumcision feast. When his mother had consumption, she was isolated from the rest of the household in the *selamlık* and, again, used the iron bedstead.[20] Aside from such special occasions, the bedstead was used for guests.[21] It is still possible to find iron beds in reception rooms in provincial cities or in villages in Turkey. Ultimately, the spread of iron bedsteads led to the new departure of using a specialised 'bed room' for husband and wife.

Such homely shifts in daily life were obvious manifestations of profound changes which came with the establishment of the Republic and increased contacts with the West in the 1920s and 1930s. In particular, Turkish women began to be recognised in the public sphere, a move that had been one of the deliberate aims of the reformers. New laws on education, participation in economic and political life and inheritance rights, which aimed to redress gender inequality, were some of the formal measures which had been taken. Despite these efforts, women's participation in public activities was still limited. The educational level of women, even among the middle and upper-middle strata was low and through the 1950s their participation in the waged economy was circumscribed. There were few women to be seen on the streets, in parks or in recreation centres. Nevertheless, it should not be claimed that upper- and middle-class women were uninterested in the westernisation movement. They showed their enthusiasm about the construction of the 'new society' through changes in their role, through being 'modern' housewives and in the reordering of their houses.

One reflection of such changes was the transformation of the *harem* to the *oturma odası* or living room and the *selamlık* to the *misafir odası* or reception room. This change was not only semantic: the *selamlık*, which had been strictly for men only and a symbol of relations of the household with the outer world, opened its doors to women. Husband and wife together received their guests in the reception room during the evenings. During the day, when men were out at work, women regularly organised *kabul günü* or Reception Days in these rooms. Such Reception Days acted as schools for modernisation for middle-class women. Manners, fashion, child-rearing practices and relations among spouses were discussed at these occasions. In the first few decades of the Republican era, participation of these women in a form of public sphere was mainly limited to such Reception Days. Thus the room which had been the central masculine domain became a window opening onto the outer world and a path for middle-class women to begin moving into a species of public life.

Reception Days differed from informal and intimate neighbourhood and familial relations. They had an official atmosphere in which women often did not bring their children and dressed in their best outfits. The Western furniture, such as armchairs and occasional tables, were not yet an internalised part of their culture and seemed to be even physically uncomfortable. This gave the feeling of being in a public place where the room was a showcase for the household and family.[22] For these rooms were not open to daily use. On the contrary, they were kept clean for guests, the doors closed to daily family activities. (In those houses without central heating this had a practical as well as symbolic function.) While the existence of such mixed reception rooms led to a closer relationship between husband and wife, it tended to exclude other household members, especially children. There were also still many men to be found in coffee-houses, on the streets or in other venues, but now husbands spent more time with their wives in visiting and accepting friends as couples in their homes.

The *harem*, too, had been replaced by the multi-purpose living room. Here the family came together for everyday occasions, when they ate meals, or rested during the day, and children studied or played. At night children and other relatives might sleep in the living rooms. These changes also led adult men to spend more time at home and with their family; for example they no longer ate their meals apart. Brothers and sisters in the family became closer, for now girls, too, went to school and some of the blatantly unequal treatment they received was modified.

Despite these changes, during these first decades of the Republic, although service personnel changed somewhat, the organisation of housework did not alter radically. The use of domestic slaves in elite households did disappear and paid household workers were used more widely. This was partly due to an increase in the supply of such labourers, especially in the cities. In a 1920 survey of widows in Istanbul, it was discovered that, among Muslims, almost 50 per cent said they worked as servants, cooks or laundry women, among Armenians and Jews around 50 per cent, and 75 per cent among Greeks.[23] In this period, too, the use of *evlatlıks* was still common. Army officers also benefited from having soldiers who did domestic work as orderlies. Such practices provided extra free domestic help and it may be argued that the spread of Western household practices could only have been established on the basis of such supplementary labour.

The first blocks of flats had been constructed several decades earlier at the turn of the century and among non-Muslim upper-middle-class families gave a prestigious address in offering a Western lifestyle. Then again, the house porters, which every block kept, were an additional communal, and hence cheap, form of domestic labour. But such flats were not widespread until the 1930s and the majority still lived in two-storey houses with gardens.[24] Middle-class housewives who had already accepted a modern lifestyle with the use of reception rooms now aspired to living in a flat, for this was taken as the outstanding indicator of modern living. A flat meant the privilege of living in a modern part of the city with people of similar advanced views. At the beginning there was no possibility of owning a flat. Ownership meant having bought the whole apartment building, which cost more than having a mansion, so that renting became the only alternative for middle-class households wanting this type of accommodation. In practical terms flats made housework easier and they usually included purpose-built larger reception rooms now called *salons*, especially when the dining table and chairs were placed there. The typical older reception room had not been big enough for a dining set and ideally the dining area should be separated from the living space with a door or at least a folding screen.

These blocks of flats were only built gradually, spurred by laws on flat ownership and housing cooperatives. But as they became more widespread their prestige gradually eroded, for mass migration from rural to urban areas had begun in earnest from the 1950s. The housing needs of the poorer migrants were only met through self-help in the form of shanty-towns at the city's margins. Low-quality blocks of flats were constructed by private building firms for sale or rent and began to be the prototypical middle-class home whose showcase was the *salon*. The remainder of the flat – two or three bedrooms, kitchen, bathroom and Turkish-style lavatory – was small and carelessly designed. Builders aimed to fit as many flats as possible onto a given parcel of land so that tiny, dark working rooms were ignored.

At the same time, the mistress of the house began to undertake most household tasks on her own. Cheap domestic labour in the form of *evlatlıks* was disappearing. Now only the wealthiest upper-class families could afford resident servants. This change was connected to the decrease in numbers of children per family as well as in attached relatives and others living in the household.[25] Housewives were confined to spending most of their day alone in these dark, small kitchens and bathrooms, while housework began to be more time-oriented. It became important to start the work after the men left the flat and finish it before they came home. Thus domestic labour lost both its communal form and visibility.

The contrast in these women's lives between the modernity they lived out in their large *salons* and the confining, unhealthy conditions of drudgery they worked under in back rooms reflects the double standards of industrial society towards women in these strata. By the end of the twentieth century some of these women have made arrangements which lessen these tensions. Changes in lifestyle, technology and architecture have reduced the time and effort of domestic work. After 1950, refrigerators and washing machines appeared in middle-class flats and houses. This has led to a moderate increase in the size of kitchens and bathrooms in new flats, while in the old, changes could be made; for example balconies were enclosed to extend kitchen or bathroom or storage spaces and the old servants' rooms were gradually converted. Housewives had to improvise by, for example, using the old Turkish-style lavatories for storing cleaning utensils. As central heating gradually increased, fetching coal and wood, dealing with dirt and dust, decreased, and more of the existing space could be used, even in cold weather.[26]

Today it is rare to find closed-door reception rooms or *salons* in middle- and upper-middle-class houses or flats. There is much less distinction between front- and back-stage activities. With fewer children in a family, there has been more concern for their overall well-being as well as education, which has been reflected in their use of household space. Giving separate rooms for each child started to be seen as important for personality development and individuality, so that keeping the *salon* only for visitors began to seem irrational and back-stage living rooms began to be converted to children's rooms. These changes in use of space both reflected and were incentives to the markedly lower birth rate in this generation. The emergence of TV sets as a central item in family life in the 1970s was also effective in opening the door of *salons* for daily use by all. This change also indicated a more complete adoption of Western furnishings as the pretentious but uncomfortable furniture of the previous era was replaced.

The significance for women of the new *salons* was changing. They no longer functioned as a 'school for modernisation', a kind of women's public space. For now there were more women going outside the home, onto the streets and with various contacts in public life. Women had become almost totally responsible for daily shopping and they took an active role in voluntary associations. They had begun to make regular contact with educational and health institutions for their children and other family members. Above all, more urban middle-class women were employed in the formal economy.[27]

Such increased contact with the outer world has lessened the significance of the former 'Reception Day', which gradually changed its form and name. Women now have 'meetings' which are informal and friendly. But evening entertainment has also altered. In the past people used to send messages to their neighbours, friends or relatives when they wanted to pay a visit. A child, acting as messenger, would trot round to the designated person's home and announce 'my parents would like to visit this evening if it is convenient'. Now the mistress of the house decides when and who may visit the family and then the *salons* can be prepared for guests.

Spatial indicators of masculine hegemony still exist in many homes, but the power of the *selamlık* has transmuted to dad's chair in the *salon*, although in upper-middle-class homes a study room for his use may be annexed to this main living room. Often the home life of the male household head is limited to the *salon*, the master bedroom and, if there is one, his study, and these rooms are decorated with great care. While there is thus still a modified form of the husband/father's prerogatives, the hierarchy between generations is now less than in the immediate past. Nevertheless, the largest room in the flat is no longer the back-stage 'living room' but the parental bedroom which often is the setting for an impressive bedroom suite. Others in the household, notably children, have very small rooms but these are now seen as their own space where they study and play as well as sleep. In this way they now have less contact with the adult family members in the *salons*. A woman who was recently asked about the use of household space recounted the transition from having a closed-door reception room to a *salon*:

> When we were living in a two story wooden house I used to feel guilty that I could not give separate rooms to my children. I wanted to move to a flat for that reason. I hoped that all the family would gather in the *salon* and watch TV together. The day we moved to our new flat the children retired to their rooms. My husband and I were so lonely in the big *salon*. I was so sorry that I cried.[28]

As far as domestic labour goes, the main source now is hiring cleaning women by the day or hour. A 1990 survey of Istanbul reveals that at least half of middle- and upper-middle-class families use such help.[29] Moreover they often also have modern household appliances. Yet women are still responsible for the management of the housework and are still often alone in their kitchen. Undoubtedly this development of household technology, accompanied by shifts in the design of new flats, has gradually benefited women's lives. Usually the kitchen will now be put adjacent to the *salon*, for example. Until recently, another common complaint had been the cramped dimensions of the kitchen. The size did increase with the widespread use of refrigerators and modern ovens but there was no space available for dishwashers, which came into use in the 1980s. Dishwashers were the new status symbols of that period, but at the same time their contribution to lessening housework was revolutionary and they also helped to keep the kitchen clean and orderly.

In new blocks of flats the deployment of kitchen and bathroom furniture is an important selling point used by builders. New kitchens are elegant and large enough for even a dining table to be placed. Such rooms have gained new functions as places to eat and even chat. In small older flats, the wall between the kitchen and *salon* may be demolished and the so-called 'American type' *salons* with kitchen included are formed. In such rooms family members share more housework tasks and once again women's domestic labour becomes more visible. While women are working in the kitchen they can talk with their husbands and children or watch television.

The menu, too, has changed in these open-plan kitchens. Traditional Turkish food, which requires much time and expertise to prepare and in the frying creates smells and the mess of spitting fat, is no longer as popular. Easy to prepare, ready-made meals, and for some people the search for 'healthy food', have come to be preferred by many. These changes mean that other family members can take over at least parts of meal preparation. While status and health reasons combined with the decline in supplies of cheap labour have contributed to the new patterns, the main impetus has come from women who are working in paid employment. Working women tend to use modern household appliances and like open-plan houses more than women who are full-time housewives. It may be claimed that working outside of the home has legitimised these women's efforts to alleviate the tensions in their lives between front-stage middle-class lady and back-stage household drudge.

Another and related dimension of contemporary, more informal, upper-middle-class culture is the way visitors are now allowed to see various parts of the flat or house. In the Ottoman period, male and female visitors could only see the *selamlık* and *harem* respectively, while in the first decades of the Republican period both men and women guests were invited into the reception room. Today visitors can go from kitchen, bathroom and children's rooms to almost every corner of the house. Indeed, giving a house tour to newcomers is customary. It may be argued that opening both the living space and the lifestyle of the family to general view can have a positive effect on a woman's position in both her family and society at large.

The relationship of women, men and children to living space in flat or house has changed along with basic shifts in social structure and culture. But such a relationship is complicated and the changes are by no means linear. Furthermore, it must be remembered that the characteristics of a house or flat may have positive or negative impact on women's identity and differ markedly according to class position Here the direction of change has been reviewed in connection with the urban middle- and upper-middle-class use of household space, for these were the groups which controlled general taste and set standards, particularly through advertising and the press. Rural houses which showed great variations by geographical location as well as socio-economic factors are not studied here.

The general separation of public and private domains characteristic of a society shifting to an industrial and urban base did not necessarily help women to develop their identity. But it has led to the elimination of much gender segregation in the spatial use of housing and has been intimately linked to reforms in the name of women's emancipation, not least the substantial gain in health, energy and time as a result of the decline in the birth rate. Nevertheless, the double standard of modern society that expects a woman to be a 'lady' outside the home and still something of a servant within it remains.

Even such a brief excursion into the daily lives and use of space in a specific, local setting can give insights into much wider questions which are often lumped together under the rubric of modernisation. It also takes on board a particular facet of this process; that is, the narrower aim of demographic historians' efforts to explain the fall in the birth rate, which has so often been based solely on quantitative measures. Both of these endeavours have been seriously flawed in their neglect of gender relations. Going to the level of such a 'microcase', which can then be recontextualised to build up a larger picture, gives a novel perspective on gender relationships themselves. When combined with a variety of other such studies, the single case may be woven into a more convincing picture, one which is genuinely inclusive.

While women played the main part in this drama of household transformation, the ideas and practices around men's expectations were always the foil against which the drama was played. The households examined here were lived in by men as well as women. Their changing configurations had as much to do with interpretations of masculinity as of femininity.[30] For, from the modern transformation of a non-Western society and the building of a nation state, to the deepest level of reproductive beliefs and behaviour, to major shifts in the meaning of work and composition of the labour force, admitting the powerful role of gender construction and identity confronts historians in coming to grips with major changes on a world-wide scale.

Notes

This study is a part of the project on 'Non-Kin Members of Households in Turkey' funded by MEAwards.

1. See Leonore Davidoff, Megan Doolittle, Janet Fink, Katherine Holden, *The Family Story – Blood, Contract and Intimacy, 1830–1960* (Longman, London and New York, 1999), p. 25.
2. Davidoff et al., *The Family Story*.
3. Alison Mackinnon, *Love and Freedom: Professional Women and the Reshaping of Personal Life* (Cambridge University Press, Cambridge, 1997), p. 50.
4. G. R. Elton, *Return to Essentials: Some Reflections on the Present State of Historical Study* (Cambridge University Press, Cambridge, 1991), pp. 117–18.
5. Deniz Kandiyoti, 'Gendering the Modern: On Missing Dimensions in the Study of Turkish Modernity', in *Rethinking Modernity and National Identity in Turkey*, ed. Sibel Bozdoğan and Reşat Kasaba (University of Washington Press, Seattle and London, 1995), p. 114.
6. Alan Duben and Cem Behar studied Istanbul Muslim households from around 1880 to 1940 and did use both demographic and anthropological approaches to family history. *Istanbul Households: Marriage, Family and Fertility, 1880–1940* (Cambridge University Press, Cambridge, 1991).
7. Edhem Eldem, 'Istanbul 1903–1918: A Quantitative Analysis of a Bourgeoisie', *Boğaziçi Journal*, 11(1–2), (1997), pp. 53–98.
8. Duben and Behar, *Istanbul Households*.
9. Kandiyoti, 'Gendering the Modern', p. 117.
10. Duben and Behar, *Istanbul Households*.
11. SIS, *The Population of Turkey, 1923–1994 Demographic Structure and Development* (State Institute of Statistics, Ankara, 1995), p. 4.
12. HIPS, *Turkish Population and Health Survey – A Preliminary Report* (Hacettepe Institute of Population Studies, Ankara, 1998).
13. Ferhunde Özbay, 'Türkiye'de Aile ve Hane Yapısı: Dün, Bugün, Yarın', *75 Yylda Kadınlar ve Erkekler – Bilanço 98*, der. Ayşe Berktay Hacımirzaoğlu (1991; tıpkı basım. Türkiye Ekonomik ve Toplumsal Tarih Vakfı Yayını, Istanbul, 1998), ss. 155–72.
14. Kayaoğlu, İ Gündağ ve Pekin, Ersu (yay. haz) *Eski İstanbul'da Gündelik Hayat*, (Ystanbul Büyükşehir Belediyesi, İstanbul, 1992).
15. This rather late circumcision tradition which is used as a passage to manhood for boys may have been inspired by the age of menarche of girls.
16. Ubicini, M. A. *Osmanlıda Modernleşme Sancısı*. Cemal Aydın (çev.) (Timaş, İstanbul, 1998).
17. Duben and Behar, *Istanbul Households*.
18. Gülsün Bilgehan, *Mevhibe* (Bilgi Yayınevi, Ankara, 1995).
19. Selçuk Esenbel, 'The Anguish of Civilized Behavior: The Use of Western Cultural Forms in the Everyday Lives of the Meiji Japanese and the Ottoman Turks during the Nineteenth Century', *Japan Review*, 5 (1994), pp. 145–85.
20. Halis Duman, *Anılarım 1908–1924* (Acar Matbaası, Istanbul, 1991).
21. In Greece the iron bed was put in reception rooms in certain households also. See Renée Hirshon, 'Essential Objects and the Sacred: Interior and Exterior Space in an Urban Greek Locality', in *Women and Space*, ed. S. Ardener, *Cross Cultural Perspectives on Women*, vol. 5 (Berg, Oxford and Providence, 1993).

22. Sencer Ayata, 'Statü Yarışması ve Salon Kullanımı', *Toplum ve Bilim*, 42 (1988), ss. 5–25.

23. C. Richard Johnson (ed.), *Istanbul 1920* (Tarih Vakfı Yurt Yayınları, Istanbul, 1995), pp. 243–69. Note that it was a non-probability sample with a sample size of 400 widows.

24. İlhan Tekeli, 'Türkiye'de Konut Sorununun Davranışsal Nitelikleri ve Konut Kesiminde Bunalım', *Konut '81* (Kent-Koop, Ankara, 1982).

25. Özbay, 'Türkiye'de Aile ve Hanc Yapısı'.

26. Even in 1973 in large cities only 10 per cent of houses had central heating. The highest was Ankara with 14 per cent. Mümtaz Peker, 'Türkiye'de Barınma Koşulları ve Gelirle İlişkisi', *Türkiye'de Nüfus Yapısı ve Nüfus Sorunları – 1973 Araştyrması* (Hacettepe Üniversitesi Yayınları D-25, Ankara, 1978), p. 165.

27. Ferhunde Özbay, 'Changes in Women's Activities both Inside and Outside the Home', in *Women in Modern Turkish Society*, ed. Şirin Tekeli (Zed Books, London and New Jersey, 1995), pp. 89–111.

28. Ferhunde Özbay, 'Houses, Wives and Housewives', in *The Housing Question of the Others*, ed. Emine Komut (TMMOB, Ankara, 1996).

29. Emre Kongar ve Taner Berksoy, *Istanbul Halkının Günlük Yaşam Biçimi ve Tüketim Davranyşlary Araştırması* (Istanbul Ticaret Odası, Istanbul, 1990).

30. Ferhunde Özbay, 'Changing Roles of Young Men and the Demographic Transition in Turkey: From Nation Building to Economic Liberation', paper presented in the Seminar on Social Change and Demographic Transition, Family Structure and Gender Relations in Muslim Societies (SOAS & UNESCO, London, 1992).

12

Paradoxes of Gender: Writing History in Post-Communist Russia 1987–1998

Irina Korovushkina

The past decade in Russia, associated with Gorbachev's reforms and continued through the neo-liberal policies of Yeltsin's government, brought about the liberalisation of political and economic life, including the removal of ideological constraints on publication and research (*glasnost*). This was followed by the rise of nationalism and disintegration of the Soviet Union and an unceasing chain of economic disasters. This catalogue of change and instability must be the context for discussion of the way gender studies have been integrated into historical disciplines in Russia over the last decade.

The paradox of gender in Soviet society is that women were emancipated without challenging the basic premises of patriarchal structure. Moreover, patriarchal attitudes and stereotypes are not only taken for granted but encouraged by both men and women. That is why there is a popular disapproval of and even hostility towards the attempts by feminists to challenge established social and cultural hierarchies. For example, one half of the women questioned by sociologists in the Russian town of Kostroma displayed negative attitudes towards the word 'feminism'.[1]

A large part of pre-Revolutionary Russian society, that consisted predominantly of peasants, can be described as literally patriarchal, in which women and younger men were subordinated to older men. In the twentieth century this society was drawn into the process of state-led industrialisation, impelled modernisation and cultural revolution. Patriarchal values, gender hierarchy and traditional division of labour within the family and society, however, persisted despite industrialisation and the involvement of women in industry during the 1930s to 1950s. An official declaration of women's equality – partly an impact of Marxist doctrine and partly a tribute to the communist vision of modernity – walked hand in hand with patronising and sexist attitudes. The party and the state treated the woman as the object rather than the subject of emancipation, granting her political rights and social benefits that could never be adequately applied in the custodial system of the Soviet state.

The Russian language, one among many others, has no equivalent word for gender. To define gender in grammar, linguists use the same word as for 'kin' (*rod*). But, unlike English, the Russian language has a neutral form for human person that does not indicate gender, *chelovek* (similar to the Greek *anthropos*). This does not preclude, however, the usage of this neutral linguistic form in a sexist context, such as 'every person may have a wife and children'; or 'women in the lives of famous persons'.[2]

Academics and social activists who use the concept of gender prefer to avoid translating the term into Russian and use its English equivalent, pronouncing 'g' as in 'gun'. The word itself and its derivations, such as *genderology, genderistics* (both terms mean gender studies), *gendernyi* (adjective form of gender), *genderist/ka* (a person who does research on gender), enriched the post-perestroika vocabulary of foreign words and evoked the abhorrence of purists of the Russian language. However, unlike many other foreign words that are being used despite the existence of Russian equivalents (e.g. killer, dealer), *gender*, along with *identity* and *mentality*, was introduced to indicate new concepts that have no parallel in the Russian intellectual vocabulary.[3] The English equivalent is used for the purpose of conciseness. 'You have to use many Russian words to translate *gender* adequately', says Zoya Khotkina, a member of the Group for Gender Studies in the Moscow Institute of Economics. Moreover, the very foreignness of the word is seen as an advantage for developing the new field. In the late 1980s, when the first Centre for Gender Studies emerged in Moscow, gender in its title was used strategically to disguise feminist activism under the scholarly jargon that many people were not aware of. While *feminism* and anything that had the word 'sex' in it were seen as dirty words, *gender* had an appeal of political neutrality that was immediately appreciated by those who had already been moving in the direction of gender studies.

The transition from a socialist to a market economy and the disintegration of the Soviet Union led to an identity crisis for Russians, of which a 'gender crisis' was an important part. The radical change in sexual roles, the breakdown of stereotypes and the fragmentation of the traditional models of femininity and masculinity accompanied the transitional period.[4] Although both men and women were confused and disoriented during this transition period, men seemed to have more problems about their masculinity because they were compelled – both by the country's leadership and by women – to perform the traditional role of breadwinners in the disintegrating economy. Women, who were officially encouraged to 'carry out their womanly mission' and stick to their traditional roles as mothers and housewives, had experienced less pressure of this kind because their income was not seen as the measurement of their femininity. Indeed, the new models of economic behaviour such as entrepreneurship, rationality, competitiveness and willingness to risk and gamble were perceived as masculine norms.

However, the lack of correspondence between the new cultural models and economic reality – in which men were an equally vulnerable economic group to women – contributed to the crisis of masculinity, the signs of which could be seen in the growth of alcoholism, crime and divorce rates in contemporary Russia. Recent discussion in the media over the introduction of the drug Viagra into Russia seems to be an excellent illustration of men's anxieties over their sexuality and masculinity.

The impact of perestroika on women has become an area of considerable debate. Economists and sociologists usually emphasise the negative effect of market reforms on women who, according to the Centre for Gender Studies, have made up between 60 and 80 per cent of the workforce made redundant in the 1990s. They also became the objects of sexual exploitation in a society where pornography and the sex trade were booming. However, the outcome of the transition period in relation to gender is not clear-cut. The market economy, in which both men and women as consumers exercise a kind of freedom that could not be controlled by the power structures, is experienced by the younger generation of Soviet people as a liberation from the paternalism of the Soviet system.

The introduction of *gender* in the late 1980s, at least in the field of women studies, did not make an intellectual revolution in Russia. Academic research in women's studies already had long-term roots in Soviet scholarly writing. However, the uses of women's studies in the Soviet Union were quite different from those in the West. On the one hand, the research was meant to build up a scientific background for the ideological claim that women in the Soviet Union have more political rights and social and economic benefits than their Western counterparts. On the other hand, emphasis on women's patriotism and heroic deeds during wars and revolutions can be seen as the construction of a Soviet woman as a loyal citizen and active supporter of the party's policies. Desperately trying to strengthen its declining popularity, the Communist Party encouraged women's studies in the 1980s. The publication of Elena Emel'ianova's book *Revolution, Party and the Women* had gone through six editions between 1982 and 1985 and was accompanied by numerous official publications that emphasised women's contribution to the building of socialism in the USSR.[5]

Gorbachev, who became the General Secretary of the Communist Party in 1984, tried to win women's support by showing sympathy with their feelings of disappointment about the 'double burden', that is, the combined strains produced by wage work, household duties and motherhood in an economy of shortage. Having urged women to make a choice between full-time employment and being a housewife, Gorbachev also encouraged their public activism, that which had been channelled through the traditional women's councils (*zhensovet*). In order to guide women's activity through official academic channels, in 1989 the Council of Ministers approved the establishment of the Centre for Gender Studies in a leading research institution, the Institute for Population Studies in Moscow. The members of the Centre, who eventually took an explicitly feminist direction in their research, were established scholars, mainly economists and social scientists, working within the Soviet academic structure.

The ideological master-narrative and party control over the academic research did not hinder publication of some well-researched and professional works on the history of the women's movement, women's education and women in medicine in the postwar period.[6] Then, too, Soviet historians who worked in the areas of medieval studies as well as the fields of folklore and ethnography usually exercised more freedom from ideological constraints. Works on social and cultural history and on population studies in the late 1970s, which touched the issues of gender, made their way despite political censorship.[7]

It must be noted that it was not only ideological and political constraints that put limits on the unbiased study of gender in historical context, but also the division of subject matters between the disciplines in the Soviet academia. The gendered character of this division is striking. The prime focus of Soviet history was the public spheres of military issues, class struggle and politics, areas which could be characterised as a 'masculinisation' of the discipline. Subjects relating to everyday life, the history of privacy, family, marriage and popular culture were presented as ahistorical and came under the rubric of other, politically less important disciplines such as ethnography and folklore studies.[8] Although this view of history as a primarily public process was not only to be found in Soviet scholarship, in the Soviet Union it persisted despite all the challenges of the perestroika era.

The period of glasnost that followed the Gorbachev reforms (1985–90) had a particular significance for historians because it allowed access to documents and facts that previously were locked away in the archives; it brought about new themes and ideas and made it easier to break away from the traditional master-narrative and ideological constraints. In this atmosphere the field of women's studies continued to develop, moving away from the former Soviet paradigm. New histories of women emerged to demonstrate that, even before the Bolshevik revolution, women in Russia played a far from insignificant role in cultural, social and political life. These histories brought into focus names that had been erased from official Soviet histories. For example, researchers studied the wives of Russian rulers and noblemen and their influence on politics between the tenth and the eighteenth century, on female rulers of the eighteenth century, and on women scholars and liberal activists of the nineteenth century.[9] In publications that demonstrated a radical departure from the Soviet master-narrative, woman was represented not as a collective being but as an individual, a unique personality, whose life was important per se without any connection to a man, a party or an idea.

These new studies stressed private rather than public arenas, ordinary rather than heroic, outrageous rather than virtuous, and the commonplace rather than intellectual and sophisticated. Bringing women into history as the legitimate agents of historical process was accompanied by rapid development of the fields and subjects that previously were perceived as non-historical, such as anthropology, history of everyday life and history of mentalities. Combining approaches of the Annales schools with theories of Mikhail Bakhtin and Iurii Lotman's school of semiotics, Russian historians launched a number of projects that focused on gender in the context of history of the family, popular culture and the history of *mentalité*.[10] After the removal of ideological taboos on such forbidden topics as sexuality, new studies on prostitution and the history of sexuality emerged. For instance, the history of prostitution in St Petersburg between the 1840s and 1940s, challenging the Soviet thesis of the prostitute as a criminal, represented a well-researched account of the social composition of St Petersburg prostitutes as well as the legal and cultural framework of prostitution in urban Russia.[11] The issue of sexual ethics and practices and how these concerned women and men were placed in historical and cultural context. Thus, attempts were made to look at Orthodox religious ethics as a constituent element of the construction of gender models and sexual behaviour in comparative perspective with Catholic models.

The revival of historians' interest in the age of the Enlightenment was a great contribution to the shifting perspective in women's studies, because this was the period when many noble women in Russia became visible in public life and produced their own narratives. A number of biographies of Catherine the Great (1764–96) and the women of her time, such as the head of the Russian Academy of Science, Ekaterina Dashkova, accompanied by the publication of primary sources of this period signified a shift from the old Soviet view. A legacy to Stalinism, the Soviet historians usually underestimated the role of Catherine II in favour of another ruler of the century, Peter I (1698–1721), energetic reformer and westerniser. In one of the post-perestroika histories of the eighteenth century, a historian described Catherine II as 'one of the most talented politicians in [Russian] history' and argued that she actually was in charge of the plot against her husband, the legitimate Russian ruler Peter III, rather than having been manipulated by the nobles who wanted to disband the unpopular emperor, as was previously believed. Moreover, challenging the popular perception of female rule as weak and incompetent, historians suggested that Catherine was a more suitable candidate to rule the country, unlike her husband, 'who neither psychologically nor mentally was fit for the difficult job of the emperor'.[12]

Without denying the importance of such empirical research, it must be admitted that a theoretical and historiographical basis is crucial for the development of the new field of gender studies. Although the Iron Curtain never completely separated Russian academics from their Western colleagues, in the past only experts had access to new Western research. And it is noteworthy that at present the enthusiastic Russian scholars who have access to Western literature on gender and apply new approaches in their research try to popularise the new field among fellow historians and fill the gaps in the methodology they apply.[13]

The development of gender is impossible without a network of communications and facilities. The rise of a provincial and national commercial press and development of the networks of new educational and scientific institutions that followed the disintegration of the Soviet Union led to a further pluralisation and diversification of historical studies. Official encouragement of the study of local history in the 1990s, from the middle of that decade meant that a half of the history syllabus at schools covered regional history. Such moves allowed provincial historians to concentrate on the social and cultural aspects of their field. Thus, narrowing down the analytical focus from large-scale narratives to micro-history contributed to bringing gender into local histories.[14] The scholars in regional universities seem to have more opportunities to introduce new programmes and courses relevant to gender than their Moscow colleagues.[15] And three summer schools for students, researchers and university teachers were organised through financial support of Western foundations, Ford and Soros, between 1996 and 1998, to discuss critical issues in promoting gender research in Russia. These schools, the first attempt to discuss gender issues at a conference level, brought together economists, historians, philosophers, anthropologists and writers from different parts of the Russian Federation, Belorussia, the UK and United States.

To sum up, the removal of ideological constraints and the revival of public interest in the issues of privacy and the incredible diversification and pluralisation of public life in Russia during perestroika and after the collapse of the Soviet Union certainly had a positive impact on the development of gender studies in Russia. Historians, although slower and more conservative than their colleagues in sociology, ethnography and cultural studies, nevertheless managed to legitimise gender as a 'useful category of historical analysis' and to challenge some of the persistent stereotypes about women in history.

The introduction of the concept of gender benefited the scholars who were not satisfied with the traditional focus on women, rather than gender, as an object of scholarly study. Already in the 1970s some of the women historians who worked on the history of the family and social movements were trying to look at the relations between the sexes rather than on the place and roles of women in society.[16] Then again, gender allowed researchers to shift attention from the political agenda to the domain of cultural and social studies. And finally, the new concept was utilised by scholars who did not identify themselves with a feminist agenda. For example, gender found a place in the works by experts in cultural studies, a booming field in the post-perestroika years.

Russian historians see their approach to gender as different from Western practice in so far as they advocate dialogue rather than a power struggle, and cooperation rather than competition between men and women. Informed by the theories of Mikhail Bakhtin, gender is described as a dialogical relationship and the goal of gender studies is seen as promoting partnership between the sexes. Such an approach, that blurs the element of power in gender relations, must be understood as a rational choice in present-day

Russia, a society striving for coherence and unity. But it can also be seen as a tactic to popularise and promote gender studies against the criticism and hostility of those who consider that gender is irrelevant in a country facing economic and political crisis.

Religion is seen as an area of productive dialogue between men and women, as well as a possible ground for reconciliation between the advocates of the gender approach and their critics. Religion, represented as one of the pillars of the patriarchy, has usually been seen as a false ally of women by feminists. The issue of 'religion and gender' is a slippery area. While gender analysis, like any other scholarly discourse, intends to cut across cultural differences, religion reasserts this difference in the form of national tradition, which has often had a strong religious dimension. In parallel with black feminists' call for separatism, women scholars of the Eastern European countries resist Western intellectual intervention, seeing it as a part of cultural imperialism. This resistance is often formulated in the rhetoric of traditional culture that has a strong national religious background.[17] These developments cannot be simply dismissed as a form of 'false consciousness', but must be evaluated in the light of its origins and political agenda.

To understand the alliance between Orthodox religion and the feminist movement that emerged in the 1970s in the Soviet Union, we should take into account the fact that for most of the twentieth century the Orthodox church in Russia, whose members were systematically persecuted and harassed by the state, was in opposition to the ruling regime. In the 1970s to 1980s many of Russia's dissident intellectuals were concentrated around the church, engaging in debates that led to a revival of Russian religious philosophy in the perestroika period. That is why it is not surprising to find in the late 1970s some Russian feminists associating themselves with this Orthodox religion, for instance organising the club 'Maria' in St Petersburg, named after St Mary.[18] The appeal of the Orthodox tradition to feminists was partly because it allowed them to find a language that could be understood by those who were in opposition to the official ideology of women's emancipation that had been experienced as ideologically biased, production-oriented and inhumane. Thus a new Christian feminism challenged the persistent stereotype of *Homo Soveticus* that was a model for both men and women as 'an abstract, one-sided pseudo-masculine ideal of personality'.[19]

The alternative to this Soviet model, argued feminists, was the Virgin Mary, the human being who transcended the limits of human existence and was deified. Contrary to Roman Catholicism, the Orthodox church emphasises the motherhood rather than the virginity of St Mary: the title 'the Mother of God' (Theotokos) rather than Virgin is more accurate in Eastern Christianity when referring to the woman who gave birth to Christ. The great popularity of Theotokos in Russia in the past and up to the present day is evident in the large number of miraculous icons of the Mother of

God and by the existence of a vast body of hymns devoted to Mary as well as churches and monasteries consecrated to her. The apparitions of Mary which were recorded in various places during the years of turmoil following the revolution of 1917 and during the Second World War (particularly in Stalingrad, the place where the Russian army had the major success over Nazi Germany) are evidence for the continued popularity of Mary throughout twentieth-century Russia. The gender aspect of the cult of Theotokos has not yet been measured, despite its overwhelming significance for understanding the culture and history of Russia on the one hand, and Russian feminist philosophy on the other hand.

What can the study of religion tell us that is new about gender in a particular culture? The following brief case-study, based on my own research, may demonstrate how the knowledge of religious history and theology can contribute to gender studies. My research has dealt with the theology and practices of Old Believers, a religious group that emerged in the mid seventeenth century as a result of the schism in the Russian Orthodox Church. Old Believers, persecuted severely for their religious beliefs, represent an intriguing case for a historian: despite their reverence for tradition, in many respects they were more modern than their Orthodox counterparts. Successful merchants, talented icon-painters and craftsmen, vigorous polemicists and restless migrants, Old Believers – the representatives of less privileged classes – were usually more literate and entrepreneurial than the average Russians.

Contemporaries commented on the high status of women in Old Believer communities where they read in church, conducted church choirs, taught children how to read and write, copied manuscripts and painted icons. The priestless Old Believers, who challenged the tradition of apostolic succession and began to elect their ministers among themselves, often gave women the chance to try a spiritual vocation as ministers and confessors. In eighteenth- and nineteenth-century Russia, which was still a serf country, Old Believer women were generally more literate, mobile and sexually liberated than the majority of their Russian female counterparts.

To understand this phenomenon, I particularly looked at the priestless faction of Old Believers in their theological writing, although this was a theology which was not a product of highly educated scholastic 'men of letters' but rather a part of popular culture. I have also studied the polemical writings on marriage produced by members of two rival communities – one that refused marriage as a church sacrament and advocated the ideal of chastity, and the other that developed new teaching on marriage, regarding it as a social contract. In analysing this theological controversy, the question might be asked: what did this argument, pro and contra marriage, actually mean for real men and women? And, in order to measure their impact, I studied the debate vis-à-vis the social practices of both communities.

The conclusions of my study were somewhat paradoxical: the teaching on celibacy encouraged women to take up Christian virtues, described as 'manliness', such as the courage to confess one's faith in the face of persecutions, asceticism in daily life, suppression of sexual desires and zeal-ousness. By representing fallen humanity as feminine, however, the advocates of universal celibacy, unlike the medieval clergy, identified femininity not with sexuality but with procreation. Thus, to overcome her 'fallen' gender, *woman* was to become *man*, by which was meant the denial of motherhood. This teaching, which in practice was applied as a licence for unsolemnised marriages and sexual freedom, was quite popular among the urban lower classes in the late eighteenth century and first half of the nineteenth century, for it liberated men and women from the control of both the church and village moral economy. The excess of women over men among the inhabitants of the dormitories of the Preobrazhenskoe commune in Moscow, a centre of 'contra-marriage' Old Believers, suggests that women were more attracted to the communal model as an alternative to marriage than men. The competitors of Preobrazhenskoe, proponents of traditional marriage, combated the universal value of celibacy and argued that mar-riage was a sacred institution established by divine power. The absence of church and priesthood in the more radical contra-marriage group did not mean that this institution was no longer relevant for Christians. They emphasised the emotional and social aspects of marriage, particularly stressing the importance of its child-rearing function. In their writings gen-der is represented in a fairly traditional way, operating within the frame-work of a 'separate spheres' discourse. However, even here the role of woman as the head of the household and the educator of children was not questioned. If we look at the family and communal practices of these communities, we can see that women, indeed, had considerable power running the household, assisting husbands in business, educating children and engaging in community work. Liberal attitudes to divorce and non-uniform nuptial practices allowed both men and women a degree of flexi-bility that was refused them in society at large; for example, generally nineteenth-century Russian divorce law was the most rigid in Europe.

In sum, the study of Old Believer theology and communal experience reveals that relations between religious discourse and social practices are not straightforward and that theology cannot be seen as a blueprint for patriarchal attitudes in a society. Moreover, religious imagery and symbolism can be seen as both liberating and oppressive depending on the different social and economic circumstances. For example, religious teaching that 'de-sacralised' both marriage and motherhood was liberating in the peas-ant moral economy, in which marriage was a primarily economic institution and childbirth was closely associated with the reproduction of the labour force. However, the same discourse became oppressive once the woman, as an individual, had considered the option of a congenial marriage and voluntary motherhood.

This case-study of Old Belief makes us think about traditional religion in a more complex way. In the patriarchal structure of traditional society, religion may often play a destabilising role because it challenges conventional social roles and provides a space for those in conflict with the system as well as some social support for the dispossessed. Many peasant men and women broke with their village commune to choose a religious vocation. For literate Old Believers, religion was not only an alternative social community but also a source of income; reading the Psalter for the departed, for example, was a relatively well-paid occupation for many of the women inhabitants of nineteenth-century Preobrazhenskoe

Thus religion cannot be seen solely as an instrument of oppression and the justification of patriarchy, but should also be studied as the 'weapon of the weak', a subaltern language and the voice of those whose experiences and dreams have been excluded from the domain of history, particularly the lower classes and women. Religion and religious tradition should not be understood as a repository of ready-made, fixed gender models which serve to cement the relationship of inequality between men and women in a given society. Rather it is a living tradition subject to change and creative interpretation. This study of Old Belief demonstrates that even the most conservative religion is sensitive to social change and outside influence. An analysis of competing religious discourses on the subject of marriage demonstrates that religion can be a communicative process in which the participants articulate their understanding of and exchange their arguments about what were conceived as unchanging gender archetypes. To study religion and gender means to engage in this communicative process without dominating so-called primitive religious world-views by our enlightened positivist standpoint.

Religious revival in present-day Russia demonstrates the outright failure of the project of socialist modernisation that tried to eliminate religion from social life and culture. However, many positive initiatives of socialism were buried under the ruins of this project. Among many, the idea of gender equality and women's emancipation was defamed, evidence of which is the lack of research on gender.

Trying to be positive about current developments in Russian historical studies one must estimate critically the gap between promise and actual outcome. If we consider these developments in comparison with other European countries, the unfavourable conclusion must be drawn that in the last decade gender in history remains, as they say in Russia, an 'unploughed field'. Some of the main problems that are being faced may be assessed as follows.

Perestroika and glasnost, indeed, stimulated historical research and evoked tremendous public interest in history. Between 1985 and 1991 the print runs of periodicals that published historical material increased rapidly; not taking into account popular journals that gave extensive space to historical topics in their pages, we can see that a professional historical journal such as *Voprosy istorii* increased its print runs 8–9 times between 1989 and 1992 while another journal, *Otechestvennaia istoriia*, doubled its readership.

However, the introduction of new details and publication of new documents was not accompanied by rethinking of the principal problems of historical analysis and methodological issues behind the writing of history. The re-evaluation of modern and contemporary Russian history, for example, has been done through a traditional conceptual framework which continues to emphasise politics, economics and ideology.

Access to new archival documents and to Western publications did not challenge the subject matter historians were dealing with. For it has been mainly the re-evaluation of recent political history that has allowed historians to rehabilitate their subject in public opinion. Due to the media frenzy and public appetite for suppressed issues of Soviet political history, social history in general, and gender history in particular, were marginalised in the late 1980s and early 1990s. The leading official journal of Russian history, *Otechstvennaia istoria*, had published only one (literally!) entry that had relevance to gender studies in the last decade – and that was, alas, by a British scholar.[20] Debates among historians about the ways of rethinking history in the late 1980s and 1990s seemed to be more preoccupied with the problem of deciding at what point in time Russian history took a wrong turn, in 1917 or in 1928, the year of Stalin's revolution. These debates that focused predominantly on the issues of class, economy and politics were not understood as containing a gender dimension.

The fact that the history of the family, marriage and childhood was for a long time withdrawn from mainstream history has had its effects on gender studies. Scholars who responded to the rising interest in sexuality, everyday life, or family and marriage often came from an anthropology background. This had an impact on their treatment of gender as a timeless, ahistorical category. A predominantly descriptive, empirical approach, which was also often uncritical about the sources used as evidence, was characteristic of ethnography, the other discipline which had covered the discussion of gender in the context of history of the family, marriage and popular culture.

For example, a romantic view of the peasantry, informed by nineteenth-century studies of folklore, persisted in the works by Soviet and Russian anthropologists. The striking contrast between romantic and social history approaches to peasant women can be illustrated by two papers on that issue presented to a conference on the *mentalité* of the Russian peasantry that took place in 1992. A Russian scholar's paper, titled 'Women's Lot', about rural women in postwar Russia, represented an emotional account of women's miserable conditions in the socialist village. The paper articulated some transparent romantic stereotypes about the peasantry, arguing that the village was morally less corrupt than the city, mainly due to the higher religiosity of rural women. An American scholar's paper on peasant women's migration in the nineteenth century, which focused on the issues of changing patterns of the rural community, female labour and the family, may be contrasted with the former for its lack of emotion and value judgements. This may be why the American researcher seemed puzzled by her Russian colleague's question: why did she not say anything 'about the problem of woman's soul'?[21]

Another example relates to the rehabilitation of Catherine II in the post-perestroika historical writings; she remains a controversial figure in Russian history. But the debate about her political activity was often presented through gender stereotypes. For example, the examination of Catherine's private life was to reveal her 'abnormal hyper-sexuality'. Such a judgement, supported with medical discourse, reveals the implicit double standards in historical writing: what is considered to be 'normal' for male rulers, that is, Peter I's and Alexander I's love affairs, is condemned for a woman performing what was considered a male role and whose similar sexual behaviour is regarded as deviant. Another approach, used in popular histories of Russian female rulers in the eighteenth century, is to represent the royal women in a sympathetic but unsophisticated light. The absence of politics from these books suggests that women remain women despite their royalty; they were charming and fun-loving persons who by chance or by intrigue happened to be on the throne.[22]

A cultural studies approach to gender, partially informed by psycho-analysis and by early twentieth-century theories of civilisation, has tried to incorporate gender as a key axis of cultural analysis. Yet this seems to generate new mythologies about femininity and masculinity instead of a deconstruction of past stereotypes. The binary models of culture, in which a 'feminine' element, associated with passive, artistic, irrational, natural, was juxtaposed to a 'masculine' one, represented as active, logical and civilised, suggest that old concepts of gender were being successfully recycled in Russia. For example, the translations of Otto Weininger's *Sex and Character*, which had introduced the idea of gender as key determinant of personality, reproduced between 1992 and 1994, were sold out as bestsellers in post-perestroika Russia, despite its hostile and derogatory view of femininity.[23]

Despite the emergence of a limited number of studies of masculinity, much of gender history still remains in the field of women's studies. *Man* is not seen as a subject of scientific inquiry unless it concerns men's sexuality. In a database of Russian publications since 1982, book titles that contain the word 'man', in the sense of a person of the male sex, (muzhchina) made up a tiny proportion of the just under 4,000 book titles pertaining to gender (5 per cent). Apparently, it is difficult to imagine a serious discussion about what is involved in the construction of masculinity and manhood yet taking place within the Russian academy. Perhaps, for this reason, the scholars who are trying to introduce it into historical studies have to hide their uneasiness under the usage of foreign words: *maskulinnos'* and *feminnost* instead of the somewhat misleading Russian equivalents, *muzhestvennost* and *zhenstvennost*.[24] An interesting attempt, though, was made to shed light on the cultural construction of particular types of masculinity within the Russian radical intelligentsia. Characteristically, this endeavour by a specialist in sexology relates the formation of a particular historical and cultural phenomenon to the suppression of sexuality, by this implying that masculinity is largely a product of psychological mechanisms deeply permeated with sexual desires.

Instead of a simple conclusion to this account of the recent developments in the field of gender and history in the Russian academic context, I would like to restate the words of a Russian MP: 'our women don't need freedom, they need sausage'. Though it may sound a dissonant note with the above analysis, it is an apparent fact that in present-day Russia the development of new areas of research depends very heavily on economics. The 'shock therapy' economic reforms and the tremendous cutting down of the budget for education and research resulted in the rapid fall of academic standards and scholarly performance. Due to a dramatic drop in salaries, scholars are forced to earn their income by increasing the number of teaching hours and by writing textbooks instead of pursuing their own research. The curtailing of funding for research institutions, libraries and archives in Russia and the general deterioration of the material conditions of individual researchers, who cannot afford to go on research trips and buy expensive books, has had a detrimental effect on quality and quantity of scholarly production.

Yet, as many Western scholars emphasise, the fact that, despite the absence of material reward and public recognition, Russians continue to pursue their scholarly work says a great deal about their commitment and enthusiasm.[25] The same must be said about scholars working on gender who despite the lack of funding from the state continue their scholarly and political activities. Some of them, living in apartments that have no fitted bathroom and sharing these quarters with a family of three generations, continue to write books and articles, to organise international conferences and to lecture for the public in their free time.

Notes

1. *Ponedel'nik*, 29, 23 July—2 August 1998, p. 1.

2. Examples from the course on 'Gender and Society' by Dr Valentina Uspenskaia, Tver' University.

3. S. Boym, *Common Places* (Harvard University Press, Cambridge, MA, 1994).

4. See N. Funk and M. Mueller (eds), *Gender Politics and Post-Communism: Reflections from Eastern Europe and the former Soviet Union* (Routledge, New York, 1993).

5. *Zhenshchiny v tylu i na fronte* (1984); *Zhenshchiny v bor'be i trude* (1985); *Zhenshchiny v budniakh velikikh stroek* (1986).

6. *Vysshie zhenskie kursy, 1878–1918* (Moscow, 1965); Z. Evteeva, *Vysshie zhenskie kursy* (Moscow, 1966); T. Tishkin, *Zhenskii vopros v Rossii, 50–60 gody XIX veka* (Moscow, 1984).

7. B. Romanov, *Liudi i nravy Drevnei Rusi* (1947); A. G. Vishnevskii (ed.), *Brachnost rozhdaemost, smertnost v Rossii i v SSSR* (Statistika, Moscow, 1977).

8. For example, the important work on the status of women in peasant society emerged in the context of the study of wedding ritual and folklore; see for example T. Bernshtam, 'Devushka-nevesta', in *Russkii nardonyi svadebnyi obriad* (Leningrad, 1978); Martynova, 'Kolybel'naia pesnia', *Russkii folklor: Issledovaniia i materialy*, (Moscow, 1975); N. Minenko, *Russkaia krest'ianskaia sem'ia v Zapadnoi Sibiri: XVIII –pervaia polovina XIX v* (Novosibirsk, 1979).

9. S. Kaidash, *Sila slabykh. Zhenshchiny v Rossii (XI–XIX vv)* (Moscow, 1989); N. Pushkareva, *Zhenshchiny Drevnei Rusi* (Moscow, 1909)

10. Odissei, 1989–96, Iu. Bessmertnykh (ed.), *Zhenshchina, brak, sem'ia do nachala novogo vremeni* (Moscow, 1993); Iu. Bessmertnykh (ed.), *Chelovek v krugu sem'e: ocherki po istorii chastnoi zhizni do nachala novogo vremeni* (Moscow, 1996).

11. N. Lebina, M. Shkarovskii, *Prostitutsiia v Peterburge* (Moscow 1994).

12. A. B. Kamenskii, *Pod sen'iu Ekateriny* (St Petersburg, 1992), p. 82.

13. L. Repina, 'Zhenskaia istoriia': problemy teorii i metoda', *Srednie veka*, 45 (1994), pp. 24–36; A. Iastrebitskaia, 'Problema vzaimootnosheniia polov kak dialogicheskikh struktur srednevekovogo obshchestva v svete sovremennogo istoriograficheskogo protsessa', *Srednie veka*, 45 (1994), pp. 36–45; O. Voronina, 'Kategorii pol/gender v filosofii feminizma', *Filosofskie issledovaniia* (1995), pp. 29–36; N. Pushkareva, 'Gendernye issledovaniia: rozhdenie, stanovlenie, metody i perspektivy', *Voprosy istorii*, 2 (1998).

14. *Traditsionnaia kultura krest'ianstva na Urale* (Ekaterinburg, 1997).

15. V. Uspenskaia (Tver' University), 'Iz shkoly rozhdaetsia shkola', *Genderland*, 2 (1998), p. 1.

16. Interview with Dr V. Uspenskaia (Tver', 10 October 1998).

17. *Zhenshchina i pravoslavie* (Moscow, 1994).

18. The feminist movement, which originated in St Petersburg in the late 1970s, grouped around the club Maria, publishing illegally the journal *Women and Russia* (editors Ju. Voznesenskaia, N. Malakhovskaia, T. Mamontova, T. Goricheva). The journal was disbanded in 1980 and its editors were forced to emigrate. For more information, see L. Alekseeva, *Soviet Dissent: Contemporary Movements for National, Religious and Human Rights* (Wesleyan University Press, 1985), pp. 354–60.

19. *Zhenshchina i Rossiia* (Paris, 1980), p. 23.

20. F. Wigzel, 'Zarisovki rossiiskogo byta XVIII–XIX vv: gadalki i ikh klienty', *Otechestvennaia istoria*, 1 (1997), pp. 159–67. After this article was completed, the first publication on gender by a Russian historian appeared in this journal. M. Pushkarev, 'Gendernyi analiz i ego primenenie k izucheniiu istorii kul'tury', *Otechestvennaia istoriia*, 1 (1999), pp. 19–29.

21. *Mentalitet i agrarnoe razvitie Rossii XIX–XX vv: materialy mezhdunarodnoi konferentsii* (Moscow, 1996).

22. E. Anisimov, *Zhenshchiny na russkom prestole* (St Petersburg, 1997).

23. O. Weininger, an Austrian psychologist, published his book in 1903 in Vienna.

24. N. Pushkareva, 'Gendernye issledovaniia', 16.

25. R. Davies, *Soviet History in the Yeltsin Era* (Macmillan, Basingstoke, 1997).

13

Conceptualising Gender in a Swedish Context

Åsa Lundqvist

Historical knowledge in general and feminist history in particular play an important role in current debates about gender relations, especially the understanding that their content, form and concrete expression varies over time and in various local as well as national contexts. But at the same time the conceptualisation of gender also displays a certain degree of historical continuity; the legacy of the past is never swept clean.

During the twentieth century, the conceptualisation of gender has evolved in relation to the development of the Swedish welfare state, a project that, more than in most other countries, has emphasised the importance of work as a means to achieve universal welfare. From the 1930s, attempts to integrate reformist projects and academic research have been important, and models from the social sciences were used as a political instrument in the struggle to reform an antiquated social structure, a project which included the relationship between women and men. Scholarly insights have continued to be mobilised in attempts to improve women's conditions in different social and cultural spheres.

But even if new scientific knowledge and political reforms did, indeed, change the conceptualisation and, at times, the practice of gender relations during the twentieth century, patterns inherited from a previous culture can be traced to the patriarchal principles inherent in the small, rural and industrial communities which were the central feature of Swedish society into the early twentieth century. These were paternalistic units where a landowner and/or founding proprietor of an enterprise, such as an iron mine, had sole power as employer and cultural leader. Such communities usually exhibited clear class distinctions and a work organisation based on a characteristic craft tradition. A specific culture was established which, as we will see, influenced the ideas of those who founded the modern welfare state and their understanding of gender.

The following discussion attempts to illuminate how the political conceptualisation of gender has developed during the twentieth century with to some extent its roots in those rural industrial communities, particularly in relation to the emerging welfare state. This development is brought to light in the analysis made by feminist historians, specifically the development of gender relations within the labour movement as well as in more general debates. Within these discussions, what kind of questions have been raised, under what circumstances and how has the past conceptualisation of gender affected the present in the Swedish context?

Swedish industrialisation began during the second part of the nineteenth century and led to a degree of urban growth,[1] but the main thrust was the development of industries within a rural village setting. In the countryside, farming and industry existed side by side in rural industrial communities that were called *brukssamhällen*. During the mid seventeenth century small industries were established in many places around the country where wood and iron were the basic products. For a long period many of these communities were more or less closed to the surrounding world and the mobility among mill and iron workers was very low. In some of the larger rural industrial communities, the workers, including the whole family, were initially not allowed to move or to be employed by another proprietor. By keeping their employees in the same place such employers were guaranteed a supply of special skills. For example smiths were particularly important and their skills were passed on from generation to generation.

The founder proprietor was always a man and, as head of the enterprise, for a long time played a patriarchal role with more or less total control over the lives of his employees. There was a form of lifetime employment for work people – men, women and children – where everyday life both inside and outside the mill was controlled. Workers were rewarded mainly in kind through subsidised housing, free food and later on a type of pension, but little money wage, a kind of remuneration termed *naturahushållning,* or 'primitive economy'. This specific culture created entire dependency on the owner of the enterprise for workers and their families. The founder proprietor was the ruling patriarch so that within these communities the hierarchical culture of dependency *also* provided a type of security. A specific culture, based on a local 'spirit of compromise', was developed since the founder proprietor and the employees were dependent on each other.

In these communities, women's and men's work was often predestined: men and boys worked within the mills, women and girls in the homes and in the fields. Many narratives from the past tell us how women were often characterised as the 'saviours' of the family economy. When the boys started working, around twelve years of age, girls stayed at home and helped their mothers with cooking, care of younger siblings, sewing, animal breeding and keeping, as well as the continual washing of the boys' and husbands' working clothes. Women used the spinning wheel to create yarn out of wool and flax, and looms to weave all the fabrics for both clothes and use in the house. Women brewed the families' drink, baked their bread and slaughtered animals. They gleaned the grain that was given to the workers as a remuneration and then ground it into flour, a particularly onerous task.[2]

Nevertheless, in the context of late nineteenth-century industrialisation, the emergence of a politically aware working-class movement, together with reforms of the political system, forced changes upon the ideas behind the old industrial communities. The primitive economy more or less disappeared when new factory owners decided to hire workers as individuals and on a contractual basis. The family structure within the working class also changed as a more modern gender division of labour was established.[3] Women became part of the industrial workforce and the strict demarcations of the past were breaking up.

With these changes a novel division between men's and women's *industrial* work emerged. Many men had more independent, more qualified and better paid jobs than women, including positions as foremen.[4] Yet at the same time working-class men and women also adopted new ideals from upper-class families, where women were seen as part of the family and home. However, in reality most working-class women could not afford staying at home or the luxury of rejecting a paid job.[5] This question became an important political issue during the twentieth century.

Since industrialisation in Sweden also developed in the countryside and within the rural industrial communities, many of the labour movement's early organisations were established there. Both general movements and the Social Democratic Party (SAP) became an important factor in Swedish politics in the early twentieth century. In alliances with the Liberal Party, later with the agrarian party, and finally on its own, the SAP formed the basis of a new era of Swedish history: the 'People's Home' (*Folkhemmet*). The main purpose was to create a state where the right to work, social security and proper housing would be granted to all citizens, both men and women. This was to be a general policy, not limited to the larger cities or densely populated areas.

Coincidentally with the formation of the Party, the industrial and social patterns of Swedish life were shifting. A more sophisticated industrial structure was emerging, trade unions were constituted and the growing aspirations of welfare policy reshaped Swedish society into a modern social democratic welfare capitalism. From the 1940s to the 1960s people enjoyed the harvest of this politics, when Sweden became one of the most well-developed welfare states in the world – some would even claim the ideal–typical welfare state.[6]

Despite this break with the premodern social structure that is associated with the rise of social democracy, and even if the fundamental motives differed between the egalitarian labour movement and the hierarchical paternalism of the original, there is a connection between the old patriarchal rural industrial community and the twentieth-century welfare state.[7] It may be argued that there was a *conceptual* similarity between these paternalistic small units and the Swedish welfare state and, especially, the idea of inclusiveness and the importance of the whole population's welfare for social cohesion.

Furthermore there were those regions where the older-style communities physically survived the emergence of the welfare state. In these reconstituted rural industrial areas, aspects of the older patterns were reproduced, but took a rather different shape. Social relations were less asymmetrical and the relationship between workers and employers had become more formal.[8] Employers were more or less forced to recognise that the workforce was organised through trade unions. Former dependency on the founder proprietor was lifted, and when the SAP came to power the older-style founder proprietor's tasks altered to develop a 'society without privileged or neglected men and women'.[9]

Ever since the Social Democratic Party (SAP) was formed in 1889, there had been a discussion within the Swedish labour movement about women's position in society. The initial ideological standpoint was inspired by international socialist ideas on equality between the sexes in the struggle for social justice. Socialism could only be achieved through cooperation between working women and men fighting together against capitalism. However, this standpoint changed in the context of practical politics.

The most contentious issue was how women could combine motherhood with gainful employment. Then, too, the heterogeneous position of working-class woman as mother, wife and worker complicated social democratic ambitions towards gender equality.[10] Men's position was constituted as more homogeneous, as they were conceptualised as workers only. Because of this dual construction, women could not be incorporated within the labour market as easily as men. As a result, the labour movement emphasised a male-breadwinner model with a housewife system.[11] And with this model went an ideal of the housewife and mother as a central premise of the early twentieth-century labour movement.

This did not mean that all members of the SAP shared the housewife ideal, especially since, at an early stage, the Social Democratic Women's movement organised primarily employed women and women who were union activists. A cleavage emerged within the movement, where employed women were contrasted with women who were housewives, a duality which caused much debate in the following years.[12] In 1932, Alva and Gunnar Myrdal, an already well known intellectual and politically active couple in the Social Democratic movement, published their *Kris i Befolkningsfrågan* (A Crisis in the Population Question), an influential book that analysed the declining birth rates of the period and suggested, for the time, a radical social policy including improvements in health care, child care and education to increase birth rates. The fact that Swedish women were giving birth to fewer children, together with the economic crisis, intensified the debate on women's conditions within the family and the workplace.

Indeed, women's political engagement during the 1930s and 1940s seems to be a key factor behind the reforms that were decided during this period, innovations such as maternity support and universal child allowances both being paid directly to the mother, as well as legal prohibitions against the dismissal of pregnant women from the workplace. Measures like these increased women's participation in the labour market and their influence on the financial situation of the family.[13] Women's political mobilisation and the reforms which followed also widened the definition of politics, for in addition to traditional concern with conditions of labour market participation, issues related to the family and household were now politicised. There was, however, strong resistance to such a shift, for the housewife and male-breadwinner ideal had continued vitality, especially in ideological discussion, but was also manifest in practical politics.

The historic compromise between employers and trade unions from 1938, combined with advantages gained through Sweden's non-participation in the Second World War, had made industry highly competitive in the early postwar phase.[14] This encouraged an intensified debate over the issue of 'equal pay' for women and men. Despite labour shortages and a booming economy, women earned on average 30 per cent less than men, a highly controversial issue within the labour movement.[15] It was not until 1960 that the SAP included a paragraph on equal wages in its party programme. Nevertheless, the debate had an impact on political practice and through these debates women's 'double role' as mothers and workers was highlighted. One concrete example that came out of these discussions was the introduction of 'home helps' (*barnvårdinnor*) providing care for sick children.[16]

During the 1950s the numbers of employed women increased, and continued to climb during the following decade. The share of married women working increased from 15.6 per cent to 36.7 per cent between 1950 and 1965.[17] Together with immigrants, a large pool of married women and mothers became an increasingly important labour market 'reserve army' in the 1950s and 1960s.[18] The stay-at-home housewife and the male-breadwinner model became even more problematic when the demands for more labour power highlighted the possibility of including women on a broad scale.

During the 1960s and the 1970s more ambitious family and labour market policies were established. There was an attempt to reorganise the traditional family constellation in order to enable women to enter the labour market, and the family became a focal object of political reforms. Significantly, in 1967, a Ministry solely responsible for the family was set up for the first time. A more gender-neutral family policy gradually emerged to ensure that the responsibility for child care as well as care for the ill and the elderly would not be solely women's responsibility.[19] As a consequence, the labour movement abandoned its traditional stance and moved to develop a dual-breadwinner model.

Some important institutional changes in gender relations are characteristic of this period. The Swedish Confederation of Trade Unions (LO) established a Family Council in 1967 based on the Women's Council,[20] the focus shifting from women to families seen as *the* problem. Social insurance and the tax system were modified. In 1970 the so-called housewife insurance was extended to men at home and, in the same year, individual taxation was introduced, a move which at the time was called the 'greatest equality reform ever'. Maternity insurance was replaced with a gender-neutral parental insurance in 1975. The marriage act was changed and the father could apply for child custody after a divorce. At the same time, efforts were made to increase the representation of women in political arenas.[21] The expansion of public services increased female employment, both indirectly by measures which enabled women with home responsibilities to go out to work, and directly since most of these services were provided by women. Thus, between the late 1960s and early 1980s, more than 500,000 Swedish women entered the labour market, of whom many had children. Undoubtedly many of the structural obstacles in the path of women's labour market participation had been swept away.[22]

The problem of 'women's two roles', first highlighted by the women of the labour movement, was widely studied by academic researchers during the 1950s and 1960s. Research on the obstacles women faced in the labour market was commissioned by the state. The analytical focus of the researchers, most often from the social sciences, was on how women's everyday lives and the demands of the labour market could be adjusted.[23] At the same time, the 'sex role debate' was emerging. The new line of thinking assumed that women's social position had been established through socialisation and could therefore be changed. Nevertheless it was acknowledged that there were structural features making women's participation in waged and salaried work problematic.[24]

In 1961, Eva Moberg, a pioneer in the women's movement, wrote *Kvinnans villkorliga frigivning* (Women's Conditional Release). This publication sparked off the Swedish gender and equality debate. Moberg claimed that the social framework for gender relations had to change in order to establish gender equality between men and women. A year later, the anthology *Kvinnors liv och arbete*[25] (The Changing Role of Women and Men) was published. This book, in many ways, marked the beginning of Scandinavian feminist research. It had a major influence on the emerging debate around sex roles, a concept which, by this time, had been established as a scientific 'truth'. In the book, Swedish and Norwegian sociologists discussed women's situation in the labour market and in the educational system. Pedagogues and psychologists discussed women's and men's different patterns of socialisation and personality development, along with a more general and theoretical discussion around the explanation of sex roles. As long ago as 1956, Alva Myrdal and Viola Klein had presented a similar paradigm in their book *Kvinnans två roller* (Woman's Two Roles), but with *Kvinnors liv och arbete*, the existence of a socially constructed concept of woman and man, femininity and masculinity, was acknowledged.

By this time the political climate within the labour movement had changed. During the 1960s the role of women in the family and in the workplace had been redefined. 'Some of the wordings in programmes and decisions of the Social Democratic Party seemed to be inspired by *Kvinnors liv och arbete*',[26] wrote Edmund Dahlström, one of its authors. Undoubtedly there were now clear connections being made between academic research and the political climate.

Towards the end of the 1960s and the beginning of the 1970s the 'New Women's Movement' developed in Sweden. As in other European countries, this movement grew out of the 'New Left', which had emerged a few years earlier. At the same time a critical feminism was being built from, on the one hand, a reformist and positivist tradition and, on the other, a gender-blind Marxism. Within this amalgam of intellectual discussion and political activity so-called 'equality politics' developed where many of the demands raised by the Women's Movement were threshed out. This was consistent with Social Democratic strategies in relation to the rise of new social movements, namely to incorporate various protest movements' demands into the established political agenda.[27] Thus discussions about women's role in society were merged into mainstream political discourse. Women's and men's unequal relationship became a reform arena now conceptualised as *equality policy*. But in the wake of these heady progressive developments a peculiar shift in the relationship between politics and research had taken place.

If we generalise, we can talk about a duality between the political conceptualisation of gender and feminist attempts to critically examine gender relations. On the one hand, equality politics stressed the problematic relations between women and men in society, but rarely, if ever, questioned or analysed the roots of these oppressive structures. On the other hand a theoretically oriented feminist research agenda arose which had thrown into question existing social structures and patterns of domination in society as well as existing research paradigms. The resulting incongruity has led to a debate concerning both the concept of equality and the premises of feminist research. The debate was intensified in 1983 when the public equality committee presented a report: *Om hälften vore kvinnor ...*[28] (If Fifty Per Cent Were Women ...). Emanating from the small number of women employed in senior positions in the academic system, the report examined the conditions for female researchers as well as the development of feminist research.

Feminist reactions to the commission's report were mixed. Many agreed that the initiative in surveying women's difficulties in establishing themselves within the academic system was a positive move. Nevertheless, they argued that the report was plagued by conceptual confusion. The incorporation of feminist research into a broader concept of *equality research* was deemed unacceptable. Equality as a concept was connected to the political sphere and did not fit more theoretical feminist discourse and could not be used in international debates. Perhaps the most salient critique centred on the purposes of the concepts: equality as a political goal did not, as feminist research did, question established political terms and conditions.[29]

By the mid 1980s the intensity of this debate had ebbed. Feminists had shown that equality politics was fundamentally uncritical of the existing patriarchal order. Many feminist researchers had looked into the consequences of equality politics where they tried to bring out the deep-seated nature of gender-based hierarchies and from there to identify impediments to equality strategies. These efforts then led to a new type of cooperation between the political and academic arenas. One such example was the report *Varannan Damernas* (roughly translated as 'Turnabout With The Ladies') whose purpose was to improve the representation of women in public organisations and in parliament. Another example was the establishment of *Kvinnomaktutredningen* (The Committee on Women's Economic Power in Society). Its aims were to survey and analyse the distribution of economic power and resources between women and men in Sweden. In some of the committee's reports different aspects of equality policy aims were closely scrutinised,[30] although, in fact, most of the in-depth accounts emerged from the field of feminist research.

As in many other European countries, the early feminist debate often focused upon the complex relationship between Marxism and feminism. Much attention was paid to the 'unhappy marriage' between these perspectives so that the relationship between concepts of patriarchy and class remained a recurrent theme among many feminists. While this primarily feminist–Marxist debate continued, from the mid eighties other perspectives were surfacing. For example poststructuralist ideas had by now reached Swedish intellectual and feminist circles. Among others, Joan Wallace Scott's perspective became very influential in the Swedish debate, as her book *Gender and the Politics of History* redefined the research agenda for many feminist historians. Above all, the peculiarly Swedish introduction of the concept *genus system* marked a theoretical shift.

The introduction of *genus* as the Swedish translation of gender from a feminist point of view, was made by the historian Yvonne Hirdman in 1988.[31] She introduced this idea to expand thinking around the question of why women generally have a lower value than men in society and how this is related to historical change. Hirdman starts out with certain premises: women have been accepted within the capitalist system through their participation in the labour market. Women have also been integrated into the democratic political system since universal suffrage was practised for the first time in 1921. However, despite this formal equality in both spheres, women are still subordinated in society.[32]

By using the concept *genus*, Hirdman wanted to identify the 'increasingly complex knowledge we have developed about "male" and "female" and how these categories are constructed'.[33] To this end she employed the concept *genus system*, which was defined as 'a structuration order of gender. This fundamental order is the precondition for other social orders'.[34] The *genus system* should be understood as a network of social action that creates a gender-bound pattern or logic.

By this, Hirdman wanted to expose a society where both everyday life and structural features are based on two premises, the separation of women and men and the masculine as the norm. These two were related since separation strengthens the normative primacy of men. Hirdman argued that the overriding conceptual value of the term *genus system* was to highlight how unequal social orders have been reproduced. In her schema the *genus system*, a complicated network of social acting that creates and reproduces patterns and connections, may be studied concretely through a *genus contract*, that is, looking at how men and women act in their everyday life. Within the framework of the *genus system*, the *genus contract* is specified and the relationships of women and men are shaped in time and space.

Hirdman was also struggling with the fact that, despite her emphasis on its dynamism, such a systemic model might be regarded as static. She was convinced that this does not have to be the case and argued that there is a transcending character to the *genus system*. Here, she introduces a biological dimension in her model: 'the human similarity between the sexes'.[35] Although the *genus system* separates men and women, there is a fundamental similarity in their conceptualisation of the world. Yet despite their common confrontation of the human condition, the system of gender differentiation is difficult to overcome. Historically it seems that only major social upheavals, such as those related to wars, can break through the pervasive setting apart of women and men in society and culture. The problem is, Hirdman argues, that when an existing *genus system* is broken down, power centres will be transferred to other areas and territories where a new system is created which reproduces the original duality in a different form.

The concept of *genus system* is historically variable. Its content can change depending on what time period is being studied, but the patterns and logic continue to be reproduced through the *genus contract*, that is, our thinking and everyday acting. The concepts of *genus system* and *genus contract* and their various manifestations have been well received among feminists in all branches of the social sciences and the humanities.[36] Undoubtedly Hirdman's thinking has played a major role in contemporary Swedish feminist historical research. Nevertheless, there are also feminist scholars who have confronted her model and found it wanting in certain respects. Among empirically oriented feminist historians, its relation to concrete historical analysis has been questioned.[37] There has also been a theoretical critique which queries the model and proposes other strategies.

In 1992, the feminist historian Christina Carlsson Wetterberg presented an alternative model.[38] Her starting point was the complex relationship between abstraction and historical reality and was particularly directed at the limits that the abstract level of the *genus system* concept imposed on concrete historical analysis. Her aim was to anchor the theoretical discussion of women's own experiences in a social context. Carlsson Wetterberg claimed that the reflecting actor was obscured in the abstractions of models like Hirdman's *genus system*. At the same time she stressed that a constructivist analysis à la Joan Wallace Scott could lead to unacceptable relativism since the connection between discourse and praxis remained undefined. Inspired by Linda Alcoff,[39] Carlsson Wetterberg tried to unite a structure-centred and actor-centred perspective. Through understanding structure as changeable, where 'people are part of the structure, fixed at a position within a larger societal context'[40] she wanted to focus on both the acting individual and her interaction with her surrounding context.

On the basis of her research into the lives and political activity of Social Democratic women, Carlsson Wetterberg claimed that women often act in a contradictory fashion, both at the ideological and practical levels. For example, they demanded that men and women should have equal treatment in the labour market while at the same time they defined the household as a female sphere.[41] Contradictions like this should, according to Carlsson Wetterberg, be explained by the heterogeneous constellation of working-class women's positions. If we could, she claimed, explain and understand the manifold differences within the Social Democratic women's collectivity, between those who brought their different experiences of life and work to the same movement, and then relate these differences to a wider societal context, we would be able to provide an 'explanatory historical analysis of women's strategies'.[42]

The action of women and men should not be forced into pre-given interpretative schemes. If we do that, the complexity of identity disappears as does our capacity to visualise variations in those identities. Instead Carlsson Wetterberg argued for a 'perspective where we ... see women and men as acting subjects in complex, historical contexts. A perspective that has as its aim to make variations within the women's collective visible, such as the way women's subordination is linked to other power hierarchies'.[43]

Norwegian feminist historian Gro Hageman recently presented another theoretical alternative.[44] She started by posing the question, 'is it possible to conceptualise gender in a way that is consistent with empirical studies of historic events and processes?'[45] Here she wanted to develop an answer partly on the basis of Hirdman's and Carlsson Wetterberg's work, but also incorporating insights from Joan Scott's poststructuralist theory. Hageman's perspective straddles the boundary between different theoretical models, accepting both the concept of discourse and that of the acting subject. She wanted to develop a theory that could grasp the 'supra-individual' at the same time as historical change and purposeful acting were included.[46]

Hageman's model, therefore, has an ambiguous relationship to Yvonne Hirdman's *genus system*. On the one hand she sympathises with Hirdman's aim of pinning down the reproductive power of existing gender structures which they both understand as a culturally changeable order.[47] On the other, she argued that it is not obvious that gender is dominant over all other social hierarchies. Instead, these orders interact. She is also sceptical about what she regards as an ahistorical universalisation at the centre of Hirdman's concept. Hageman argued that the 'iron law of genus', a phrase introduced by Hirdman in order to show the rigidity of the *genus system*, does not accord well with historical pluralism or historical actors: 'What kind of changing perspective is possible if historical processes are ruled by iron laws and the result is more or less predictable?'[48]

Hageman agrees with Carlsson Wetterberg on a number of points. She argues that Carlsson Wetterberg's wish to take the historical actor's own contextual experiences and behaviour into account in the analysis is a preferred strategy. Nevertheless she also raises some questions concerning Carlsson Wetterberg's approach to the structural constraints placed on actors. All human action is not based on individual choices and reflections. Instead, actors are part of social and cultural frames that are carriers of our society. These frames cannot always be reflected upon and chosen.[49] Hageman also questions Carlsson Wetterberg's critique of the poststructuralist analysis of individual experiences and interests. In this, her starting point is Scott's resistance to the idea of a specific female experience as creating a monochrome feminine identity rather than interpreting the subject's experiences as 'discursively constituted'. But Hageman raises further the question, 'where do resources come from that enable the creation of independent actions?'[50]

In uncovering these contradictions at the conceptual level, Hageman's analysis points to the importance of research into empirical historical problems. Yet, working historians are hard-pressed to find concrete examples of a way out of such a dilemma. Hageman herself states that a solution may not be possible. She also asks if this really is necessary or even desirable: 'A great deal of the dynamism of historical research lies in the difficulty in negotiating the tension between the determined and the transcending and between continuity and change'.[51] However, in conclusion, she comes down on the side of Scott's poststructuralist position as preferable in feminist historical analysis since it takes 'social interaction as a starting point (to create knowledge), rather than the individual subject'.[52]

Throughout the political history of the Swedish welfare state, there have been many attempts at reforming the role of women, in the family as well as in the labour market. Beyond this twentieth-century reformism, the legacy of the past sometimes becomes visible. Using the old rural industrial communities as a metaphor of historical continuity, we might find an interesting path to the historically constructed notion of gender.

The old rural industrial communities emphasised work as a key category in order to integrate workers (i.e. male workers with their families) within the community, embodied through the 'local spirit of compromise'. These communities had been marked by a strong gender division of labour, where men were constituted as part of working life and women were constructed as a part of the family and the home. This tradition has proven to be tenacious.

The local 'spirit of compromise' stemming from rural industrial community life survived the industrialisation as an *idea*, especially the idea of inclusiveness and the importance of welfare for social cohesion. It could be argued that, in doing so, a deeply gender-biased practice was following this specific legacy. The labour movement's emphasis on work (i.e. gainful employment) as a key category for social life and for human dignity led to a complicated relationship between women as mothers and women as workers. This contradiction has not been resolved in our time despite the high labour market participation rates among Swedish women. It is on the basis of this contradiction that 'women' have been constructed as a target for political reforms where new reform areas such as 'family' and 'equality' have emerged.

The changes in the conceptualisation of gender within the political system are also reflected in the academic sphere. Women's complex position between on the one hand the family and on the other the labour market has been emphasised, although from different perspectives and using different theoretical models. Studies of women's position in society conducted before the 1970s were based on empirical surveys and were often done in connection with political reforms. Current feminist studies of the development of the welfare state and its effects on gender relations instead take the cleavage between the reform ideals and the realities of women in Swedish society as their starting point. By analysing the social basis of these contradictions, a complex theoretical discussion has emerged within feminist research, shown in the debate around Hirdman's concept of the *genus system*. In other words, Swedish feminist research has moved from being a part of the political system towards a critical reflection of the limits and possibilities of reforming Swedish society in general and its welfare state in particular, without losing feminism's political orientation.

Notes

I would like to thank Leonore Davidoff for her encouragement, and constructive and insightful comments on previous versions of the chapter. Without her this chapter would not have been written. Mats Benner and Christina Carlsson Wetterberg read and commented upon an early version of the chapter.

1. Urbanisation in Sweden began rather late and took a very long time. Approximately 75 per cent of the population lived outside urban areas as late as 1913.

2. Christer Ericsson, *Vi är alla delar av samma familj: Patron, makten och folket* (Carlssons, Stockholm, 1997), pp. 97–9.

3. Anita Göransson, *Från familj till fabrik: Teknik, arbetsdelning och skiktning i svenska fabriker 1830–1877* (Arkiv, Lund, 1988); Ulla Wikander, *Kvinnors och mäns arbeten: Gustavsberg 1880–1980* (Arkiv, Lund, 1988).

4. Anita Göransson, *Från familj till fabrik*, p. 269. Lena Sommestad argues that the conditions for agricultural working women were different since they always had been a part of working life, although their work changed depending on different phases. Lena Sommestad, 'Jordbrukets kvinnor i den svenska modellen', in *Gender, Work and Welfare: Report from a seminar 14 June 1996*, ed. Anne Lise Ellingsæter and Gro Hageman (Institutt for samfunnsforskning, 1996), pp. 20–36.

5. Ulla Wikander, *Kvinnor och mäns arbeten*, p. 219.

6. Gøsta Esping-Andersen, *The Three Worlds of Welfare Capitalism* (Polity Press, Cambridge, 1990).

7. Maths Isacson, 'Bruket och folkhemmet', *Häften för kritiska studier*, 3 (1991), p. 42; Christer Ericsson, *Vi är alla delar av samma familj*, pp. 228–31.

8. Thommy Svensson, 'Japansk företagsledning och svenska bruk – en felande länk', *Arkiv för studier i arbetarrörelsens historia*, 33 (1988), p. 21.

9. Maths Isacson, 'Bruket och folkhemmet', p. 44.

10. Christina Carlsson, *Kvinnosyn och kvinnopolitik: En studie av svensk socialdemokrati 1880–1910* (Arkiv, Lund, 1986), pp. 272–7.

11. Christina Carlsson, *Kvinnosyn och kvinnopolitik*, p. 6; Yvonne Hirdman, *Med kluven tunga: LO och genusordningen* (Atlas, Stockholm, 1998), pp. 10–11.

12. Gunnel Karlsson, *Från broderskap till systerskap: Det socialdemokratiska kvinnoförbundets kamp för inflytande och makt i SAP* (Arkiv, Lund, 1996); Ylva Waldermarsson, *Mjukt till formen, hårt till innehållet. LO:s kvinnoråd 1947–1967* (Atlas, Stockholm, 1998).

13. Ann-Sofie Ohlander, 'The Invisible Child? The Struggle for a Social Democratic Family Policy in Sweden, 1900–1960s', in *Maternity and Gender Policies: Women and the Rise of the European Welfare States 1880s–1950s*, ed. Gisela Bock and Pat Thane (Routledge, London and New York, 1991), p. 69.

14. For an overview of this specific period, see *Äventyret Sverige: En ekonomisk och social historia* (Utbildningsradion och Bra Böcker, Stockholm, 1995).

15. Yvonne Hirdman, *Med kluven tunga* (Atlas, Stockholm, 1998), p. 400.

16. Diane Sainsbury, *Gender, Equality and Welfare States* (Cambridge University Press, Cambridge, 1996), p. 192.

17. Yvonne Hirdman, 'Genussystemet', in *Demokrati och makt i Sverige* (SOU 1990: 44), p. 87. Hirdman organises the history of the Swedish welfare state into three phases where she distinguishes the conceptualisation of gender within the labour movement: *husmoderskontraktet* (housewife contract) 1930–1960, *jämlikhetskontraktet* (equality contract) 1965–1975/80 and *jämställdhetskontraktet* (gender equality contract) 1975/80 to the present.

18. Edmund Dahlström, 'Debatten om kön och familj under svensk efterkrigstid', in *Kvinnors och mäns liv och arbete*, ed. Joan Acker et al. (SNS förlag, Stockholm, 1992), p. 18.

19. Barbara Hobson, 'Kön och missgynnade: Svensk jämställdhetspolitik speglad i EG-domstolens policy', in *Ljusnande framtid eller ett långt farväl: Den svenska välfärdsstaten i en jämförande belysning*, ed. Agneta Stark (SOU 1997: 115), p. 198.

20. See: Ylva Waldermarsson, *Mjukt till formen, hårt till innehållet. LO:s kvinnoråd 1947–1967* (Atlas, Stockholm, 1998) for an indepth discussion of the council's history and its effect on the labour movement.

21. Christina Berqvist, *Mäns makt och kvinnors intressen* (Acta Universitatis Upsaliensis, Uppsala, 1994).

22. Hobson, 'Kön och missgynnade', p. 199.

23. Andreas Lund, *Kvinnor i industriarbete: Studier och debatt 1953: 3* (SNS förlag, Stockholm, 1954).

24. Harriet Holter 'Berättelser om kvinnor, män, samhälle; kvinnoforskning under trettio år', in *Kvinnors och mäns liv och arbete*, ed. Joan Acker et al. (SNS förlag, Stockholm, 1992), pp. 56–7.

25. Annika Baude et al. (eds), *Kvinnors liv och arbete* (Prisma, Stockholm, 1962).

26. Edmund Dahlström, 'Debatten om kön och familj under svensk efterkrigstid', p. 22.

27. Gunnar Olofsson, *Klass, rörelse, socialdemokrati* (Arkiv, Lund, 1995).

28. *Om hälften vore kvinnor* (SOU 1983: 4).

29. Anna-Lena Lindberg, 'Rundabordssamtal: Om hälften vore kvinnor', *Kvinno-vetenskaplig Tidskrift*, 3 (1983) pp. 6–8.
30. SOU 1997: 144, SOU 1997: 115. Many of the articles that focus on women's pos-ition within the Swedish welfare state are inspired by Jane Lewis's thoughts on women's relationship to paid work, unpaid work and to welfare. See, for example, Jane Lewis, 'Gender and Welfare regimes: Further Thoughts', *Social Politics*, 2 (1997), pp. 161–77.
31. In Sweden, most feminist scholars had used the term *socialt kön* (social sex) as a translation of the English word *gender*. The introduction of the *genus system* by Yvonne Hirdman was presented to a broader feminist audience in 1988. Before that she had discussed the concept in an anthology written within the *Maktutredningen* (Power Commission, 1987). See Yvonne Hirdman, 'Makt och kön', in *Maktbegreppet*, ed. Olof Petersson (Carlssons, Stockholm, 1987), pp. 188–206; Yvonne Hirdman 'Genussystemet – reflexioner kring kvinnors sociala underordning', *Kvinnovetenskaplig tidskrift*, 3 (1988), pp. 49–63. Hirdman's model has been presented and discussed in many forums and there are a number of interpretations. The following discussion is my interpretation of the article written in 1988.
32. Hirdman, 'Genussystemet – reflexioner kring kvinnors sociala underordning', p. 50.
33. Hirdman, 'Genussystemet', p. 51.
34. Hirdman, 'Genussystemet', p. 51.
35. Hirdman, 'Genussystemet', p. 58.
36. Among others, feminist economic historian Ulla Wikander claims that 'we will in the overall perspective discover that one of the most important organising principles in society, apart from class, race and religion, is genus. It is all about a difference between men and women that is culturally, socially and economically created, accord-ing to a so-called genus system' (Ulla Wikander, 'Kvinnohistoria – vetenskap om makt och relationer', *Kvinnovetenskaplig Tidskrift*, 3–4 (1989), p. 42). Ulla Wikander also used the term *genus history*, a research perspective that studies not only the power relationship between women and men but also the relationship between women.
37. See, for example, Renée Frangeur, *Yrkeskvinna eller makens tjänarinna? Striden om yrkesrätten för gifta kvinnor i mellankrigstidens Sverige* (Arkiv, Lund, 1998).
38. Christina Carlsson Wetterberg, 'Från patriarkat till genussystem – och vad kommer sedan?', *Kvinnovetenskaplig Tidskrift*, 3 (1992), pp. 34–48.
39. Linda Alcoff, 'Cultural Feminism Versus Poststructuralism: The Identity Crisis in Feminist Theory', *Signs*, 3 (1988).
40. Wetterberg, 'Från patriarkat till genussystem', p. 43.
41. Wetterberg, 'Från patriarkat till genussystem', p. 44.
42. Wetterberg, 'Från patriarkat till genussystem', p. 45.
43. Wetterberg, 'Från patriarkat till genussystem', p. 46.
44. Gro Hageman, 'Postmodernismen en användbar men opålitlig bundsförvant', *Kvinnovetenskaplig tidskrift*, 3 (1994), pp. 19–34.
45. Hageman, 'Postmodernismen', p. 20.
46. Hageman, 'Postmodernismen', p. 26.
47. Hageman, 'Postmodernismen', p. 22.
48. Hageman, 'Postmodernismen', p. 23.
49. Hageman, 'Postmodernismen', p. 25.
50. Hageman, 'Postmodernismen', p. 31.
51. Hageman, 'Postmodernismen', p. 31.
52. Hageman, 'Postmodernismen', p. 32.

14

Gender and the Categories
of Experienced History

Selma Leydesdorff

In the last few decades several feminist historians have argued that women's history and oral history have points of connection.[1] Oral historians began to query whether the role of methodological debates derived from oral history might enhance a new discussion on the creation of sources and the subjectivity in sources – a set of questions that has been taken up by many feminist scholars; in addition oral historians early joined those who critiqued the narrative structure of historical writing. They also focused attention on the value of micro-histories, which have become much more common now than such histories were in an earlier phase of women's history. Oral history, like sociology and anthropology, has shown the value of localised examples and detailed case studies of small groups. This trend is also becoming visible in women's history of pre-contemporary periods. From the very beginning, international oral history conferences devoted a substantial number of sessions to women's history, repeatedly exploring the theme of the disappeared, silenced, or oppositional voices of women.

But many who practise oral history are wondering where to move the field in the future. Much of our work has been the writing of history grounded in the analysis of a presumably representative segment of a particular population, based on the assumption that studying a small sample by using qualitative methods can yield important new insights. In a sense oral historians' theoretical posture is akin to sociologists', but with one major difference: their careful consideration of the dimensions of time and memory. Because time and memory are inherently volatile, however, they make arguments concerning the representative nature or empirical value of a given sample complicated. At the same time, gender has been inscribed in the field, rendering women and constructions of femininity and masculinity central objects of study.

In order to combine the analytical strategy of sociology, history, and the study of gender, an alternative has been found in the method of life stories through which a whole life is told by means of an interview employing careful techniques. In creating life stories, an individual's experiences are contextualised within a wider web of meanings. Analysis will, for example, take into account not only gender but also inter/transgenerational transference and the role of genre in storytelling. For many years already, we have tried to decipher the differences between female and male memory; we have also probed the differences in speech patterns between women and men as well as female and male narrative genres.[2] We have often come to the conclusion that the differences among women can be greater than those between the sexes. By looking closely at individual lives, we have become aware that the context of the nation-state, so important for most writing of history – which is generally concerned with how the equality of different groups of citizens is problematised – is replaced by new contexts, which present religion and civilisation as key concepts. Any historian who has written a life story will undoubtedly know how many contextualisations, besides the category of gender, are possible within the interpretation of a single interview. And how sometimes categories other than gender are more important, even when one is writing the life of a woman.

Although the fields of women's history and oral history tend to overlap they have also remained quite separate, while the influence has flowed mostly in one direction. Oral history has been shaped by women's history, but in this essay I wish to explore the other side of the equation.[3] At times one gets the impression that the preceding discussion regarding the problems of oral history and the uses of life stories are not known to women's historians, despite their obvious relevance to many crucial feminist concerns. These include the fragmentations of life embedded in women's (auto)biography, the representation in history of everyday life, the narrative structure of historical discourse, and especially the role of subjectivity in the construction of the historical past. One explanation for this apparent ignorance about methods and ideas embraced by oral historians could be that the older generation of feminist historians heard stories that defied feminist expectations and organising principles. The stories they were told included details of daily life, domestic contentment, and the acceptance of motherhood – as well as stories of powerlessness or empowerment that conformed to a then-current feminist model that demonised the ubiquity of women's involuntary confinement in the private sphere.[4]

Contemporary women's history has become a significant part of the field of oral history: in the proceedings of conferences one finds many forms of feminist oral history, while there is also a wealth of monographs based on collective oral histories.[5] There is also a strong feminist influence on oral histories and life stories of the family.[6] Similarly a lively interaction has occurred with cultural anthropologists – employing methods and approaches that are dear to feminist theory – who initiated debates about the manner in which the world is configured by people who are interviewed.[7] It is true that some oral-history anthologies have reached a wider feminist audience.[8] But feminist scholars tend to ignore the bulk of oral-history literature. Only work with clear theoretical implications such as that of Liz Stanley (who might not call herself an oral historian) has found a place in what we might call – with a sense of irony – the 'canon'.[9]

There are many explanations for the one-sided nature of the conversation between oral historians and women's historians, but I would venture that the major reason is the fact that so much oral history concentrates on the local level, refuses a larger theoretical framework, and looks somewhat narrowly at a particular group of women or a single region. Sometimes wider conclusions can be drawn from such research (about, for example, the power relations involved in representing memory). But the focus remains on the particular empirical sample. Oral history shares this problem with many studies in anthropology where, in the same way, studies that transcend the particularity of the local context are scarce. In a recent volume of *Frontiers*, Susan Armitage complains about this issue when she writes: 'Usually the number of people interviewed is small, the interviewers are beginners, and the research is conducted under the time and other constraints of dissertation pressure. And because so much work is academic and is shaped by current academic styles, the emphasis is sometimes more on the interviewing interaction and its difficulties than on what the narrator actually says.'[10] Continuing the discussion in the same journal, Sherna Berger Gluck points out that oral historians are now overcome with doubt where earlier they relied, naively, on a sense of gender solidarity and a simplistic feeling of 'insider-ness'. As she notes: 'I would put considerably more faith in the ability of some of my male colleagues in oral history to apply what we often referred to as feminist principles than I would some women who are more bound by race, class, gender, and sexual orientation'.[11]

Berger confesses that she is bored by the regionalism and the dominant practice of gathering stories in a mostly uncritical fashion, wondering how 'oral history can be both a scholarly and an activist enterprise, [how] it can change our knowledge but also empower people and contribute to social change'.[12] She takes note that for many feminist oral historians (of whom a number have left the field), attention has shifted to memory, representation and meaning. But for others a political motivation remains primary; the wish to give a voice to women from a silenced class, ethnicity or region is a reason to write oral histories and a way for academics to be socially engaged.[13] It is true: the idea of listening to voices that are not usually heard is still a powerful political incentive.

I want to consider the points raised by Armitage and Gluck by thinking about ways in which oral history can be converted into a scholarly enterprise that is both exciting and more challenging. Of course the field has been provocative at times, when subjectivity and historiographical methods have been debated, but now it feels as if oral history as a distinct mode of inquiry has stagnated. Hence, I agree with the discontent articulated in the discussion in *Frontiers*. I would like to add that the outcome of the current debates in oral history has been the introduction of gender as an analytical category – but that is no longer enough.

Gender itself must be rethought in light of what oral historians are telling us.

Oral histories often constitute a very small study about the social existence of a certain group, sometimes reflecting the group's mentality and interactions with the outside world. Most such work does not even deal with issues of interaction and subjectivity. Although a lot of insight can be gathered from an examination of changing patterns of femininity across generations as well as female memories and representations of the past, much of the current scholarship records details and anecdotes without reaching for a more critical or theoretical conceptualisation. Unfortunately oral historians are no better in this regard than other historians. But when the limitations of approach have been transcended, as in the discussions about subjectivity in interviews, oral historians are accused of 'being difficult'. For example, a fierce attack from quite a traditional historical perspective came from the women's historian Joan Sangster. In the *Women's History Review*, in 1994, she criticised the widely used reader *Women's Words* by Sherna Gluck and Daphne Patai.[14] This volume was one of the first systematic efforts to analyse women's language across a wide geographical area; the authors argued that the interview is not only a linguistic but also a social and psychological event. Sangster, however, warns against 'overstating the ultimate contingency, variability, and "fictionality" of oral histories and the impossibility of using them to define a women's past as "real and knowable"'.[15] Following Louise Tilly, she pleads against creating a polarity between subjectivity and social relations. She sees a split between the older generation of oral historians who 'accepted the "transparency" of their interviewees' accounts and the new, "complex" approach influenced by theory'.[16]

However, I argue that reverting to the old social history paradigm does not provide a solution. In life stories we have learned valuable lessons about the convergence of histories, about the ways of dealing with the past, and about representation and subjectivity; these various insights have added to our historical knowledge. Although we have to move beyond the esoteric level – discussing the representation of five women in a mining community, for example, arguing about interrelations – oral history's problems cannot be solved by stating either naively or cunningly that everything must be placed within a social and material context. It is also clear that the problems of endowing an individual life with a framework are by no means only challenges to the oral historian. Biography inflects and intrudes on all kinds of history.[17]

I am convinced that many of the problems described here are not peculiar to the women's history contingent within oral history. In the life-story approach in oral history and sociology, a number of authors have tried to overcome what might be called 'traditionality'. Within the social sciences more generally, there have been efforts to create new forms of representation and to overcome the limits of quantitative thinking. Barbara

Laslett and Barrie Thorne have shown in *Feminist Sociology: Life Histories of a Movement* that many well-known feminist sociologists have struggled with the fact that (semi-)quantitative research no longer answered the questions their feminist experience prompted them to ask.[18] Life stories have shown how biased sociological questions can be, and have given us new sensitivities and methodologies to help us study other cultures and people with minority status.

The plea for 'real history' has not forestalled the ongoing debates about how interviewer and interviewee interact in the creation of a source – which can then be seen not only as a text but also as a confrontation of different subjectivities. But the importance given to interaction and shared subjectivity has sometimes become an impediment to listening carefully. On occasion it has emerged that, whether intentionally or inadvertently, the interviewer has dominated the record. Hence Luisa Passerini, Paul Thompson and I pleaded several years ago for a politics of plurality. This would start by recognising how much our feminist voice, always present in the analysis, is a Western voice imposed on the 'other'. We argued that listening carefully to the plurality of voices might give us the ability to render account of the differential significations at work in other cultures. But this can splinter and fragment notions of gender. What we understand to be gender as an analytical tool is formulated through Western women's experiences and thought. Recognising this pluralises gender at the same time. Living in purdah may seem horrific to a Western woman, but within certain cultural contexts it may provide a satisfying, and secure woman-centred existence.

Thus we might have to ask whether the experiences we listen to can be categorised as resulting from a distinct set of gendered dictates. Is gender enough to tell us about the manifold experiences of the past, even if the category is used flexibly and includes the politics of locality as defined by Sandra Harding? Or, as Liz Stanley has suggested, if gender is understood as a historical moment in a display of changing contradictions?[19] The way we now conceive of the rootedness of human experience in material conditions as well as shaped by individual and collective significations and memories, is far removed from earlier notions employed by oral historians. While we may have added gender as a category to our research, the 'plurality of voices' compels us to think about 'genders'.

Recently I taught a class of women from many countries such as Sudan, Senegal, Mali, and Ethiopia among others, and I used Joan Scott's article on gender as a fundamental category of analysis. What ensued made me aware again of the enormous differences among women. My students perceived a discrepancy between the unitary concept of gender proposed by Scott and the idea of plurality of voices I had previously emphasised and celebrated. African and other students identified more closely with the men from their own regions than with women from the Western world, and wondered if different analytical categories could be devised. They queried why other relations of power were not presumed to be just as fundamental. This argument, of course, has been central to post-colonial studies, but my students expressed it with personal urgency.

Those are some of the problems within the field of oral history at the present moment. The big question is: where do we go from here? Will the oral history of gender continue to be the small-scale enterprise with the added prism of gender, in which we look at how men and women construct masculinity and femininity in their reifications of the past? Or can we imagine creative steps that move beyond this impasse, so we can conceptualise the myriad subjectivities and experiences that emerge in our stories? In what follows I want to review the possibilities of overcoming the problems of research at the micro-level. I will explore the current intellectual quandaries and boundaries of oral history in the hope of demonstrating how these might be addressed and expanded.

My ideas have been greatly influenced by Michael Walzer's *On Toleration* and his descriptions of the problems arising when several cultures try to live together but fail to accept one another.[20] This is what happens in our world. Another significant work for me has been Benjamin R. Barber's *Jihad versus McWorld.*[21] The author describes two oppositional trends that are unfolding simultaneously in the contemporary world. The first is cultural fragmentation, which is often anti-modern, while the second involves economic unification, integration of technologies, uniformity and what he calls the 'McWorld' of computers, the global economy and international entertainment. Bill Gates has recently called it McWord, giving the phenomenon a new dimension. Both of these tendencies erode, Barber argues, not only the nation state but also democratic processes. His complex and insightful argument sheds light on the oral historians' predicament: much oral history already deals with cultural fragmentation, but we should perhaps pay equal attention to the tendency toward world-wide cultural standardisation. And since historical practice should foster democracy, insofar as it can give a voice to those who have been silenced, I propose a new use of historical studies as a counterweight to the cultural homogenisation inherent in 'McWorld'.

Some years ago I collaborated briefly with the multinational corporation and electronics giant Philips, and found they were firmly convinced that regional identity was one of the pillars of social cohesion in the future. The aim was to design a new way to stimulate local participation in the writing of history and of course to sell: Philips viewed history as an instrument for establishing community and identity in a scattered and disintegrating world. So a shared past, or rather shared storytelling about the past, could strengthen social ties. The aim was the design of a utensil (not a computer; it was to be something new) with which people could engrave their own history in the collective memory of a community, whether it was a street, a neighbourhood, a city or a region. This project was intended to be part of the cultural programme of the European Community by which social citizenship would be redefined in terms of local community. It was an ambitious programme in which women's needs and participation were both valued and viewed as endemic. So this was how McWorld asked for help from an academic life/oral historian.

I never really believed in the idea, precisely because this idea of re-inforcing local and regional identity is diametrically opposed to the rapid globalisation of a world-wide community of people who consume culture and change cultural identifications by becoming transnational citizens of the world. I would argue that this opposition calls into question our ideas about community and identity. Any fixation on the local and the familiar becomes sterile and can be coopted into a political agenda to which feminism is opposed. This vocabulary directly bolsters the many forms of xenophobia that haunt the right-wing fringes of contemporary European politics.

The major question is: how do we combine a commitment to the transcultural with a critical view of the mesmerising influence of fashion, international film and modern culture? Can we write a history that will acknowledge the transcultural and still be of use in helping people to articulate an identity, something for which they rely heavily on history?

Throughout history, transcultural and transnational persons have existed. Transcultural is not transnational; some Chinese and many Jews exemplify transnational people but have kept their culture, even if they adapted socially to the societies that host them. Slavery and colonialism also created diverse blends of the two. In this kind of transformation of culture women have their own role. The degree to which one moves beyond one's own culture has become a political and a personal challenge, and in some circumstances a struggle. However, modern media, communication, and transport have given the transcultural new meanings and emphasis. In addition to migrants, refugees, and elite expatriates, middle-class people with no special reason to leave their countries now travel all over the world. Speaking about different cultures has become fashionable and part of daily life. Even if we are not travelling, we take in stimuli from all over the world. Our lives are no longer regionally confined.

Despite such apparent unification, people cling to their own culture and customs. They seem to need a sense of their own history and their own culture. This need is especially strong among migrants who have not abandoned their traditional way of life to adopt mass culture. On the contrary, many often negotiate endlessly between their own cultural prescriptions and the regional cultural demands of their host society. This practice, again, is not new but has simply become more widespread, finding its articulation since the 1930s in a very poignant literature of migration, in which there is a distinctive female presence. A telling example can be found in the francophone stories embedded in the culture of the Maghreb, describing nostalgia, adaptation to a new language, and cultural resist-ance.[22] Another instance is the literature produced by Chinese émigrés, among whom Amy Tan may be the most ambivalent.[23] Very often this literature is biographical or autobiographical. But in the contemporary global situation it is not only the life story of migrants that exudes a polyphonic and unstable resonance. Rarely now do I interview individuals who could actually be considered 'authentically working-class' or endogenous people. Reciprocity with other cultures always lingers.

I foresee that in our interviews we will listen increasingly to the stories of people who could be characterised as quintessential 'other' and will convey a cultural medley.[24] I am convinced that the strength of life stories lies in their ability to help us to analyse a kaleidoscope of cultural representations. Oral history and life stories derive their strength from accommodating the uniqueness of the individual experience. They offer an alternative to behavioural sciences which, in their efforts to make general statements, are powerless to deal with the tremendous variety of experiences and cacophony of voices. Merely presenting an experiential polyphony, however, will not suffice, even if a single life story can at times provide greater insight into the pains and pleasures of cultural transformation than a sample of many lives. As historians and social scientists, we will be asked to present some coherent thoughts on representation if we want the validity of our methods to be acknowledged.

In the social sciences this task is even more difficult than in history. The French sociologist Daniel Bertaux, for instance, has tried in his work on Russia to generalise from a multitude of individual life stories[25] about the mechanisms of class and genealogy under the former communist system. He and Paul Thompson have attempted in the *On Generations*[26] to look at the role of different generations in cultural transmission, as well as the symbolic meanings of money and the role of the family in social mobility. The tensions between the aggregate and the individual are also visible in the work of the French sociologist Pierre Bourdieu, who in his *La Misère du Monde*[27] gives us many life stories but interprets them in a comprehensive sociological framework. His book provides valuable insight into the lives of immigrants and working-class people who meet each other in the streets, at schools, or at other impromptu social gatherings.

The same tension is visible in the contribution of oral history and life stories to the paradigms of so-called development studies. In *Listening for a Change: Oral Testimony and Development*, Hugo Slim and Paul Thompson argue that we need to know the voices and histories of the subjects of development.[28] Oral history can tell us what it feels like to be at the edge of development. The authors assert that speaking out can be an act of protest against the fact that people are not consulted enough, since the main debate takes place in documents they do not write and in meetings they do not attend. In certain societies women's voices are especially hidden: relegated to the realm of 'gossip' if acknowledged at all. Yet women are often the anchors of the households or farm economies. Their patterns of speech differ from those of men, as do the times and places in which it is socially acceptable for them to speak. Interviews with women in private settings (i.e. in the home and communal areas or their places of work) can illuminate hidden spheres of experience and private life.[29] The authors insist that if we dare to question conventional social-scientific terms of reference, such as representative sampling, our understanding of looking at these unexplored private and familial areas of experience can be enhanced. Somewhere in this avalanche of information, and in spaces designated as transnational and transcultural domains, our challenge is located. However, the transnational and transcultural domains are not just positioned in the so-called Third World: what we learn from the different perspective of that world compels us to rethink our cultural assumptions and to listen more carefully, while questioning, too, many commonly held assumptions about meaning and processes of representation.

By focusing on specific themes – such as the culture of the Jewish poor in the city of Amsterdam during the first half of the century – my work has inherently been more open to cultural difference than the research of many colleagues. But I look back and become doubtful.[30] Did I conduct interviews correctly? Even though I was an insider I nonetheless framed the interviews as an outsider? What happened when I imposed my academic standards? Yvette Kopijn has recently shown the extent to which cultural dictates determine the ways we conduct an interview.[31] To escape this problem, Mary Chamberlain argues that it is crucial to interview families, not just women.[32] Suad Joseph has shown the extent to which subjectivity is an imposed construct, even within the intimacy of small-scale fieldwork.[33] Our Western assumptions mould and shape our expectations. One of my students, who is from Senegal, told me that in her region a respectful way to welcome a guest is by talking – just talking. The longer one talks the more respect one shows to one's guest. I suggested that she return for a second visit in order to structure the interview. But she explained that the talking would start again in the same courteous and routinised way at every subsequent visit. This forced us to think about other strategies.

Pierre Bourdieu has recently written that, until a few years ago, his focus on traditional notions of what was and is supposedly representative about a particular culture had prevented him from noticing and problematising those places in society which defy description, hard to describe and even harder to imagine in any kind of coherent fashion. Passerini, Thompson and I argue that women's history can change our overall understanding of history.[34] 'Every female voice is potentially dissonant to existing histories. Dissonances are part of the continuing "modernisation" of the music and art of our time: and the multiplicity and plurality of the narrating voices.' The oral history method helps us not only to improve our understanding of the intellectual and ideological climate of a particular era, even decades after it has passed, but also offers grounds for criticising common notions of what constitutes 'reality'. The stories flow in a relentless stream and the information inundates most of us.

What information do we absorb and how? When listening to life stories, we are confronted with a narrative that conveys the way people think they have experienced their lives and certain events. The primacy of the narrated character of human experience is as crucial to oral history as it is to feminist theory and the feminist movement. The epistemological connection here – one of many – lies in the importance attributed to subjectivity in the narrative as a source of understanding, knowledge and ultimately democracy. Yet most of the problems concerning the epistemological value of narrated experience persist. What do we mean when we use this term? How useful is narrated experience for our understanding? Are we dealing with an essential experience transmitted to us by words, but potentially in many contradictory ways? How much do we understand of the meaning of those words? We are not the same person as the one we interview, and in most cases we do not derive from the same social background, nor do we share a similar cultural or emotional universe. Words spoken by another can have quite a different symbolic meaning and may represent feelings that differ greatly from the ones we think they imply. The other person's experiences also become interwoven with our own lives during an interview; the impressions we absorb are in part the product of our creativity and imagination. Here, the same epistemological problem occurs as the one observed by anthropologists, who are well aware that the experience of the 'other' is inevitably refashioned by the researcher.[35]

In the case of women from other cultures the status of narrated experience becomes even more complicated still. As historians we often deal with overt and covert relations of power, and the embodiment of power favours us. Stories are often chosen and concocted for our hearing and have been packaged in narratives and genres designed to please us as oral historians by telling us what an interviewee thinks we would like to hear. The interaction is combined with a subtle but inevitable conflict between interviewer and narrator. These tensions become visible when we analyse transcripts. They express feelings and personal histories while also trying to reveal a profound sense of cultural difference in another or a past world: one encountered in the present and one in which the old and the new are being negotiated. In essence, the contexts and experiences being articulated reflect ambivalence and ambiguity, in itself often painful and lacking expressive form. However trusted and accepted the interviewer may be, he or she is perceived as having power denied to many of those interviewed. The story of the experience is also an act of imagination and inventive negotiation on both sides. These accounts turn the past into the present and turn memory into reality. The interviewees have difficulty escaping the confines of their cultural 'we'; as a modern-day interlocutor may not be able to abandon her late twentieth-century biases. Part of the solution is the creation of a life story couched in the genres of migration, nostalgia, anticipation of the future, and a critique of the rules and regulations preventing what is hoped for.

As instances of possible ways forward through the thicket of dilemmas we face, I will describe two projects in progress. The first brings out clearly the problems of the transnational research; the second, though not intrinsically a life-story project, also involves oral history.

Some years ago the Belle van Zuylen Instituut in Amsterdam joined with a European NGO to start a comparative study of the lives of young migrant women in six European countries: Germany, Spain, Sweden, France, Great Britain, and the Netherlands. We have made use of life stories to look for differences and similarities in the experiences of those we interviewed, and studied the ways in which adjusting to the host culture has affected them. Very little is known about the existence of young women after immigration to Western Europe: in contrast to young men, they are not considered 'problematic' because they are not seen to be involved in petty crime or misdemeanours. At the same time we know, for instance, that Hindu girls in the Netherlands have an astonishingly high suicide rate, but we do not know why. We can speculate of course, but no one seems to have asked the girls themselves in order to find answers to this and many other questions. We have conducted interviews in all six countries in order to obtain preliminary results.

Our first serious problem is the variety of languages. To discuss each other's interviews, we need to raise massive sums to have the transcripts translated. We expect to obtain such funding in the future, but thus far we do not yet know what kind of information we have collected. In the beginning, we formulated endless global questions and fields of interest. Now we are having great difficulty determining how to compare individual lives, and wonder whether they can be usefully juxtaposed at all. Will this effort ensure comparable interviews, or will we end up with a kaleidoscope of lives, culminating merely in a report revealing that life for women caught between two cultures is difficult, and that they manage as best they can? Or a report in which gender means divergent things in different cultural contexts and interactions? Individual country reports remain an option, but the original challenge was to do much more. There is also the problem that some of the interviews have been conducted with assistance from interviewers coming from the same non-endogenous culture as the interviewees, and may therefore have yielded a totally different kind of information. In such cases the balance of power differs profoundly from interviews conducted by academics with academics who represent the host society. In short, talking about overcoming our limitations and accepting the challenges of the transnational and transcultural is easier in theory than in actual research.

The second project is about the meaning of Islam in the lives of migrant and non-migrant women. The Dutch Ministry of Development Cooperation is sponsoring this long-term research enterprise as part of a larger study of women and Islam. Our role involves collaboration with the Royal Tropical Institute (the former Colonial Institute). In six countries (Bangladesh, Sudan,

Ethiopia, Yemen, Mali, and Senegal) women will conduct life-story interviews about the meanings that Islam has for them. These will be compared to stories of those who migrated to the Netherlands. We hope to be able to elucidate the meaning of Islam and religion in the lives of the women interviewed so that we may devise tools for empowerment by mobilising the tenets of the Islamic religion. The focus will be on reproductive rights and the co-equal right to education. An advantage of this project's design is that we will work with women from the culture of the interviewees. However, it also shows the problems that can arise with such policy-oriented research. Empowerment politics is the only way to get such massive research off the ground. No small academic group will be able to work together with local NGOs without governmental support and access to diplomatic channels. Still, I am looking forward to studying the possible transformations of religious meaning, representation and symbolism in these two contexts. Since migrants to the Netherlands will also be interviewed, I anticipate comparing the interviews made in the new and the old societies, and am especially curious to see whether new genres of storytelling have resulted from migration.

Participating in this project has offered a unique opportunity to listen to and read material that would otherwise never have become available. Such research is extremely difficult to plan (one needs a network of contacts in many countries) and very expensive. Yet already people who are reading about women and Islam have learned from their statements that wearing a veil is not simply a sign of oppression, as some naive politicians want us to believe, but a much more complex act. We have been able to learn more about its many layers because they have spoken, and because we have listened.[36]

In sum it must be obvious that the transnational and transcultural approach still makes critical use of oral history. I would like to challenge the competition between visions of the world by introducing the often unheard speech of women. In research that links the small, local and regional focus to new patterns of history writing, we can include a plurality of voices. In so doing, we will be forced to listen more carefully to those who have no ready-made history of their own but rather a whole different range of 'histories'. As modern historians we positively need to hear those voices in order to challenge our own notions and understanding of history. This is more than the introduction of gender into a traditional framework. It asks for a new definition not only of the meaning of such voices but ultimately of our own.

Notes

Frances Gouda and Siep Stuurman have been critical commentators, helping me to strengthen language and argument. For help in revising the language of this chapter I thank Caitlin Adams.

1. A very early reference was made by Michelle Perrot at a UNESCO meeting in 1984 of international experts: 'Theoretical Frameworks and Methodological Approaches to Studies on the Role of Women in History as Actors in Economic, Social, Political and Ideological Processes'. See M. Perrot, 'Making History: Women in France', in *Retrieving Women's History: Changing Perceptions of the Role of Women in Politics and Society*, ed. J. Kleinberg (Berg, Oxford, 1988), pp. 41–60.

2. See for instance R. Ely and Alyssa McCabe, 'Gender Differences in Memories for Speech', in *Gender and Memory: International Yearbook of Oral History and Life Stories*, vol. IV, ed. S. Leydesdorff, L. Passerini, and P. Thompson (Oxford University Press, Oxford 1996), pp. 17–31.

3. There are exceptions to such generalisations. For instance *Frontiers, A Journal of Women's Studies* had three volumes on feminist oral history in 1977, 1983, 1998.

4. See S. Leydesdorff, L. Passerini, P. Thompson, Introduction, in Leydesdorff et al., *Gender and Memory*, p. 2.

5. See for instance Mary Nash's fascinating book *Defying Male Civilization: Women in the Spanish Civil War* (Arden Press, Denver, 1995). There are also autobiographical books which build a collective memory through a variety of individual stories, such as L. Gulati, *In the Absence of their Men* (Thousand Oaks, New Delhi, and Sage, London, 1993). Or, to take another genre, A. Baker, *Voices of Resistance: Oral Histories of Moroccan Women* (State University of New York Press, New York, 1998).

6. See for instance E. Roberts, *Women and Families: An Oral History, 1940–1970* (Blackwell, Oxford, 1995).

7. See for instance Lila Abu Lughod, *Writing Women's Worlds: Bedouin Stories* (University of California Press, Berkeley, 1993); D. L. Wolf (ed.), *Feminist Dilemmas in Fieldwork* (Westview Press, Colorado, 1996), especially the article by V. Matsumoto, 'Reflections on Oral History: Research in a Japanese American Community', pp. 160–70; and A. James, J. Hockey and A. Dawson, *After Writing: Culture, Epistemology and Praxis in Contemporary Anthropology* (Routledge, London and New York, 1997).

8. S. Gluck and D. Patai (eds), *Women's Words: The Feminist Practice of Oral History* (Routledge, London, 1991); Personal Narratives Group (eds), *Interpreting Women's Lives: Feminist Theory and Personal Narratives* (Indiana University Press, Bloomington, 1989).

9. The same is true for some feminist literary studies, where (auto)biography is discussed. One of the most important books showing this interaction is R. Ganier, *Subjectivities: A History of Self–Representation in Britain, 1832–1920* (Oxford University Press, New York and Oxford, 1991). I was also inspired by F. Lionnet, *Autobiographical Voices: Race, Gender, Self-Portraiture* (Cornell University Press, Ithaca and London, 1989). For an extensive review article, see L. Marcus, 'Border Crossings: Recent Feminist Auto/biographical Theory', in S. Leydesdorff et al., *Gender and Memory*, pp. 187–95.

10. 'Susan Armitage to Sherna Berger Gluck', in S. Armitage and S. Berger Gluck, 'Reflections on Women's Oral History: An Exchange', in *Frontiers, A Journal of Women's Studies*, 19 (1998), p. 2.

11. Armitage and Gluck, *Frontiers*, p. 5.

12. Armitage and Gluck, *Frontiers*, p. 3.

13. Luisa Passerini, Paul Thompson and I have also noticed this: 'It has been crucial to hear female voices, whether in politics or in women's groups, discussing present or past experiences. The rediscovery of female voices in history has affirmed the need for female voices now, and vice versa' (Leydesdorff et al., Introduction, in *Gender and Memory*, p. 6).

14. S. Gluck and D. Patai, *Women's Words*. I still think of this book as path-breaking (and I still teach from it), especially the ways they have made visible how difficult it is to listen. The other 'old' book I still use is *Interpreting Women's Lives*, edited by the Personal Narratives Group.

15. Joan Sangster, 'Telling our Stories: Feminist Debates and the Use of Oral History', in *Women's History Review*, 3 (1994), p. 13.

16. Sangster, 'Telling our Stories', p. 15.

17. See for instance Natalie Zemon Davis, *Women in the Margins: Three Seventeenth-Century Lives* (Harvard University Press, Cambridge and London, 1995).

18. B. Laslett and B. Thorne, *Feminist Sociology: Life Histories of a Movement* (Rutgers University Press, New Brunswick, New Jersey, and London, 1997).

19. L. Stanley, 'Writing the Borders: Episodic and Theoretic Thoughts on Not/belonging', in *Knowing Feminism*, ed. L. Stanley (Sage, London, 1997) and L. Stanley, 'Recovering Women in History from Feminist Deconstruction', in *Women's Studies International Forum*, 13 (1990).

20. As he says in *On Toleration* (Yale University Press, New Haven and London, 1997), the way in which toleration is not only a principle but also a political practice has many consequences for everyday life and the ways we cope with cultural pluralism: 'Cultures and religions have marked themselves off by distinctive practices in these matters [he refers to family arrangements and gender roles] and then have criticised the practices of "others". But a virtually universal male domination sets limits to what could be argued about' (p. 60). This has given me a lot of ideas about framing my interviews in migrant communities.

21. B. J. Barber, *Jihad vs. McWorld* (Random House, Toronto, 1995). See also G. Kepel, *Allah in the West: Islamic Movements in America and Europe* (Cambridge University Press, Cambridge, 1997).

22. The best-known is Assia Diebar, but there are many others; for example my favourite, by Merlene Amar, *La Femme sans tête* (Gallimard, Paris, 1993).

23. Amy Tan, *The Joy Luck Club* (Ivy Books, New York, 1993).

24. I developed this in S. Leydesdorff, 'Genres of Migration', in *Caribbean Migrations, Globalised Identities*, ed. M. Chamberlain (Routledge, London, 1998), pp. 81–95. See also in this volume H. Lutz, 'The Legacy of Migration: Immigrant Mothers and Daughters and the Process of Intergenerational Transmission', pp. 95–109.

25. Forthcoming as a joint book by D. Bertaux and P. Thompson in the series 'Memory and Narrative' (Routledge, London and New York).

26. D. Bertaux, and P. Thompson, *Between Generations: Family Models, Myths and Memories* (Oxford University Press, Oxford, 1993).

27. P. Bourdieu, *La Misère du Monde* (Seuil, Paris, 1993).

28. H. Slim and P. Thompson, *Listening for a Change: Oral Testimony and Development* (Panos, London, 1993).

29. M. Mukhopadhyay, *Legally Dispossessed: Gender, Identity and the Process of Law* (Stree, Calcutta, 1998); L. Antherjanam, *Cast Me Out of Your Will: Stories and Memory* (Stree, Calcutta, 1998).

30. S. Leydesdorff, *We Lived with Dignity: The Amsterdam Jewish Proletariat 1900–1940* (Wayne State University Press, Wayne State, 1994).

31. Yvette J. Kopijn, 'The Oral History Interview in a Cross-Cultural Setting', in *Narrative and Genre*, ed. Mary Chamberlain and Paul Thompson (Routledge, London, 1998), pp. 142–60.

32. Mary Chamberlain, *Narratives of Exile and Return* (Macmillan, London, 1997).

33. S. Joseph, 'Relationality and Ethnographic Subjectivity: Key Informants and the Construction of Personhood in Fieldwork', in *Feminist Dilemmas*, ed. Wolf, pp. 185–215.

34. S. Leydesdorff et al., *Gender and Memory*.

35. L. Stanley, 'Writing the Borders: Episodic and Theoretic Thoughts on Not/Belonging', in *Knowing Feminism*, ed. Stanley.

36. Much of the credit for this project goes to Maytrayee Mukhopadhyay, author of *Legally Dispossessed*, and to her team at the Royal Tropical Institute.

15

Writing Gender into History and History in Gender: *Creating A Nation* and Australian Historiography

Joy Damousi

'The creation of nations has traditionally been seen as men's business', write the authors of *Creating A Nation.* 'We wish to challenge this view of history', they state boldly, 'by asserting the agency and creativity of women in the process of national generation'.[1] By declaring this aim of interrogating the frameworks within which national history has been understood and women's role within it, Patricia Grimshaw, Marilyn Lake, Ann McGrath and Marian Quartly were breaking new ground in writing Australian national history.

While previous works had questioned the absence of women in the national landscape, this project sought to rewrite the enterprise of national history itself:

> This book starts from the premise that gender is integral to the processes that comprise the history of Australia – that political and economic as well as social and cultural history are constituted in gendered terms … It explores the appropriation of women's procreative powers by men in their assertion that they gave birth to the nation … It also considers the difficulty encountered by women who attempted to carve a place for non-party women's interests in a political system organised around the conflict between capital and labour, between employers and workers.[2]

This approach signified an important departure point from national histories written before or since, because it not only diverged from existing accounts of adding 'women to Australian history', but, more boldly, unsettled received notions of how national histories could be imagined. Women's agency is situated at the centre of a range of contexts and situations. The process of nation building is examined, whether 'giving birth to babies, or in refusing to do so, in sustaining families and multi-cultural communities, creating wealth, shaping a maternalist welfare state or in inscribing the meanings of our experience in culture'.[3]

In this article, I trace the production and reception of *Creating A Nation* and then consider more broadly, the impact of 'gender' on the writing of Australian history. I argue that whilst there has been an impressive volume of feminist history published over the past twenty-five years, and with it has come an important shift towards its acceptance within the historical profession, it has become a specialist field where many texts and arguments have become marginalised and have found only a limited audience outside of feminist circles.

The history of *Creating A Nation* can be seen as a microcosm of the place of women's history in general. The concept of a gendered national history of Australia was first raised in 1986, and took almost eight years to write. The coming of the bicentennial celebrations of 1988 which marked the 200 years of white invasion and domination, spawned many histories. Away from the specialised field of women's history, in the area of national histories, the connection between gendered and nationalist identities had not been made. In these national histories *women* are included in narratives, but the integration of questions of gender are eschewed. In texts such as the four volumes of the *Oxford History of Australia*,[4] the four volumes of the people's *People's History*[5] and five chronological volumes of *Australia: A Library*, the experiences of women and Aborigines are included, and the four authors of *Creating A Nation* contributed to these volumes. But the interrelatedness of gender with other issues, such as race, nationalism, war, and the state was not established.[6] The 'nation' was thus framed in these texts within a conventional paradigm and women are players in the action. Women are thus there, but 'gender' as a category of analysis, as a cultural construct and as a process is not incorporated.[7]

This sort of analysis also applies to single-volume national histories. Both John Rickard's *Australia: A Cultural History*,[8] and the more recently published David Day's *Claiming A Continent: A History of Australia*,[9] offer creative and engaging histories. Day's account is especially concerned with racial questions and the decimation of Aboriginal culture is at the centre of his narrative. Whilst women are provided with a voice and a role, national and gendered identities are separated and seen as unrelated.

The addition of 'women' to these histories reflects the fact that over the past thirty years in Australia, feminists have made an impressive and significant foray into historical writing. Historians have been prepared to 'add women' to their historical accounts, and 'recover' women's activities and past experiences. There is a comfort with, and support of, the empirical contribution women's history has made to historical writing. Beyond this, it seems, they flounder. Even in accounts which have attempted to question the seamless narrative of many national histories, gender is located exclusively where women are found. Few general histories consider the possibilities of integrating gender not only as a 'set of lived relations' but as a 'process' and 'symbolic system' which incorporates questions of language, space, and identity, as a means of shaping a more creative, innovative and complex narrative. This is the case I would argue, because there remains an unease about feminist theory – for to engage with questions of 'gender' is to understand how knowledges are constructed, how they are contested, change over time and are unstable and contingent. The integration of 'gender' within the broader parameters of historical writing is reflective of this wider anxiety and, in some cases, indifference. Although gendered history has at times been embraced, paradoxically its reception has also been ambivalent and ambiguous.

Published in 1994, *Creating A Nation*, represents the zenith of the influence of feminist history in Australia. It was no coincidence that it was conceived in the year Joan Scott's pathbreaking article, 'Gender As A Category of Analysis' was published, which was to transform the writing of women's history.[10] Scott's bold proclamation that women's history needed to move beyond what she perceived as its descriptive nature, and that historians should focus on the ways in which meanings have been constructed through language, continues to arouse heated controversy and discussion.[11] Each of the authors had been influenced by these debates. Before the emergence of *Creating A Nation*, they had published extensively in the field of gender history and remain amongst its leading practitioners. Ann McGrath had opened new directions in Australian history through her work in Aboriginal history and race relations, especially in regard to colonialism and Aboriginal women.[12] Marian Quartly had introduced innovative approaches to colonial history, but from the point of view of white governors,[13] whilst Patricia Grimshaw had pioneered research on demographic aspects of the colonial family.[14] Through her writings on femininity and war, masculinism in the 1890s, nationalism, maternalism and citizenship, Marilyn Lake offered interpretations which altered existing debates of historical writing in Australia.[15]

In preparing the general history, the authors had a burgeoning body of Australian feminist literature to draw upon, which had established a substantial amount of material on Australian gender history from the 1970s to the early 1990s.[16] The achievement was so pronounced that, in April 1996, the leading history journal *Australian Historical Studies* devoted an issue to the celebration of twenty-five years of feminist scholarship in Australia. In the period before *Creating A Nation* was published, central texts appeared which had placed the feminist agenda within historical scholarship, covering areas of labour history, cultural history, race relations, the state, war, and biography. Jill Matthews estimated that in the period between 1991 and 1995, there had been almost forty books published in the field of Australian feminist history, as well as a substantial number of articles.[17]

But paradoxically, despite this flurry of publishing, 'gender' has not always been considered as an interactive, relational category, or as having relevance to a range of categories and situations. This is not to say that gender has been entirely ignored by non-feminist historians. Some have

recently woven the insights of feminist historiography within their narratives, and have integrated a gender analysis with a deft and subtle hand.[18]
Others have attempted to include some of the insights of feminist engage-
ments, especially in relation to histories of national identity, race relations
and post-colonialism.[19] Despite the contribution and importance of these
recent histories in shaping understandings of race and nation, there is scope
for further work to be done in considering post-colonialism and its relationship to, and intersection with, issues of gender.[20] After all, the literature by
feminists in the general field of imperialism and gender is now extensive in
Australia, as it is elsewhere. These questions of the interconnectedness of
race and gender have most recently been explored by Marilyn Lake in her
examination of the relationships between white feminists and Aboriginal
women, and by Patricia Grimshaw in her consideration of colonialism and
gender relations.[21]

The defining characteristic of *Creating A Nation* was its attempt to draw
these threads together, and integrate race and gender in historical writing
by examining the sexual dynamics of racial politics. Neither at the time
of publication, nor indeed since, has any national history so systematically
attempted to integrate class, gender and race within a framework of exploring women's subjectivity, identity and agency. While earlier histories of
women had attempted to write women's experience into Australian history,
they left the prevailing masculinist and nationalist frameworks intact.[22]
Creating A Nation sought to overtly and explicitly redefine understandings
of 'nation' and its multiplicity of power, and to situate women firmly within
the process of nation-building. In these respects, the book was distinct from
existing feminist histories.

Creating A Nation begins with an account of an Aboriginal birth, where
the common but different experiences of women are emphasised, and
the theme of women giving birth to nations is introduced. It is a powerful
and profound opening which explores black–white encounters within a
gendered context. The white colonists who invaded the land eventually
destroyed Aboriginal communities and this story is told through a prism of
race as well as that of class and gender relations.

This theme drives and shapes the narrative. When Australia becomes
federated in 1901, women still cannot vote in several states, whilst the White
Australia Policy is fully enshrined in national law. Nationalist mythologies
are formed in wartime and the masculinist myths became anchored in
these mythologies. Across two centuries, questions of motherhood, paid and
unpaid labour, the role of the state in shaping women's lives, the experiences
of urban and rural women, marriage and separation, sexuality and women's
public and private lives, are some of the themes which are explored in
relation to the intersection of gender, class, and national identities.

There are three areas which distinguish *Creating A Nation* as a *national*
history. First, while other histories have attempted to integrate class, race
and gender into their narratives in ways which have rewritten Australian

history in particular ways, this is the first – and thus far the only – general history which is framed conceptually around gender and its relationship to class and, especially, to race. At the core, 'creating a nation ... always involves conflict in the encounter between diversity and the incitement to national uniformity'. These nationalist mythologies have 'always been gendered'.[23] This book is the first to pay attention to these dynamics in this way and prioritise gender. It has not – as some critics point out – just added women into the narrative. In prioritising relations between men and women, the authors place great importance on the *process* of gender relations. Secondly, agency is at the heart of the project – where individuals act, rather than are acted upon. While both are included, this is not a history where people are mere pawns in a historical argument; they are actors in their own right. Thirdly, whilst the literature on Aboriginal history was well established before the writing of *Creating A Nation*, the intersection between race and gender is integrated as in no other national history.

Given its attempts to reconceptualise a different approach to national history, how was *Creating A Nation* received within the academic community? Despite a general sympathy with the overall project, some reviewers showed an alarming hostility to the approach adopted by its authors.

Foremost among these critics was John Hirst. Hirst, a leading historian of colonial Australia, whose work on convict society had sparked debate about whether convicts in colonial New South Wales were slaves, accused the authors of exaggerating the claims made for women and accentuating the differences between men and women. Hirst identified the key dilemma in the feminist approach to history as being women's absence from public events. The 'higher purpose' of history, he argues, is to 'explain the processes of change, why one form of society gives way to another, why nations, empires and civilisations rise and fall'. When history attempts to explore change, it 'inevitably concentrates on people of power and influence'. But feminists declare that 'women have been excluded from power and that they must have an equal place in history'. Since feminism's 'claims about the past treatment of women are true, its claims on history cannot be realised'.[24] The authors of *Creating A Nation* are thus caught in a bind. 'Defining the nation, ruling the nation and defending the nation have been done mostly by men', he argues. 'Prima facie it is unlikely that women, generally excluded from the public realm, would have exercised the influence claimed for them here'. He continues by arguing that 'No matter how able the historian, it is impossible to write an intelligible history of the nation and sustain this feminist claim for female influence'.[25]

Hirst represents the feminist history project as one which lurches from failure to failure. He argues that the search for powerful women was undertaken, but having failed to find any, feminists then embarked on uncovering women in social movements like strikes and demonstrations. But these women were not to be found in their own right. In what could only be described as patronising in the extreme, Hirst then notes that, feminists

> struck gold. They joined their concern to the broader interest in social history, no longer defined as history with the politics left out, but as the social order considered as a whole. Every social order embodies a relationship between men and women; how that relationship is fixed and contested is one of its key constituents. To study this relationship and its changes means that women and men must be given equal attention ... The way to bring women into history was to focus attention not on women, but on gender, how the sexes are given their identity and place.[26]

The way feminists could bring women into history, he observes, was to focus attention not on women, but on *gender.*[27] Hirst finds this insistence on gender objectionable. 'Gender is ... always relevant. This is so large a claim that it is well nigh useless for normal purposes.' What 'normal' purposes are supposed to be, remains unexamined. His logic reads rather oddly, as well: 'Just because male domination has been so complete, gender, which is what feminists want to talk about, will not be an important factor in explaining variety and change in the past'.[28] Hirst fails to see masculinity and men as *gendered* constructions and so cannot appreciate that the public sphere is defined by such considerations. He not only shows an unyielding naivety in his understanding of the meaning of the term and its theoretical evolution, but seems confused about what feminist historians are arguing for in its application. Both these are suggested in his attack on several specific points tackled by the respective authors.

Hirst assesses each individual contribution in his review. He praises Quartly, whose chapters deals with colonial society up until 1860, because she is 'unembarrassed in depicting official male authority as the shaping force in early Australian society'. Grimshaw, who covers to 1912, makes 'occasional strident claims for the importance of gender which are not sustained' and a 'loss of intelligibility in that obviously important things are happening off stage'.[29] Lake, who covers from 1912 to the present, is guilty of the flaw that she tends to 'push men and women further apart than they really were in order to create her gender dynamic'.[30] He takes particular offence at Lake's argument that while soldiers are said to have given birth to a nation, metaphorically at Gallipoli, women really gave birth to the nation. Once again, they were usurped. Hirst then goes on to make the startling ahistorical, essentialist claim that:

> Lake should not need to be told that women giving birth is a most unlikely process to be celebrated as a national symbol, since childbirth is a natural process not varying from nation to nation or between tribe, empire and nation.[31]

Gender is not the only term Hirst uses loosely in a muddled way. He erroneously argues that 'the authors share the postmodern view that the development of national symbols is a process of exclusion, since people not represented in the symbols feel their identity is denied'.[32] Hirst then claims that the authors have not considered the role women played in the home, and that they do not recognise the 'existence of companionate marriage' to the extent that it existed. He takes issue with the authors' apparent reluctance to highlight the domestic realm, and their apparent view that, 'men were in charge of the public realm, from which women were excluded, and they were in charge of women in the home, to which women were confined – and yet women were major actors in Australian history!'[33]

In *Creating A Nation*, Ann McGrath's contribution is comprised of three chapters interspersed throughout the text. While Hirst acknowledges that her account of Aboriginal life in Sydney after 1788 is 'elegant and moving', he claims that she is not 'very interested in the changing gender relations within Aboriginal society since 1788' and 'explains that for Aborigines their oppression as a race was the chief determining factor in their lives, for both men and women'. What Hirst calls 'this allowance of subsidiary importance of gender' would not be 'permitted' in the rest of the book.[34] The authors just can't get it right, it seems. 'The only point which jarred with me', he asserts, 'was a ritual condemnation of European cultural arrogance, which sits rather oddly in a chapter which could only have been written because of the close and sympathetic attention paid to the Aborigines by the officers of the First Fleet'.[35]

Marilyn Lake was the only one of the authors who responded directly to Hirst's claims. She challenged his paradigms and assumptions, suggesting that his remarks and criticism came from a particular view of history. In her defence of the approach adopted in *Creating A Nation*, Lake made explicit the efforts she and the others had made in 'subverting the distinctions between women's history and national history'. She points to what Hirst, because of a theoretical naivety, could not grasp:

> This history presents an account of the past in which the interaction of masculinity and femininity is the dynamic force in history, a motor of historical change. It suggests that a national history that does not see gender relations as integral to the processes and relationships that form the nation is inadequate to the task ... women are no longer restricted to a walk-on 'role': rather, like men, they are cast as major actors with diverse parts.[36]

Hirst doesn't appreciate, notes Lake, that the particular construction of citizenship as 'sexually differentiated' needs to be further articulated and explored. Above all, once gender is understood, then masculinity can be identified as shaping the 'meaning of national identity'. Moreover, women have actively participated in 'defining the meaning and possibilities of the Australian experience'.[37] For Lake, the attack on a feminist reading of Australia's past was not surprising. 'The cry used to be that women were taking men's jobs; now we are stealing their history', she observes. Male, traditional historians felt threatened because this 'new feminist writing has entered the heartlands of traditional history'. These preoccupations in the book were a product of the shifting debates about nationhood. The bicentennial of 1988 inspired *Creating A Nation*, but it emerged in time for the republican debate, at a time when Australians were considering the formation of a new republican identity. Although a staunch republican himself, Lake maintains that Hirst urges us to claim our Australianness, but does so by defining the nation in masculine terms.

It is difficult to gauge how widespread Hirst's views were or are within the broader historical profession. Perhaps there are supporters of Hirst's view that 'feminist historians claim too much for [gender]; they insist that historians who ignore gender can't be doing their job'.[38] It is important to appreciate the view that if one is told one *has* to incorporate a particular view, then this is absolutist, and such an insistence may go beyond a demand for recognition in prescribing how history *must* be written. A lack of consideration about gender has, however, led to women being ignored and misrepresented – as is evidenced in Hirst's characterisation of child-birth as a 'natural process', not varying across time and place.[39] More significantly, however, Hirst's argument implies that there is a neutral place in history where gender dynamics (or class, or race) do not exist, or are insignificant. Therefore, these variables cannot be seen to impact on the course of events, or do so without relevance to each other. One reviewer of national histories simply rendered *Creating A Nation* invisible in his survey of Australian national histories.[40]

Other critics took issue with the book for different reasons. Lyndall Ryan, while claiming it an 'exciting and challenging text [which] takes Australian feminist history in a bold, new direction', argues it did not recognise regional differences between women, and the separation of white women's narratives from those of Aboriginal women. This 'precludes any discussion of how and why white Australian women saturated themselves in racist discourse in the twentieth century'.[41] Commenting in *Australian Historical Studies*, Kay Saunders similarly argued that 'whilst an innovative and challenging examination', the authors have detached the Aboriginal story from the main narrative, and have thus 'not placed race at the centre of their analysis from the outset as they have gender and class'.[42] Ann Curthoys praised it, claiming that it 'demonstrates clearly that asking feminist questions has made Australian history much richer, more complex, and more interesting'. It is a 'significant' book, which signals the shift from 'women's history to a general Australian history foregrounding the relations between men and women'.[43] In theoretical terms, however, Curthoys found difficulties where it 'sometimes reverts to a more simplistic and artificially distinct set of analytic categories'.[44] Yet, it was the most thorough attempt to date to make 'feminist and Aboriginal perspectives interconnect and inform one another'.[45] Curthoys argued that 'the lack of historiographical material marred the book, the narrative style was conventional and its contribution to interpretive and theoretical debate unnecessarily limited'.[46] Others agreed. Stephen Garton was perhaps more critical of the overall project, noting that despite the claims of the authors, this was not a 'self conscious nor a sustained analysis of the "creation of a nation"'. Instead, it was a good account of a nation's history with the role of women and Aborigines given adequate recognition, but 'nation' is presented as a passive concept, it is something that simply exists.[47] Garton and Raelene Frances argued that it needed a broader historiographical engagement.[48] The criticism that a broader engagement with historiography is lacking misses the point about audience. Writing for a general, as well as for an academic audience – which *Creating A Nation* aimed to do – raises the question of the extent to which one can integrate historiographical content, and how theoretical concerns can be incorporated.

Gender history has produced some of the most exciting and innovative historical research published in Australia. But, paradoxically, it occupies an ambiguous place in Australian historiography. As it has transpired, perhaps Hirst's view that it is enough for women's experiences to be documented, as a necessary but peripheral aspect of the main action, has assumed ascendancy in some quarters. There seems to be little sense that gender needs to be integrated beyond an acknowledgement that women should be added to the mix, in order to embrace new dimensions of historical inquiry. It has in some respects become ghettoised, for although it has been added to history, it has not yet transformed the writing of it.

Despite a smattering of reviews, *Creating A Nation* did not create the controversy or arouse the intense interest that surrounded books like *Class Structure in Australian History*, published in 1982, which inspired heated debate about how a history of Australia through a class analysis can be written. Marxism and, more recently, post-colonialism, it could be said, have had a broader influence and have been more enthusiastically embraced and debated within the writing of history than has feminism. Perhaps Lake is right in arguing that national histories in particular are perceived to be the preserve of male historians. She predicted correctly when she wrote in 1988 that 'feminist historians should strive, one and all, to capture the fortress of the "general history". We should expect the ensuing battle for possession to be fierce'.[49]

Historians are inescapably the product of their time and place. Since 1994, the debates in historical discourse have taken different directions, in response to wider and broader historical events. In Australia, in recent times, because of developments in the campaign for Aboriginal self-determination, it is race which has seized the political ground. Alarmingly, issues of class and gender have to some extent been seen to be unrelated to these debates. In this climate, the reception of 'gender' as a category of analysis has been ambivalent. Whilst 'women' have been considered important, and are added to many recent histories, issues of 'gender' – of masculinity and femininity, of sexuality, of identities – are left to feminists to unpack and explore. The recognition that men act as agents of masculinity to construct and sustain cultural, social and political institutions remains a striking absence in historical accounts. What we see here is an evident ghettoisation of feminist history, where there is an audience and a space made, but it has been hived off to the degree that it can be ignored, let alone incorporated within historical paradigms. We all welcome the multiple histories which are now being written which capture a range of complex dimensions to historical understandings. But there remains a sense that there are times, places and situations which are gender neutral. There is no such neutral place where historians can retreat to and insist that there is no gender at play. It is an illusion to think that we can separate the complexity of these intersecting power dynamics; such an omission replicates power structures and denies the historical complexity of how they evolved in an interrelated way.

Outside of the specialist field, few texts follow what was editorialised in the first issue of *Gender & History* in 1989 – that the creation and reproduction of gender is not only a 'set of lived relations but is also a symbolic system', it is a 'process, changing over time'.[50] In her review of *Creating A Nation*, the cultural theorist Meagan Morris observed that what is offered in this text is 'vivid, complex, dynamic, and, above all, legitimate' history, not just a 'feminist challenge to yesterday's orthodoxy, but an effective move to displace it'.[51] Internationally, as well as locally, it represents the only attempt to incorporate men and masculinity in the framework of general national history, thus stressing that society as a whole is coded with gendered meanings. It is hoped that more practitioners will take up the challenge that this perspective offers, with less reservation, and aspire to subvert existing paradigms which unsettle the notion of a gender neutral historical space, and thus contest the very practice of writing national histories.

Notes

I wish to thank Leonore Davidoff, Marilyn Lake and Stuart Macintyre for their important suggestions and very useful comments on earlier versions of this chapter.

1. Patricia Grimshaw, Marilyn Lake, Ann McGrath and Marian Quartly, *Creating A Nation: 1788–1900* (McPhee/Gribble, Melbourne, 1994), p. 1.

2. Grimshaw et al., *Creating A Nation*, p. 4.

3. Grimshaw et al., *Creating A Nation*, p. 4.

4. See the following in *The Oxford History of Australia* (all published by the Oxford University Press, Melbourne): Jan Kociumbus, *Possessions, 1781–1860*, vol. 2 (1992); Beverely Kingston, *Glad, Confident Morning, 1860–1900*, vol. 3; (1986); Stuart Macintyre, *The Succeeding Age, 1901–1942*, vol. 4 (1986); Geoffrey Bolton, *The Middle Way, 1942–1988*, vol. 5 (1990).

5. Verity Burgmann and Jenny Lee (eds), *A Most Valuable Acquisition* (McPhee/Gribble, Melbourne, 1988); *Making A Life* (McPhee/Gribble, Melbourne, 1988); *Staining*

the Wattle (McPhee/Gribble, Melbourne, 1988); *Constructing A Culture* (McPhee/Gribble, Melbourne, 1988).

6. D. J. Mulvaney and J. Peter White (eds), *Australians to 1788* (Fairfax, Syme and Weldon, Sydney, 1987); Alan Atkinson and Marian Aveling (eds), *Australians 1838* (Fairfax, Syme and Weldon, Sydney, 1987); Graeme Davison, J. W. McCarthy, Ailda McLeary (eds), *Australians 1888* (Fairfax, Syme and Weldon, Sydney, 1987); Bill Gammage and Peter Spearitt (eds), *Australians 1938* (Fairfax, Syme and Weldon, Sydney, 1987); Ann Curthoys, Tim Rowse and A. W. Martin (eds), *Australians from 1939* (Fairfax, Syme and Weldon, Sydney, 1987).

7. Jill Matthews, '"A Female of All Things": Women and the Bicentenary', *Making the Bicentenary, Australian Historical Studies*, 23 (1988) pp. 90–102.

8. John Rickard, *Australia: A Cultural History* (Longman, Sydney, 1988).

9. David Day, *Claiming A Continent: A History of Australia* (Angus and Robertson, Sydney, 1996).

10. Joan Wallach Scott, 'Gender: A Useful Category of Historical Analysis', in Joan Wallach Scott, *Gender and the Politics of History* (Columbia University Press, New York, 1984), pp. 28–52.

11. For a discussion of the influence of Scott's work, see Robert Shoemaker and Mary Vincent, 'Gender History: The Evolution of a Concept', in their *Gender and History in Western Europe* (Arnold, London, 1997), pp. 9–11. For a recent discussion see Lisa Duggan, 'Theory in Practice: The Theory Wars, or, Who's Afraid of Judith Butler?', *Journal of Women's History*, 10 (1998), pp. 9–19.

12. See Ann McGrath, 'The White Man's Looking Glass': Aboriginal–Colonial Gender Relations at Port Jackson', *Australian Historical Studies*, 24 (1990), pp. 189–206; '"Beneath the Skin": Australian Citizenship, Rights and Aboriginal Women', in *Women and the State: Australian Perspectives*, ed. Renate Howe, a special edition of the *Journal of Australian Studies*, 37 (1993), pp. 99–114.

13. See Marion Aveling, 'Imagining New South Wales as a Gendered Society 1783–1821', *Australian Historical Studies*, 25 (1992), pp. 1–12; Marian Quartly, 'Mothers and Fathers and Brothers and Sisters: The AWA and the ANA and Gendered Citizenship', in *Women and the State: Australian Perspectives*, ed. Howe, pp. 22–30; Patricia Grimshaw, 'A White Woman's Suffrage', in *A Woman's Constitution: Gender and History in the Australian Commonwealth*, ed. Helen Irving (Hale & Iremonger, Sydney, 1996).

14. Patricia Grimshaw, Chris McConville, Ellen McEwen (eds), *Families in Colonial Australia*, (Allen and Unwin, Sydney, 1985).

15. See Marilyn Lake, 'Mission Impossible: How Men Gave Birth to the Australian Nation – Nationalism, Gender and Other Seminal Acts', *Gender & History*, 4 (1992), pp. 305–22; 'The Independence of Women and the Brotherhood of Man: Debates in the Labor Movement Over Equal Pay and Motherhood Endowment in the 1920s', *Labor History*, 63 (1992), pp. 1–24; 'A Revolution in the Family: The Challenge and Contradictions of Maternal Citizenship in Australia', in *Mothers of a New World: Maternalist Politics and the Origins of Welfare States*, ed. Seth Koven and Sonya Michel (Routledge, London, 1993), pp. 378–95; 'The Politics of Respectability: Identifying the Masculinist Context', *Historical Studies*, 22 (1989), pp. 116–31; 'Female Desires: The Meaning of World War II', in *Gender and War: Australians at War in the Twentieth Century*, ed. Joy Damousi and Marilyn Lake (Cambridge University Press, Melbourne, 1995).

16. See for instance, to name just a few, Raelene Frances, *The Politics of Work: Gender and Labour in Victoria, 1880–1939* (Cambridge University Press, Melbourne, 1993); Gail Reekie, *Temptations: Sex, Selling and the Department Store* (Allen and

Unwin, Sydney, 1994); Beverly Kingston, *Basket, Bag and Trolley: A History of Shopping in Australia* (Oxford University Press, Melbourne, 1994); Penny Russell, *A Wish of Distinction: Colonial Gentility and Femininity* (Melbourne University Press, Melbourne, 1994); Katie Holmes, *Spaces in her Day: Australian Women's Diaries of the 1920s and 1930s* (Allen and Unwin, Sydney, 1995); Deborah Oxley, *Convict Maids: The Forced Migration to Women of Australia* (Cambridge University Press, Melbourne, 1996); Paula Byrne, *Criminal Law and Colonial Subject: New South Wales, 1810–1830* (Cambridge University Press, Melbourne, 1993); Joy Damousi, *Depraved and Disorderly: Female Convicts, Sexuality and Gender in Colonial Australia* (Cambridge University Press, Melbourne, 1997); Diane Kirkby, *Barmaids: A History of Women's Work in Pubs* (Cambridge University Press, Cambridge, 1997).

17. Jill Julius Matthews, 'Doing Theory: Australian Feminist/Women's History in the 1990s', *Australian Historical Studies*, 27 (1996), p. 55.

18. Kim Humphreys, *Self life: Supermarkets and the Changing Cultures of Consumption* (Cambridge University Press, Melbourne, 1998); Stephen Garton, *The Cost of War: Australians Remember* (Oxford University Press, Melbourne, 1997).

19. See, for example, Tom Griffiths, *Hunters and Collectors* (Cambridge University Press, Melbourne, 1996); Chris Healy, *From the Ruins of Colonialism* (Cambridge University Press, Melbourne, 1997); Tim Rowse, *White Flour, White Power: From Rations to Citizenship in Central Australia* (Cambridge University Press, Melbourne, 1998).

20. See Cathy Colbourne, Vijaya Joshi and Christina Twomey, 'Gender and History in Australian History in the 1990s', *Australian Feminist Studies*, 12 (1997), pp. 344–56.

21. Marilyn Lake, 'Feminism and the Gendered Politics of Antiracism, Australia 1927–1957: From Maternal Protectionism to Leftist Assimilation', *Australian Historical Studies*, 29 (1998), pp. 91–108.

22. See Miriam Dixson, *The Real Matilda* (Penguin, Melbourne, 1975); Anne Summers, *Damned Whores and God's Police: the Colonisation of Women in Australia* (Penguin, Melbourne, 1975).

23. Grimshaw et al., *Creating A Nation*, p. 2.

24. John Hirst, 'Women and History: A Critique of *Creating A Nation*', *Quadrant*, 34 (1995), p. 36.

25. Hirst, 'Women and History', p. 38.

26. Hirst, 'Women and History', p. 37.

27. Hirst, 'Women and History', p. 37.

28. Hirst, 'Women and History', p. 38.

29. Hirst, 'Women and History', pp. 38–9.

30. Hirst, 'Women and History', p. 39.

31. Hirst, 'Women and History', p. 40

32. Hirst, 'Women and History', p. 40

33. Hirst, 'Women and History', p. 42

34. Hirst, 'Women and History', p. 43.

35. Hirst, 'Women and History', p. 43.

36. *Weekend Australian*, 18–19 March 1995, p. 26.

37. *Weekend Australian*, 18–19 March 1995, p. 26.

38. Hirst, 'Women and History', p. 37.

39. Hirst, 'Women and History', p. 40.

40. Geoffrey Bolton, 'Anglocentric Immaturity', *Australian Book Review* (1996), pp. 34–5.

41. *Australian Feminist Studies*, 21 (1995), p. 230.

42. *Australian Historical Studies*, 26 (1995), p. 306.
43. Ann Curthoys, *Labour History*, 68 (1995), p. 197.
44. Curthoys, *Labour History*, 68 (1995), p. 197.
45. Curthoys, *Labour History*, 68 (1995), p. 198.
46. Curthoys, *Labour History*, 68 (1995), p. 198.
47. Curthoys, *Labour History*, 68 (1995), p. 202.
48. Curthoys, *Labour History*, 68 (1995), p. 204.
49. Marilyn Lake, 'Women, Gender and History', in *Australian Feminist Studies*, 7 and 8 (1988), p. 9.
50. See Editorial, 'Why Gender and History', *Gender and History*, 1 (1989), p. 2.
51. *Meanjin*, 53 (1994), p. 372.

NOTES ON CONTRIBUTORS

Efi Avdela is Associate Professor of Contemporary Social History at the University of Athens. She has published in Greek, English, French and Italian on gender and work, the history of feminism, and teaching history. She is a member of the editorial committee of the Greek feminist journal *Dini*.

Kathleen Canning is Arthur F. Thurnau Professor and Associate Professor of History, Women's Studies and German at the University of Michigan. Her first book, *Languages of Labor and Gender: Female Factory Work in Germany, 1850–1914*, was published by Cornell University Press in 1996. She is also the author of several essays, including 'Feminist History after the "Linguistic Turn:" Historicizing "Discourse" and "Experience"', *Signs*, 9 (1994) and 'Gender and the Politics of Class Formation: Rethinking German Labor History', *American Historical Review*, 97 (1992). She is currently working on a new book project, entitled *Embodied Citizenship: Gender and the Crisis of Nation in Germany, 1918–1930*. Kathleen has served as North American co-editor of this journal since the autumn of 1998.

Joy Damousi is Senior Lecturer in the Department of History at the University of Melbourne. She is author of *Women Come Rally: Socialism, Communism and Gender in Australia, 1890–1955* (Oxford, 1994); *Depraved and Disorderly: Female Convicts, Sexuality and Gender in Colonial Australia* (Cambridge, 1997); and the forthcoming *Labour of Loss, Mourning, Memory and Bereavement in Wartime Australia* (Cambridge, 1999).

Megan Doolittle has taught history of the family, social policy and social history at the University of Essex, Open University and the University of North London. Her research has focused on fatherhood in nineteenth-century England, and she was a co-author of *The Family Story: Blood, Contract and Intimacy 1830–1960* (1999) with Leonore Davidoff, Janet Fink and Katherine Holden.

Marco Aurélio Garcia is Professor in the Department of History of the Institute of Philosophy and Humanities of the Universidade Estadual de Campinas (UNICAMP), São Paulo, Brazil.

Irina Korovushkina was born in 1970 in the Soviet Union, graduated from the Urals State University (1992), then took an MA in Central and Eastern European History (Budapest, 1994), followed by a PhD in History at the University of Essex (1998). She is currently working as a Research Fellow in the Department of History, University of Essex, on the project *Religion and Survival: Old Believers in the Urals during Stalin's Revolution, 1928–41*. She has published a number of articles on gender and religion in Russian and Soviet history.

Selma Leydesdorff is Director of the Belle van Zuylen Onderzoeks Instituut, Amsterdam, and the author of numerous works in gender and oral history, including *We Lived with Dignity, The Amsterdam Jewish Proletariat 1900–1940* (1994) and, with Luisa Passerini and Paul Thompson (eds), *Gender and Memory: International Yearbook of Oral History and Life Stories*, vol. IV (1996).

Ilana Löwy is a senior researcher at the Institut National de la Santé et de la Recherche Scientifique (INSERM), Paris. She was trained as a scientist and a historian of science, and is interested in the history of biology and medicine, interaction between laboratory and clinics, and gender issues. She has recently published *Between Bench and Bedside: Science, Healing and Interleukin-2* (Harvard University Press, 1997) and she is a co-editor of *La Construction du naturel: les sciences et le genre* (Archives d'Histoire Contemporaire, in press).

Åsa Lundqvist is a doctoral student at the Department of Sociology, Lund University. Her main research interest concerns historical sociology. In her thesis she studies the historical sociology of a rural industrial community during the twentieth century, its relation to the development of the Swedish welfare state and its gender relations.

Michele Mitchell is an Assistant Professor in the Department of History and the Center for Afroamerican and African Studies at the University of Michigan, Ann Arbor, USA. Her article '"The Black Man's Burden": African Americans, Imperialism, and Notions of Racial Manhood' will appear in the *International Review of Social History*'s 1999 supplement.

Ferhunde Ozbay teaches in the Sociology Department at Booazici University, Istanbul, Turkey. She is editor of *Women, Family and Social Change in Turkey* (UNESCO, Bankok, 1990) and has published articles on gender, social history and demography. Recently she has been working on the history of domestic labour in Turkish households.

Jane Rendall is Senior Lecturer and co-director of the Centre for Eighteenth Century Studies at the University of York, UK. Among her many publications are *The Origins of Modern Feminism* (1985), *Women in an Industrializing Society* (1990), and, with Catherine Hall and Keith McClelland, *Defining the Victorian Nation* (1999). She is an active member of the Women's History Network, and is currently interested in the ways in which the Enlightenment in Scotland and England affected the situation of middle-class women and influenced women writers.

Michèle Riot-Sarcey teaches History at the University of Paris VIII, Saint-Denis, and is the author of numerous works in French women's history, including *La Démocratie à l'épreuve des femmes* (1994), and *Le Réel de l'utopie* (1998).

Mrinalini Sinha is Associate Professor of History at Southern Illinois University at Carbondale and is the North American co-editor for *Gender & History*. She is the author of *Colonial Masculinity: The 'Manly Englishman' and the 'Effeminate Bengali' in the Late Nineteenth Century* (1995), and has edited and introduced a new edition of Katherine Mayo's *Mother India*, which was first published in 1927 (1998). She is currently completing a monograph on the implications of the massive international controversy generated by Mayo's *Mother India*.

Christine Stansell, Professor of History at Princeton University, is the author of *City of Women: Sex and Class in New York, 1789–1860*. Her book *American Moderns: New York Bohemia and the Creation of the Twentieth Century* will be published in the spring of 2000 by Metropolitan Books/Henry Holt, New York.

Index

Printed and bound by CPI Group (UK) Ltd, Croydon, CR0 4YY